Margaret Debbadi
Siobhan Matthewson
Series editor:
Peter Marshman

INT

COMPUTING
FOR LOWER SECONDARY

STAGE
8

COMPUTER SCIENCE

DIGITAL LITERACY

INFORMATION TECHNOLOGY

HODDER EDUCATION
AN HACHETTE UK COMPANY

The Publishers would like to thank the following for permission to reproduce copyright material.

Photo credits

p.4 *l* © antoniodiaz/Shutterstock, *rt* © nd3000/stock.adobe.com, *rc* © Maciek905/stock.adobe.com, *rb* © Besjunior/stock.adobe.com; **p. 8** © Aflo/Shutterstock; **p. 10** *t* © Terovesalainen/stock.adobe.com; **p. 11** © AGPhotography/stock.adobe.com; **p. 12** *t* © Kaspars Grinvalds/stock.adobe.com, *b* © Maksym Yemelyanov/stock.adobe.com; **p. 17** © Stockphoto-graf/stock.adobe.com; **p. 45** © Mego-studio/stock.adobe.com; **p. 46** © WavebreakMediaMicro/stock.adobe.com; **p. 50** © Vermicule design/stock.adobe.com; **p. 51** © Ohmega1982/stock.adobe.com; **p. 53** *t* © Bagotaj/stock.adobe.com, *b* © Artem/stock.adobe.com; **p. 57** © Gina Sanders/stock.adobe.com; **p. 59** © Beebright/stock.adobe.com; **p. 61** © Andrea Danti/stock.adobe.com; **p. 68** © Gdarts/stock.adobe.com; **p. 89** © Tim/stock.adobe.com; **p. 95** © MCStock/stock.adobe.com; **p. 126** © Rawpixel.com /stock.adobe.com

b = bottom, *c* = centre, *t* = top

Every effort has been made to trace all copyright holders, but if any have been inadvertently overlooked, the Publishers will be pleased to make the necessary arrangements at the first opportunity.

Although every effort has been made to ensure that website addresses are correct at time of going to press, Hodder Education cannot be held responsible for the content of any website mentioned in this book. It is sometimes possible to find a relocated web page by typing in the address of the home page for a website in the URL window of your browser.

Hachette UK's policy is to use papers that are natural, renewable and recyclable products and made from wood grown in well-managed forests and other controlled sources. The logging and manufacturing processes are expected to conform to the environmental regulations of the country of origin.

Orders: please contact Bookpoint Ltd, 130 Park Drive, Milton Park, Abingdon, Oxon OX14 4SE. Telephone: +44 (0)1235 827827. Fax: +44 (0)1235 400401. Email education@bookpoint.co.uk Lines are open from 9 a.m. to 5 p.m., Monday to Saturday, with a 24-hour message answering service. You can also order through our website: www.hoddereducation.com

ISBN: 9781510481992

© Margaret Debbadi and Siobhan Matthewson 2020

First published in 2020

This edition published in 2020 by

Hodder Education,
An Hachette UK Company
Carmelite House
50 Victoria Embankment
London EC4Y 0DZ

www.hoddereducation.com

Impression number   10 9 8 7 6 5 4 3 2 1

Year   2024 2023 2022 2021 2020

Cover photo © musicman/Shutterstock.com

Illustrations by Aptara, Inc.

Typeset in FS Albert Regular 12/14pt by Aptara, Inc.

Printed in Slovenia

A catalogue record for this title is available from the British Library.

Contents

Introduction

About this book

This Student Book will continue to support your progression in computing and in the ongoing development of the skills needed to progress to specific curriculum areas such as IGCSE Computer Science and IGCSE ICT. Building on the skills developed in the previous book in this series you will further develop the technical skills needed to engage effectively in the digital world of today. It supports the curriculum areas of digital literacy, computer science and information technology:

- **Digital literacy** focuses on the impact of digital technology in today's society. It promotes understanding of the impact of the digital world with an emphasis on maintaining safety and well-being online.

- **Computer science** is the study of computational thinking and the creation of computer programs to solve problems. It also explores how a computer interprets and carries out instructions.

- **Information technology** looks at how to use computer programs to solve problems. It takes into consideration both usability (how well a program works) and accessibility needs (whether or not everybody is able to use the program effectively).

Units

This Student Book has six units:

8.1 Computer systems: The inside track introduces students to the inner workings of computer systems. It investigates the use of binary number representation and the use of logic gates for processing and decision making through a scenario around a space station holiday resort and robotic hosts that support guests during their stay.

8.2 Networks and communication: Across the world in an instant introduces the concept of networks and methods of electronic communication. The chapter uses the concept of an e-commerce application to investigate how organisations make effective use of electronic platforms to support world-wide communication.

8.3 HTML and CSS: Getting your head straight focuses on the development of web page content using HTML and CSS. In this chapter the focus is on the production of standardised web page presentations through the use of internal, inline and external CSS.

8.4 High level programming language: Expert story telling provides an introduction to high level programming through the development of an interactive adventure game using the programming language Python.

8.5 Spreadsheet modelling: Model my merch further develops skills in the use of spreadsheet applications. This chapter explores the use of more complex formula structures to support data analysis, decision making and the use of graphical presentations. It also investigates how data input can be controlled using validation methods and cell formatting.

8.6 Relational database: SegwayThere encourages further understanding of the use of database applications by introducing the concept of relational databases to effectively store data. It provides a more in-depth look at controlling data input and ensuring effective management of data output using complex queries and report structures.

How to use this book

In each unit you will learn new skills by completing a series of tasks. Each unit starts with some information followed by a list of the learning objectives that you will cover. These features also appear in each unit:

Learning Outcomes

This panel lists the things you will learn about in each unit.

SCENARIO

This panel contains a scenario which puts the tasks into a real-world context.

Do you remember?

This panel lists the skills you should already be able to do before starting the unit.

Learn

This panel introduces new concepts and skills.

Practice

This panel contains tasks with step-by-step instructions to apply the new skills and or knowledge from the 'Learn' panel.

KEYWORDS

Important words are emboldened the first time they appear in a unit and are defined in this panel. They also appear in the glossary.

This panel suggests a simple task to check your understanding.

These speech bubbles provide hints and tips as you complete the tasks.

DID YOU KNOW?

This panel provides an interesting or important fact about the task or theme.

Computational Thinking

This panel highlights tasks in the unit which involve one of the key areas of computational thinking:

Pattern recognition: the identification of repeating tasks or features in a larger problem to help solve more complex problems more easily.

Decomposition: breaking larger problems down into smaller more manageable tasks. Each smaller task is examined and solved more easily than a larger more complex problem.

Abstraction: ignoring details or elements of a problem which are not needed when trying to solve a problem.

Algorithmic thinking: providing a series of instructions which include details on how to solve an identified problem.

Generalisation: the process of creating solutions to new problems using past knowledge and experience to adapt existing algorithms.

Evaluation: the process of ensuring that an algorithmic solution is an effective and efficient one – that it is fit for purpose.

Go further

This panel contains tasks to enhance and develop the skills previously learnt in the unit.

Challenge yourself

This panel provides challenging tasks with additional instructions to support new skills.

Final project

This panel contains the final tasks of the unit which encompass all the skills developed. It can be used to support self/peer assessment and teacher assessment.

Evaluation

This panel provides guidance on how to evaluate and, if necessary, test the Final Project.

Student resources are available at www.hoddereducation.com/student-resources

Robots and AI

Robots and **artificial intelligence (AI)** are used more and more to help us complete everyday tasks, with future developments now including studies of how humans interact with machines and how machines can mimic human behaviour. For example:

Robotics	Artificial intelligence
A humanoid robot called Atlas, created by Boston Dynamics, combines AI and robotics to tackle urban obstacle courses called 'parkour'.	Voice-activated assistants such as Siri and Alexa use machine learning and AI to help provide high quality interactions with human users.
'Soft robotics' is the next generation of robots; they will be made of soft materials with a wide range of motion which can more closely mimic human movement.	Many online shopping applications use AI to track users' internet searches to target advertising. They also make suggestions for purchase when the user is next online.

In this unit you will learn:

→ about the use and impact of robotics and artificial intelligence in the travel industry
→ that data is stored and manipulated in **binary** format inside computing devices
→ how to use binary representation to store positive numbers
→ that alternative representations such as **hexadecimal (hex)** can be used to represent data (including colour representations)
→ how to convert numbers from decimal format into binary and hexadecimal number systems
→ how to perform simple additions and multiplications using binary values
→ how sound files are stored in computer systems.

SCENARIO

SpaceVaca is a new travel agent. It specialises in providing trips to a holiday resort on a space station. The company wants to offer holiday makers a realisic space adventure where robots are used to staff the resort and welcome guests.

Your challenge is to research how robots and artificial intelligence (AI) can be used to help humans run the hotel. You will consider the pros and cons of using technology in this way. Once you have identified potential areas where robots and AI can be used, you will design a 'robo-host' which will be used to perform tasks, such as welcome new guests to the hotel.

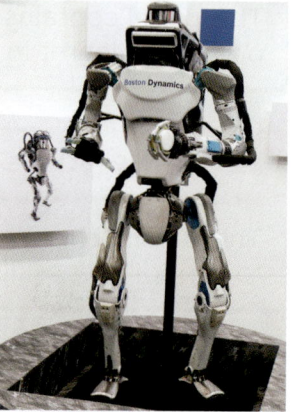

▲ Atlas the Parkour Robot. Have a look on the Boston Dynamics website for some great videos.

KEYWORDS

robot: a machine designed to automatically carry out a pre-programmed task without human intervention

Give an example of what a robot can be used for.

artificial intelligence (AI): the study of machines and application of algorithms designed to carry out tasks in a way which copies the way humans think

binary: a number system which uses combinations of two digits (0 and 1) to represent all numbers. Used to represent data in computer systems

hexadecimal (hex): a number system which uses a combination of 16 digits (0–9 and A–F) to represent all numbers

Before you can design the robo-host you will need to consider how data is stored, manipulated and transferred around a computer system.

Do you remember?

Before starting this unit, you should be able to:

✔ add two numbers together
✔ multiply two numbers together
✔ use a spreadsheet to enter basic numbers and formula
✔ enter a URL into a web browser to access a specific web page
✔ list a range of input and output devices used with computers and other digital devices, for example using keyboards or microphones or touch screens for input, screens or speakers for output
✔ list a range of sensors used to provide inputs to computers and other digital devices, for example temperature sensors, humidity sensors, light sensors or motion sensors.

You should also know that:

✔ images can be represented in bitmap format
✔ you can use flowcharts to illustrate the steps involved in solving a complex problem
✔ data can be input and output using a range of devices including sensors
✔ sensors and input and output devices can be used to provide data and receive information from digital devices
✔ spreadsheets can be used to record data and carry out calculations using formulas.

DID YOU KNOW?

The word 'robot' comes from a Czech term 'robota' which means 'forced labour' or 'drudgery'. Robots are used in, for example:

• manufacturing (for example, when building cars)
• space exploration (for example, when unmanned robots collect samples from other planets)
• healthcare (for example, to help conduct surgery when the doctor and patient are in different locations)

Robotic holiday

Learn

When we think of robots we may think about how they are used in car assembly plants, space travel or even medicine. It's unlikely we would think about using robots and AI in the travel industry. However, when we combine robotics with AI we can create a machine that mimics the way humans think and act. A robot can work out solutions to problems and learn from past experiences as well as carry out the steps to complete a task. For these reasons, robots are increasingly being used to help travellers in the travel industry.

Hotels and the travel industry also use AI; sometimes we do not even realise we are interacting with a machine. **Chatbots** allow us to make bookings or ask questions online, even when hotel or travel agency staff are not available. Chatbots are now being used by some health care organisations to ensure patients have constant access to medical support.

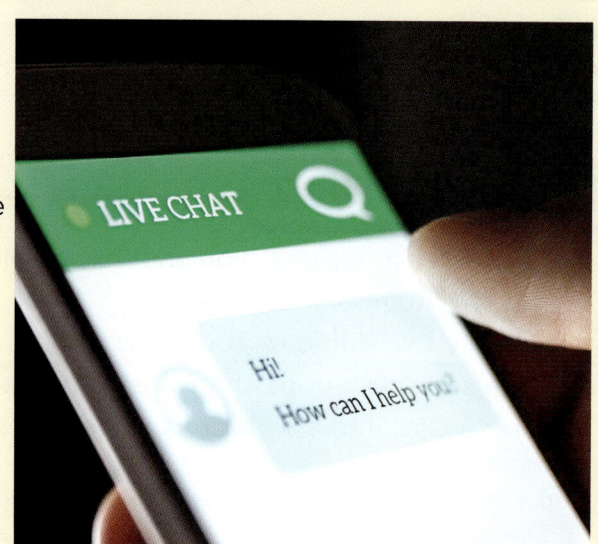

In some countries, robots are used to help with airport security to detect concealed weapons. You may have even seen people walking through airport lounges being followed by their automated suitcase!

Using technology this way has its pros and cons. For example:

Pros	Cons
• Robots do not get tired, they can work 24 hours a day, seven days a week. • Many tasks are completed more quickly by robots. • Tasks are completed to the same standard at all times. • Robots do not need to be paid. • Tasks are completed without error. • Robots can work in dangerous environments. • Robots can be programmed to interact in many different languages.	• High cost of development and maintenance. • Complex programs needed for their operation. • Need to be reprogrammed if task changes; cannot easily handle changes in tasks. • May be prone to bugs. • Security concerns; electronic devices can easily be hacked. • Staff will need to be retrained. • Some staff may lose their jobs. • Robots are unable to express emotions and provide empathy in the same way humans can.

Practice

With a partner, discuss the possible ways robotic technology and AI could be used by SpaceVaca. Think about, and make notes on, how a robot might be used:

➤ at the point where the customer accesses the SpaceVaca website to make a booking
➤ when the customer makes their booking and pays for their holiday
➤ when the customer arrives at the hotel
➤ during the customer's stay at the hotel
➤ when the customer checks out and leaves the hotel.

You could think here about food, drink, payment, health care.

Produce a poster advertising SpaceVaca and the robotic and AI services it provides for its customers. Your poster can be digital or hard copy. It should include a range of graphics and make people want to visit the space station for a holiday.

KEYWORDS

chatbot: a computer program designed to mimic a human conversation

Tell your partner about an experience you had using a chatbot.

empathy: the ability to understand the feelings of another person

Your poster should tell a story to show:

➤ how the customers will use robotic technology and AI for at least three tasks during their stay or when booking their holiday
➤ how the customer will benefit from using robotic technology and AI for each task
➤ a warning for each task about some possible difficulties or disadvantages of using robotic technology and AI to complete each task.

Collecting traveller input

Learn

Digital processing systems such as mobile phones, tablet computers or gaming stations are made up from a combination of electronic hardware devices (such as keyboards, microphones, touch screens, sensors) and software which tell the hardware devices how to operate. For the system to be useful to the user, there must be a way of providing input (such as voice input or text input via a keyboard) to the system. This input is then processed using a computer program and the output is presented to the user.

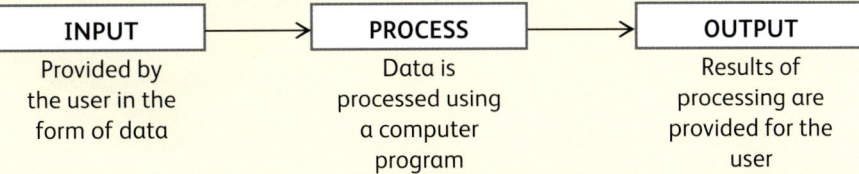

INPUT	PROCESS	OUTPUT
Provided by the user in the form of data	Data is processed using a computer program	Results of processing are provided for the user

There are many ways users can provide input to and receive output from digital systems. Some of the most common input and output devices used with digital devices today are listed below.

Input devices	Output devices
• Microphone • Touch screen (menu options or keyboard entry) • Sensors • Scanners (image scanners, biometric scanners) • Trackpads (to move cursors on screen)	• Touch screen for output display • Speakers for sound output • Printers

Users can provide instructions to computer systems in a number of ways.

➤ Users can enter commands from a limited list of instructions that the system recognises.
  • Commands could be selected from a menu using a cursor and a pointing device such as a mouse (or the user's finger, as with the **smart fridge** example shown here).

KEYWORDS

digital processing system: any system that processes digital data (that is, data in the form of 0s and 1s)

smart fridge: a fridge with internal cameras and sensors which detects what products are stored inside and allows users to keep track of contents; using internet connections they can suggest potential recipes for users based on the contents of their fridge

- Simple instructions from a limited list could be typed into the device or selected using a keyboard, such as your television remote control or a touch screen keyboard on a tablet or a gaming console.
➤ Users can use their own **natural language** (the language spoken by humans, using full sentences and phrases without breaking down instructions into key words or abbreviations) to enter commands into the computer system.
  - Instructions could be spoken into the device using a microphone; for example, the way we issue instructions to Siri or Alexa.
  - Instructions could be typed into the device using a keyboard using natural language. For example, we can type full sentences into internet search engines to find relevant content.

KEYWORD

natural language: the language spoken by humans; for example English, Chinese, Vietnamese, Japanese, Spanish

Practice

➤ With a partner, discuss the range of ways you can use your mobile phone. Consider the ways you can provide input and receive output from your mobile phone.

➤ When you have finished your discussion, your teacher will give you a copy of a diagram for you to complete to help you illustrate your findings.

➤ A smart fridge can be used to help with keeping track of food in the household, ordering shopping, and planning recipes.
Discuss with your partner how AI and robotics could be used in future homes. Design a robot which can be used in the future to help you complete everyday tasks.

➤ Draw a picture of your robot and write a short description to explain:
  o the task it is designed to help you complete
  o the input and output devices it will use.

Processing voice input

Learn

Complex programs which use AI are often needed in systems where users can enter instructions using natural language. For example, when we use voice-activated instructions with our mobile phones, we tend to speak in full sentences.

But how do these programs work out what the user's instruction is? Look at the diagram below; we can see what happens when a user speaks an instruction into a digital device such as Google Assistant on a mobile phone.

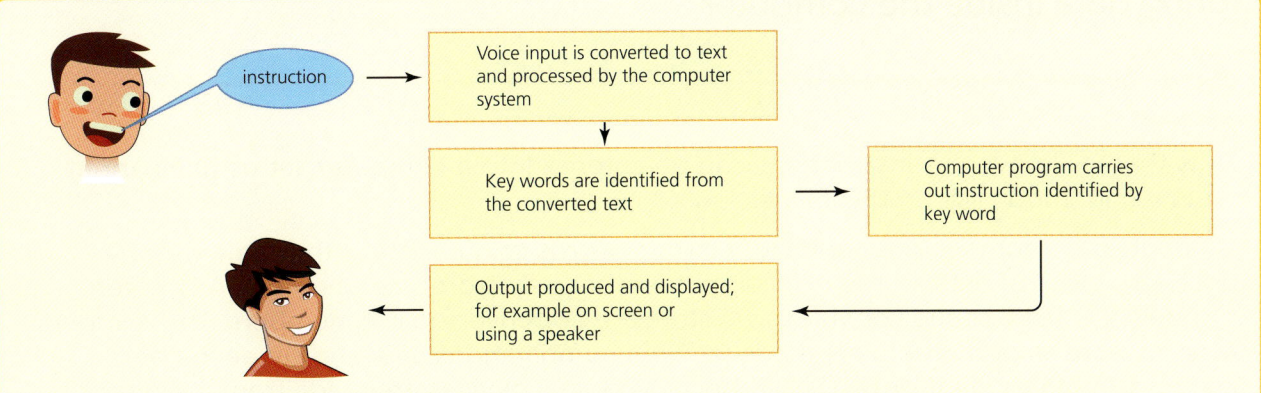

➤ Instructions are converted to text and the key words identified.

➤ The key words can then be looked up in a list of possible commands.

➤ The instructions relating to those key words are carried out.

➤ Output is produced.

Practice

➤ With a partner, create a table similar to the one shown below. Your table should contain list of digital devices you use each day. Beside each device, identify possible uses and then the input and output devices for each use. Decide if you enter commands using natural language or from a fixed list of commands when completing that task. An example has been given to help you.

Device	Use	Input device	Output Device	Natural language or Fixed command set
Mobile phone	Searching the internet	Touch screen keyboard	On screen display	Natural language

Game developers are looking at how voice activation can be used to control video games. Modern remote controls, such as those provided with Apple television, and tools such as Amazon Alexa, accept voice entry from users. This allows users to carry out many tasks, such as:

change television channels	schedule recordings	search for television shows
order goods online	search for information	book a taxi

➤ Select one of the tasks listed above and recreate the diagram from the previous Learn panel to include:
  o the input instructions a user might use to successfully complete the task
  o the key words the computer would use to help it understand the task
  o the steps the computer might take to complete the task
  o the output the computer would provide to confirm completion of the task.

Storing data inside the computer

Learn

Now that we know how instructions can be entered into a computer, let us think about what it might look like on the inside.

Computers do not recognise and store letters, words or numbers in the same way we do. Every piece of data stored in a computer is actually stored as a number. Any letters, symbols, pictures, sounds or videos we store are all converted into numbers. The numbers used to store all of this data are made up from combinations of 1s and 0s; each 1 or 0 is known as a **binary digit** or **bit**. This is because digital devices are made from millions of tiny switches called **transistors**. Each switch can only have one of two values: 1 (ON) or 0 (OFF).

When data is stored inside a computer, the bits used to represent data can be grouped and processed together in larger units as shown in this diagram. (You might recognise some of the terms used in the diagram; we use them to help describe how large a file is and the storage capacity of storage devices.)

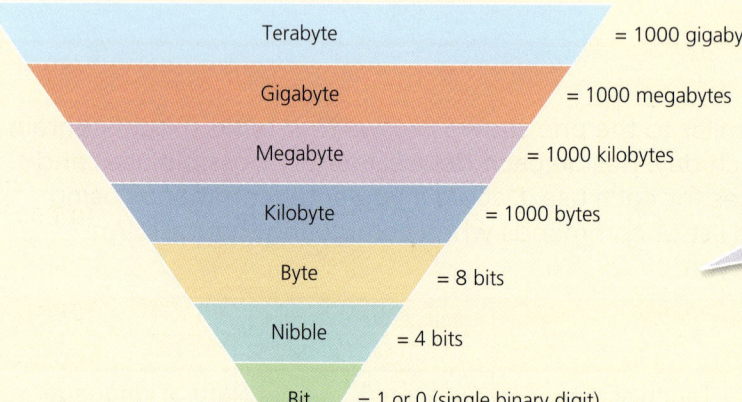

Terabyte = 1000 gigabytes

Gigabyte = 1000 megabytes

Megabyte = 1000 kilobytes

Kilobyte = 1000 bytes

Byte = 8 bits

Nibble = 4 bits

Bit = 1 or 0 (single binary digit)

8 bits grouped together is called a **byte** and can be used in computers to represent a single character of text on a computer, e.g. the following combinations of 1s and 0s (01000001) is used to represent the letter 'A' on most computer systems.

Practice

With a partner create a rhyme or poem which can be used to help you remember the terms associated with units of storage from the diagram shown above.

Illustrate your poem with graphics to give an example of each unit of storage; for example, a bit is 1 or 0 so you could show those numbers or an image of a transistor (or switch) used to represent 1 or 0. Or you could use an image of an external hard drive storage device to represent 1 TB (terabyte) of storage capacity.

KEYWORDS

binary digit: 0 or 1, the smallest unit of data represented by a computer

bit: short for binary digit

transistor: a tiny switch that can be activated by electrical signals. If the transistor is ON it represents 1, when it is OFF it represents 0

byte: a group of 8 bits, often used to represent a single character in a computer

Using binary to store text

Learn

If our digital devices are storing all of our data as 1s and 0s, then how do we use binary to represent the letters and characters which make up the words and phrases we enter into the computer?

The set of characters that can be represented on any device is known as its **character set**. The character set is made up from all of the letters, numbers, punctuation symbols and **special characters** represented on a device. Each character will be represented by a distinct set of 1s and 0s.

Most devices use a common code so that the characters can easily be transferred from one computer to another. One of the most commonly used codes is the **American Standard Code for Information Interchange (ASCII)** (this can be pronounced as 'as-kee').

ASCII is a 7 bit code used to represent all of the keys on a standard keyboard. The table below shows some of these 7 bit codes. However, as computers normally store information in 8 bits, an extra bit is added to the beginning of the ASCII code to make it up to 8 bits. Each byte contains a unique combination of 0s and 1s to represent each character on a standard keyboard.

> Remember there are 8 bits in a byte.

ASCII character	Binary	ASCII character	Binary	ASCII character	Binary	ASCII character	Binary
Space	0100000	8	0111000	P	1010000	h	1101000
!	0100001	9	0111001	Q	1010001	i	1101001
"	0100010	:	0111010	R	1010010	j	1101010
#	0100011	;	0111011	S	1010011	k	1101011
$	0100100	<	0111100	T	1010100	l	1101100
%	0100101	=	0111101	U	1010101	m	1101101

When a key is pressed on a keyboard the ASCII code for that character is generated using a group of eight electrical pulses. For example pressing R on a keyboard causes 8 transistor switches to be on or off in a particular pattern shown in the diagram.

Pressing 'R' on a keyboard will generate the 8-bit ASCII code 01010010 (remember the eighth bit is just an extra 0 at the start) which can be processed by the computer.

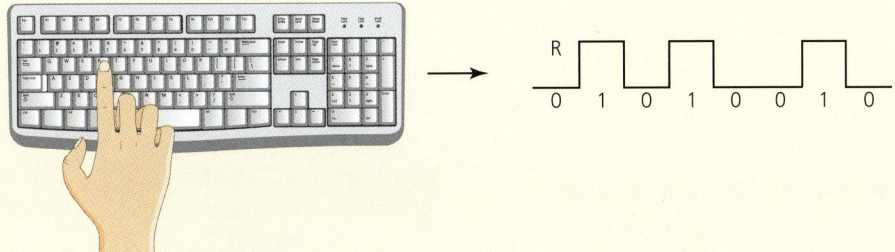

Further examples: 'H' = 0100 1000 and 'i' = 0110 1001, so the word 'Hi' would be represented as the following pattern of 1s and 0s 0100 1000 0110 1001.

Practice

Search the internet for a list of ASCII codes used to represent the letters A-Z and a-z. Show how the following words would be represented in ASCII.

➤ school
➤ computer

Pattern recognition

Examine the list of ASCII codes found during the previous practice task. What patterns do you notice with the characters? Discuss these with a friend.

Abstraction

The combinations of binary values listed below all represent phrases or questions that some guests have said to the robo-host. Using the ASCII code charts you have found on the internet, translate these binary values into English for the manager of the space station.

✪ 0100 0100 0110 0101 0110 1100 0110 1100 0110 1111

✪ 0101 0111 0110 1000 0110 0001 0111 0100 0111 0100 0110 1001 0110 1101 0110 0101 0110 1001 0111 0011 0110 1001 0111 0100 0011 1111

Decomposition

A guest has just asked the robo-host the following two questions.

✪ Can I check in now?
✪ What is my room number?

Use your ASCII code table to create the binary code the robo-host would use to represent these questions.

Use the process of decomposition to break down this problem.

✪ You may wish to look at one character at a time.
✪ Does the same character appear twice? How can you speed up the process of translating the words?

If you have time, send some messages to your friend using the ASCII code.

Remember that the table shows the 7 bit codes but the values shown here are the 8 bit versions, with an extra bit at the beginning!

Think about how long it took you to translate these messages. Your computer is carrying out billions of these conversions per second!

Using binary to store numbers

Learn

When we enter numbers into a digital device we may need to perform calculations using those values. For example, using a spreadsheet application to add two numbers together.

When numerical values are used for calculations computers cannot use the ASCII code to carry out these calculations. Instead the numbers are stored in **binary number format**. The binary number system got its name because it uses two symbols, '1' and '0'.

The prefix 'bi' means two. Just like a bicycle is called a bi-cycle because it has two wheels.

Decimal number system

Before we think about how binary numbers are represented let us revise the **decimal number system**. The decimal number system is the formal name for the numbers that we use every day.

Every number we want to represent in the decimal number system is made up from the ten digits 0, 1, 2, 3, 4, 5, 6, 7, 8, 9. When you were younger you used units, 10s, 100s, 1000s, and so on, to help you understand the value of numbers greater than 9. For example, when we refer to the number 2409, what we actually mean is:

Thousands 1000		Hundreds 100		Tens 10		Units 1
2		4		0		9
= 2 × 1000		= 4 × 100		= 0 × 10		= 9 × 1
2000	+	400	+	0	+	9

Each column heading is worked out by multiplying the previous heading by 10. So, if we added another column to the table, its heading would be Ten thousands (1000 × 10 = 10 000).

Each column can only contain one of the digits 0-9. But depending in which column that digit is placed, it could mean, for example, 9, 90, 900, 9000 and so on. This is known as **place value**.

So, the number 2409 is actually calculated as 2000 + 400 + 0 + 9.

Decimal is also known as **base 10** due to the fact that it contains 10 distinct digits (0–9).

KEYWORDS

binary number format: numbers represented using 1s and 0s

decimal number system: number system using the digits 0, 1, 2, 3, 4, 5, 6, 7, 8, 9

place value: the numerical value a digit has as a result of its position in a number; for example, the number 24 actually represents (2 × 10) + (4 × 1)

base 10: another term for decimal as it is based on 10 digits

Practice

Rewrite the following numbers using the table layout from the previous page to show how the place values of a digit can alter its overall value in a number. Your teacher will provide you with a copy of these tables in the document **Place Value Revision Exercise.docx**.

➤ Nine thousand
➤ Nine hundred and nine
➤ Seven thousand nine hundred and nine
➤ Seventy four

Binary number system

Learn

We have seen that binary has only two digits 0 and 1. For this reason, the place value column headings in binary increase in multiples of 2 and each column can only contain 0 or 1.

So, for example, here is a binary number: 10010110_2. The subscript lets us know the number is a binary number. Here is what this actually means:

When working with more than one number system it is a good idea to use a subscript to distinguish one from the other. For example, if this number were written with a subscript 10 (10010110_{10}), the number would be ten million, ten thousand, one hundred and ten.

Each column heading value is worked out by multiplying the previous heading by 2							
64×2	32×2	16×2	8×2	4×2	2×2	1×2	
128	64	32	16	8	4	2	1
1	0	0	1	0	1	1	0
$= 128 \times 1$	$= 64 \times 0$	$= 32 \times 1$	$= 16 \times 1$	$= 8 \times 0$	$= 4 \times 0$	$= 2 \times 0$	$= 1 \times 0$
128	0	0	16	0	4	2	0

the digit or bit to the left hand side of the number is known as the Most Significant Bit (MSB) as it has the largest place value.

the digit or bit to the right hand side of the number is known as the Least Significant Bit (LSB) as it has the smallest place value.

So, the number 10010110_2 represents $128 + 0 + 0 + 16 + 0 + 4 + 2 + 0$ which is 150_{10}. We use a subscript 10 to let us know that this is a decimal value.

Now that we understand how the place values work, we can easily convert any binary number into decimal. Binary is often referred to as base 2 (think about decimal being known as base 10 to help you understand why this might be the case).

Here are two more examples:

Example 1: 10110000_2

128	64	32	16	8	4	2	1
1	0	1	1	0	0	0	0
$= 128 \times 1$	$= 64 \times 0$	$= 32 \times 1$	$= 16 \times 1$	$= 8 \times 0$	$= 4 \times 0$	$= 2 \times 0$	$= 1 \times 0$
128	0	32	16	0	0	0	0

So, $10110000_2 = 128 + 32 + 16 = 176_{10}$

Example 2: 00001111_2

128	64	32	16	8	4	2	1
0	0	0	0	1	1	1	1
= 128 × 0	= 64 × 0	= 32 × 0	= 16 × 0	= 8 × 1	= 4 × 1	= 2 × 1	= 1 × 1
0	0	0	0	8	4	2	1

So, $00001111_2 = 8 + 4 + 2 + 1 = 15_{10}$

We still use 1 byte (or 8 bits) to represent 15_{10} in binary even though we do not really need the first four bits of this byte (which are set to zero). This is because computers normally store data in **fixed length** groups of 8 bits. In the past, computers could only process 8 bits at a time.

So, even though we only need 4 bits to store the number 15 we always represent binary numbers using all 8 bits, including all of the zeroes.

> When binary numbers are being stored in memory, each bit is represented by a transistor which can either be OFF or ON to represent 0 or 1.

When we think about how the number 15 is stored in computer memory we could also think of it as being stored using transistors as:

OFF	OFF	OFF	OFF	ON	ON	ON	ON

Practice

Use the tables below to show how the following binary numbers would be represented in decimal format.

(a)

128	64	32	16	8	4	2	1
1	0	0	1	1	1	0	0

(b)

128	64	32	16	8	4	2	1
0	1	1	0	0	1	1	0

(c)

128	64	32	16	8	4	2	1
0	0	0	1	1	1	1	0

(d)

128	64	32	16	8	4	2	1
1	0	0	1	0	1	1	0

(e)

128	64	32	16	8	4	2	1
1	1	1	1	1	1	1	0

KEYWORDS

Most Significant Bit (MSB): the digit to the left hand side of the number; the bit with the largest place value

Least Significant Bit (LSB): the digit to the right hand side of the number; the bit with the smallest place value

fixed length: having a set number of bits to represent a value; for example, numbers in binary are normally shown using 8 bits

Algorithms and decomposition

⭐ The hotel manager cannot understand how decimal numbers can be stored in computer memory as 0s and 1s and asks you to explain this process.

o Open a blank spreadsheet file and save it as **Binary Conversion**.

o Set up a spreadsheet similar to the one show below.

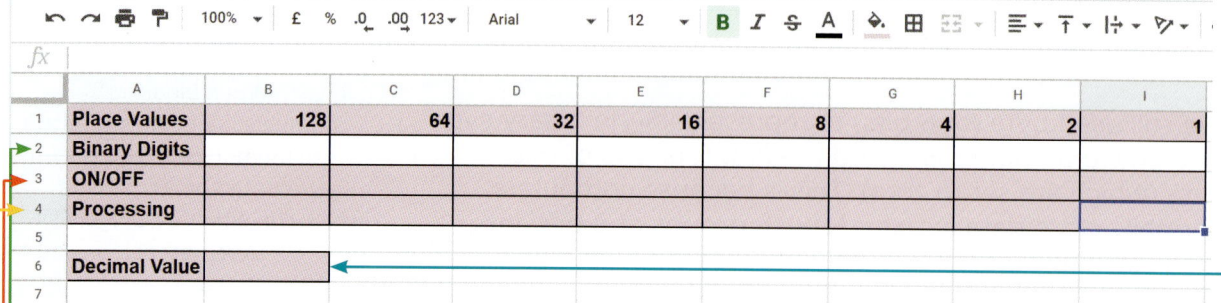

	A	B	C	D	E	F	G	H	I
1	Place Values	128	64	32	16	8	4	2	1
2	Binary Digits								
3	ON/OFF								
4	Processing								
5									
6	Decimal Value								
7									

Binary Digits: Each cell in this row contains one bit. The 8 bits together can represent a binary number which is stored in computer memory.

ON/OFF: This row shows the ON/OFF pattern for each transistor used to store the binary digit shown in the row above.

Processing: This row calculates the decimal value of each bit entered in row 2 by multiplying the bit stored by its place value in the number.

Decimal Value: Calculates the number stored by adding together place values multiplied by either 1 or 0 depending on the bit stored in each memory location.

o In cell I:4, enter a formula that will correctly convert the binary digit entered in cell I:2 into its decimal equivalent.

o Replicate this formula across the row, from cell I:4 to B:4, to calculate the decimal values for all bits in the binary number entered.

> All formulas should start with =
>
> The formula in cell I:4 should perform the following calculation cell I:2 * cell I:1

	A	B	C	D	E	F	G	H	I
1	Place Values	128	64	32	16	8	4	2	1
2	Binary Digits	0	0	0	0	1	1	1	1
3	ON/OFF								
4	Processing	0	0	0	0	8	4	2	1
5									
6	Decimal Value								

o Add a formula to cell B:6 which will calculate the decimal value being stored.

> To do this add all of the values in cells B:4 to I:4. You could use the spreadsheet function SUM here.

o Enter a set of 8 binary digits into the spreadsheet to test it works correctly; for example, we know that 00001111 should generate the decimal value 15.

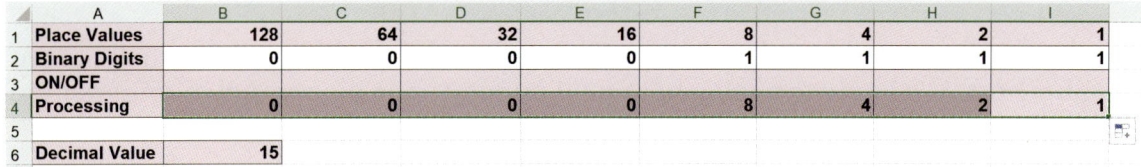

	A	B	C	D	E	F	G	H	I
1	Place Values	128	64	32	16	8	4	2	1
2	Binary Digits	0	0	0	0	1	1	1	1
3	ON/OFF								
4	Processing	0	0	0	0	8	4	2	1
5									
6	Decimal Value	15							

⊗ We can use the ON/OFF row in the spreadsheet to see how this binary number would be stored by a computer using 8 transistors. Each transistor can be switched ON or OFF.

o Enter the following formula into cell B:3:

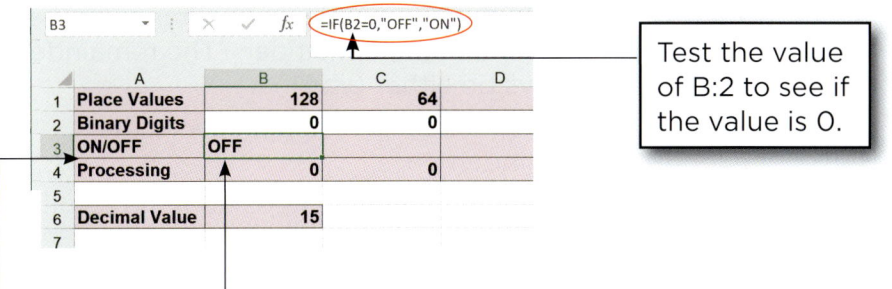

B3 fx =IF(B2=0,"OFF","ON")

Test the value of B:2 to see if the value is 0.

	A	B	C	D
1	Place Values	128	64	
2	Binary Digits	0	0	
3	ON/OFF	OFF		
4	Processing	0	0	
5				
6	Decimal Value	15		
7				

If the value in B:2 is 0, the transistor should be switched OFF to represent 0.

If the value in B:2 is not 0, the transistor should be switched ON to represent 1.

o Replicate this formula across the spreadsheet from cell B:3 to I:3 to work out if each of the other 'transistors' would be ON of OFF.

o Test your spreadsheet using the binary code for 27 (00011011).

o Entering 00011011 should produce the following results.

	A	B	C	D	E	F	G	H	I
1	Place Values	128	64	32	16	8	4	2	1
2	Binary Digits	0	0	0	1	1	0	1	1
3	ON/OFF	OFF	OFF	OFF	ON	ON	OFF	ON	ON
4	Processing	0	0	0	16	8	0	2	1
5									
6	Decimal Value	27							

⊗ Ask a friend to test your spreadsheet with binary number representations they have calculated themselves. Ask them to complete this table to show the output from your spreadsheet. Your teacher will provide you with a copy of a table to complete, with these headings:

Binary number entered	ON/OFF transistor pattern	Decimal value generated

Decimal to binary

Learn

Humans arriving at the space station hotel will need to be able to communicate with the robo-host. We know the robo-host only understands binary. Any numbers input into the robo-host must be converted from decimal into binary.

The easiest way to convert a number from decimal format into binary is by using the 'divide by 2' method.

We have already shown how the number 176_{10} would look in binary format. Let us look at how the 'divide' by 2 method does this conversion.

$176 \div 2$	=	88	remainder	0
$88 \div 2$	=	44	remainder	0
$44 \div 2$	=	22	remainder	0
$22 \div 2$	=	11	remainder	0
$11 \div 2$	=	5	remainder	1
$5 \div 2$	=	2	remainder	1
$2 \div 2$	=	1	remainder	0
$1 \div 2$	=	0	remainder	1

➤ Divide the original decimal number by 2 and write down the remainder. (The remainder will always be either 0 or 1.)

➤ Divide the result by 2 and record the remainder.

➤ Repeat the first two steps until the result of the division by 2 is 0.

➤ Write out the binary result from left to right starting with the **last** remainder produced: 10110000

For example, a guest will think of their room number as being the decimal number 176 but the robo-host will store this in binary format as 10110000_2.

Algorithmic thinking and abstraction

A guest arriving at the space station hotel must provide the robo-host with their room number so their bags can be taken to their room.

Using the flowchart on the right, your task is to design an algorithm which can be used to convert decimal numbers provided by guests into binary format so the robo-host can understand them. Flowchart statements have been provided but three are unnecessary. Use the process of abstraction to remove the unnecessary steps and then complete the algorithm by placing the remaining steps in the correct position in the flowchart.

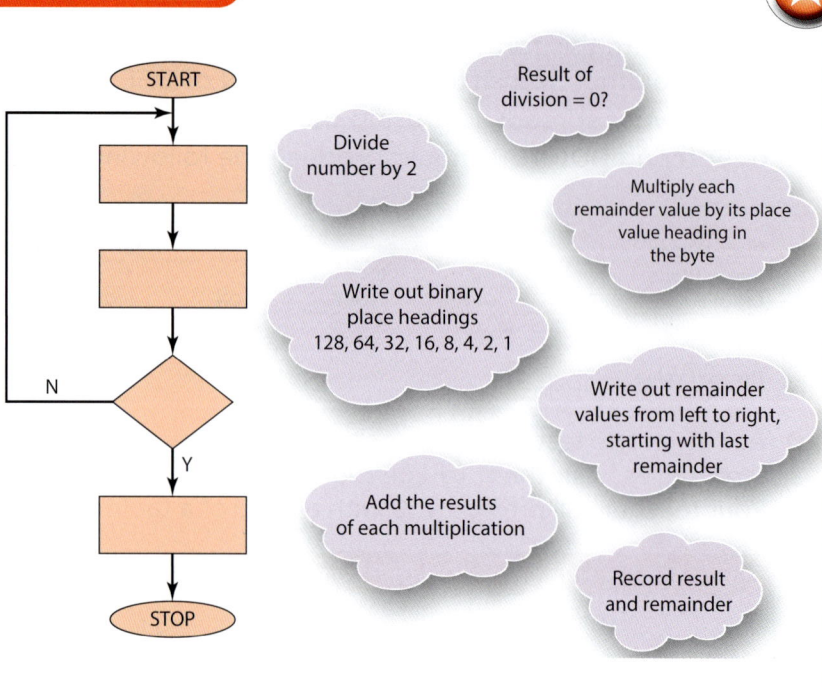

START

Divide number by 2

Result of division = 0?

Multiply each remainder value by its place value heading in the byte

Write out binary place headings 128, 64, 32, 16, 8, 4, 2, 1

Write out remainder values from left to right, starting with last remainder

Add the results of each multiplication

Record result and remainder

N

Y

STOP

Practice

The robo-host has provided the hotel manager with some information about hotel guests but it has output some of the information in binary format.

Help the hotel manager by converting binary numbers below so they contain the correct decimal value.

> Look carefully at the subscript value before carrying out your conversions, not all values are in binary format. Use your spreadsheet/algorithm from the previous practice task to help you with this.

- There are 00010111_2 guests booked into the restaurant tonight.
- To date, there are 10110100_2 bookings for next year.
- There have been 00110111_{10} queries about bookings for next year.
- There are 11001100_2 staff working in the space hotel today.

The robo-host needs to record details of how many guests are staying on each floor on the space station. A staff member entered the following digital values using a touch screen. Convert the highlighted decimal values into 8 bit binary values for the robo-host. Show your working out:

> Use your spreadsheet/algorithm from the previous practice task to help you with this.

Floor 1

32 guests

Floor 2

127 guests

Floor 3

54 guests

Floor 4

76 guests

Binary calculations

Learn

The robo-host will be used to complete a range of tasks for guests and staff during their stay at the space station hotel. For example, it could help the manager work out how many guests are staying in the hotel at any one time, or it could calculate a total bill for guests at the end of their stay.

It is quite easy to add binary numbers together – the hardest calculation you have to do is $1 + 1$.

We all know that $1 + 1 = 2$. But how do we represent 2 in binary?

Remember, the number 2 is written in binary as 10_2.

128	64	32	16	8	4	2	1
0	0	0	0	0	0	1	0
$= 128 \times 0$	$= 64 \times 0$	$= 32 \times 0$	$= 16 \times 0$	$= 8 \times 0$	$= 4 \times 0$	$= 2 \times 1$	$= 1 \times 0$
0	0	0	0	0	0	2	0

> Remember that binary only uses two digits 0 and 1 so the biggest number we could ever produce by adding two digits together is 2_{10} or, in binary, 10_2.

This is what we are doing when we add binary values:

Stage 1

Binary place values

2	1
0	1

$+ \quad 0_{(1)} \quad 1$
$\underline{\qquad\qquad}$
$\qquad 0$

Stage 2

2	1
0	1

$+ \quad 0_{(1)} \quad 1$
$\underline{\qquad\qquad}$
$\quad 1 \qquad 0$

> Adding $1 + 1$ gives us an answer of 0 and we carry the 1 across to the next column.

> We then add the carry to any other values in the column. In this case there are none, so we write down 1 under the next place value heading.

In binary addition, when adding two numbers, you come across the following possible outcomes:

➤ $0 + 0 = 0$

➤ $1 + 0 = 1$

➤ $1 + 1 = 0$ carry 1 (which is 2 in decimal or 10 in binary)

➤ If the carry value is added to a column that is already adding $1 + 1$ then you get:

$1 + 1 + 1 = 1$ carry 1 (which is 3 in decimal or 11 in binary)

Now look at some more complicated binary additions:

Example 1: $010_2 + 011_2$

Binary place values	4	2	1
	0	1	0
+	$0_{(1)}$	1	1
	1	0	1

Decimal calculation

$\quad 2$
$+ 3$
$\underline{\qquad}$
$\quad 5$

Remember: $1 \quad 0 \quad 1_2 = 5_{10}$

$4 + 0 + 1$

Just like adding in decimal, we start on the right hand side and continue adding and carrying until all columns are complete.

Example 2: $011_2 + 011_2$

Binary place values	4	2	1
	0	1	1
+	0(1)	1(1)	1
	1	1	0

Decimal calculation

$$3$$
$$+\ 3$$
$$6$$

Remember: 1 1 $0_2 = 6_{10}$

$4 + 2 + 0$

Look at the second column in this calculation. With the carry, we are now adding 3 binary digits and the answer is $1 + 1 + 1 = 11_2$ (3). So, we write down 1 and carry 1 to the next column.

Practice

Complete the following 8-bit binary additions to test your knowledge of this content.

Part 1

Calculate the results of these 8-bit binary additions and convert each answer into decimal.

(a)

	0	1	0	0	0	1	0	1
+	0	0	0	0	1	0	1	0

(b)

	0	0	1	0	0	1	1	0
+	1	0	0	1	0	0	1	0

(c)

	0	0	0	1	1	0	1	1
+	1	1	0	0	0	1	1	0

Part 2

Show how the following calculations could be carried out in binary format:

(a) 12 + 2

Calculate the binary for 12 using the method shown in the *Learn* box on page 22.

Calculate the binary for 2.

Add the two binary values together.

	128	64	32	16	8	4	2	1
Binary for 12								
Binary for 2								
Result								

(b) 32 + 10

Calculate the binary for 32.

Calculate the binary for 10.

Add the two binary values together.

	128	64	32	16	8	4	2	1
Binary for 32								
Binary for 10								
Result								

Hexadecimal number system

Learn

When programming the robo-host it can be difficult to write out lines of binary code as all of the 1s and 0s can be confusing. Some computer programmers often use a more human-friendly method of re-writing binary values. One of these methods is the **hexadecimal** (hex) number system.

Hex	Decimal	Binary	Hex	Decimal	Binary
0	0	0000	8	8	1000
1	1	0001	9	9	1001
2	2	0101	A	10	1010
3	3	0011	B	11	1011
4	4	0100	C	12	1100
5	5	0101	D	13	1101
6	6	0110	E	14	1110
7	7	0111	F	15	1111

The hexadecimal number system (also known as **base 16**) uses the characters 0–9 and A–F; that's 16 characters in total.

The table shows how the hexadecimal characters correspond to the decimal and binary values.

A 4 bit number is called a **nibble**. The largest 4 bit number is 1111_2 or 15_{10}. This means one hex character can represent a nibble.

A byte has 8 bits. We can split each byte into two nibbles and represent each one using a hexadecimal character. This allows us to represent a byte with 2 hexadecimal characters.

> A nibble is four bits – half a byte.

For example, the number 215_{10} can be represented as 11010111_2 in binary.

Write 215_{10} as an 8 bit binary value.	1101	0111
Split the byte into two nibbles …		
… and treat each nibble as a separate number.	1101	0111
Show the decimal value for each nibble.	13	7
Show the hexadecimal value for each nibble.	D	7

> 0111_2 is 7_{10} in decimal; 7_{10} is 7_{16} in hexadecimal

> 1101_2 is 13_{10} in decimal; 13_{10} is D_{16} in hexadecimal

So, 11010111 can be re-written in hex as $D7_{16}$.

To prove this is correct, let us take $D7_{16}$

	D	7
Take the hex values.		
Calculate the decimal value for each.	13	7
Convert the decimal into binary nibbles.	1101	0111
Bring the two nibbles together to form 1 byte.		
	1101	0111

Use the place values method shown on page 21 to convert from binary to decimal.

$11010111_2 = 215_{10}$ which was our original number.

Practice

Using the processes outlined in the previous section, carry out the following decimal to hex and hex to decimal conversions.

(a) Convert the number 129_{10} into hexadecimal.

Write 129_{10} as an 8 bit binary value.		
Split the byte into two nibbles …		
… and treat each nibble as a separate number.		
Show the decimal value for each nibble.		
Show the hexadecimal value for each nibble.		

(b) Convert the number 170_{10} into hexadecimal.

Write 170_{10} as an 8 bit binary value.		
Split the byte into two nibbles …		
… and treat each nibble as a separate number.		
Show the decimal value for each nibble.		
Show the hexadecimal value for each nibble.		

(c) Convert the number $B3_{16}$ to decimal.

	B	3
Take the hex values.		
Calculate the decimal value for each.		
Convert the decimal into binary nibbles.		
Bring the two nibbles together to form 1 byte.		

_____ $_2$ = _____ $_{10}$

KEYWORDS

base 16: another name for hexadecimal because it is based on 16 characters

nibble: a 4 bit number

(d) Convert the number AD_{16} to decimal.

Take the hex values.		A	D
Calculate the decimal value for each.			
Convert the decimal into binary nibbles.			
Bring the two nibbles together to form 1 byte.			

_____ $_2$ = _____ $_{10}$

Other uses for hexadecimal

Learn

In computing systems, the hexadecimal number system has proven very useful. One of the most well-known uses for hexadecimal is for specifying colours on web pages in HTML.

All colours on a website are combinations of shades of red, green and blue, or RGB. Red, green and blue can each have 256 different levels of intensity, which are indicated by numbers between 0–255_{10}. In binary these numbers range from 00000000–11111111. In hex however these numbers range from 00–FF.

Web browsers specify colours using the format #RRGGBB (Reds, Greens and Blues) where the # is used to show the number is in hex. Using this system two hex digits are used for each colour: so #FF0000 uses all Red with no Green or Blue.

In binary this would be:

R	R	G	G	B	B
F	F	0	0	0	0
1111	1111	0000	0000	0000	0000

As one number the hex value #FF0000 is $111111110000000000000000_2$.

Instead of having to type in long binary numbers when changing the colour of text on a web page, a programmer can write the short hexadecimal code. These six digit hexadecimal numbers can represent $16\,777\,216_{10}$ different colours.

> Think how long it would take to edit colours on a web page if you had to enter the binary code for each colour, and how easy it would be to make a mistake.

> There are 256 red × 256 green × 256 blue = 16 777 216 total colours.

Some examples are shown below.

Maroon #800000	Red #FF0000	Orange #FFA500	Yellow #FFFF00	Olive #808000
Purple #800080	Fuchsia #FF00FF	White #FFFFFF	Lime #00FF00	Green #008000
	Navy #000080	Blue #0000FF	Aqua #00FFFF	Teal #008080
	Black #000000	Silver #C0C0C0	Grey #808080	

Practice

Convert the following binary number representations into their colour names by splitting each number into nibbles and working out the hex vale for each nibble.

➤ $111111110000000011111111_2$

➤ $100000001000000010000000_2$

➤ $111111111111111111111111_2$

Decomposition and pattern recognition

The manager of the space station would like you to design an icon which can be displayed on a touch screen display on the robo-host.

Customers will press the icon to complete standard tasks such as:
- ✪ Check-in
- ✪ Request room service
- ✪ Book a table in the restaurant
- ✪ Book a shuttle taxi home

The icon will be made up from a bitmap image. The pixels in the image will be coloured using a 4-bit binary code. Each of the 4 bits displayed can also be represented in their hexadecimal equivalent.

Before designing your icon you will need to complete a colour mapping grid. This grid includes the hex values 0–F and the decimal equivalent of each hex value. You must assign a colour to each hex value and then calculate the binary equivalent for each hex character. You can assign any colour you wish to each hex value but you will need to assign 16 colours in total.

You should then complete the icon design using the binary code for each pixel colour.

✪ Open the file **BinaryDesigns** provided by your teacher. It contains an electronic copy of a grid with a key for you to complete.

o Use the key to devise your own colour chart to assign a colour to the hex characters shown.

o On the grid, design your own icon for the task you have selected but enter the codes for your selected colour using the appropriate 4-bit binary combination instead of the hex code. For example:

On my colour key, I am using F_{16} to represent the colour RED.

Hex	Decimal	Binary	Colour
F	15	1111	RED

My icon has a 10 pixel red line across the top. Therefore, I have shown the code for RED in binary in each of the pixels in the top line:

1111	1111	1111	1111	1111	1111	1111	1111	1111	1111

o Give your completed key and grid to a partner and ask them to colour it in for you.

o Discuss with a partner which method (binary or hex) is better for colour encoding and why?

Decomposition

You will need to use the process of decomposition to help you solve this problem and break down this challenge into these stages:

✪ Assign a colour name to each hexadecimal value in the grid.

✪ Calculate the binary representation for each hexadecimal value in the grid (and, therefore, each colour).

✪ Design your icon using any of these colours.

✪ Find the colour that you wish to use for a pixel.

✪ Find the hex equivalent for the colour.

✪ Convert the hex into binary.

✪ Record the binary value in the correct pixel location on the grid.

What about the sound?

Learn

Today, most digital devices accept input from users, via microphones, in the form of spoken words. They can also provide speech output to the user via speakers. The robo-host uses voice recognition to identify guests when taking orders or giving them access to their rooms. When a sound is produced, it creates what we call an **analogue** sound wave such as the one shown below.

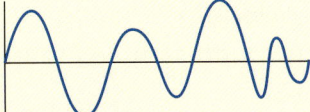

Computers do not store data in analogue format so the sound must be converted into digital format which can be stored as bits. Converting analogue signals into digital is carried out by a device called an **analogue to digital convertor (ADC)**.

ADCs take samples of the sound wave at fixed intervals in time. The number of samples taken each second is called the **sample rate**. The sample rate is measured in 'number of times per second' which is known as **hertz (Hz)**. So, for example, if the sample rate was 1Hz this would mean that only one sample was taken per second.

The diagram below shows an analogue sound wave which has been sampled 20 times in one second.

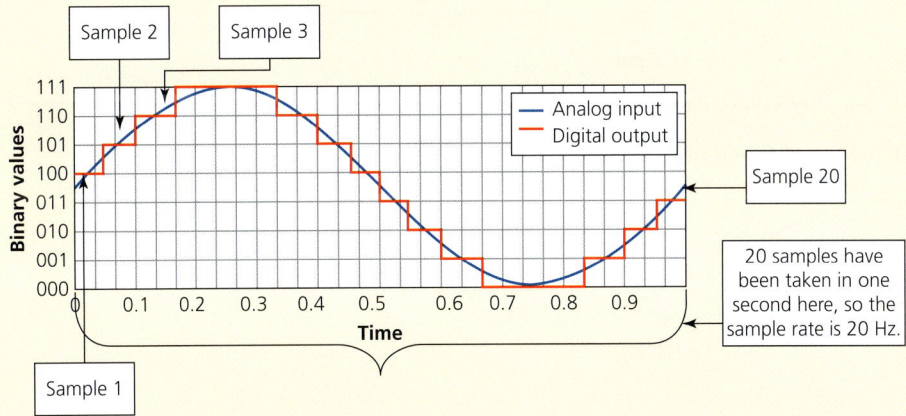

Each sample has been represented using three binary digits as shown using the values on the *y*-axis of the graph shown above. For example:

Sample 1 = 100

Sample 2 = 101

Sample 3 = 110

... and so on, up until

KEYWORDS

analogue: a continually varying signal, for example a sound signal

analogue to digital converter (ADC): used to convert analogue signals, such as the human voice, to digital signals

sample rate: the number of sound samples taken each second

hertz: a unit of measurement which tells us how many sound samples were taken in a single second

> Sample 20 = 011
>
> In this example we are using 3 bits to store each sound sample. The number of bits used to store each sound sample is called the **bit depth**.
>
> The more samples taken and the more bits used to record each sound sample, the better the quality of the digital sound file.

KEYWORD

bit depth: the number of bits used to store a single sound sample

Practice

The robo-host needs to ensure that guests' sound samples are not confused. A decision needs to be made regarding how many bits should be used for each sound sample. Your teacher will give you a worksheet to allow you to complete this task.

Complete the sampling of the sound wave shown below. The sample rate is 10 Hz.

10 samples per second.

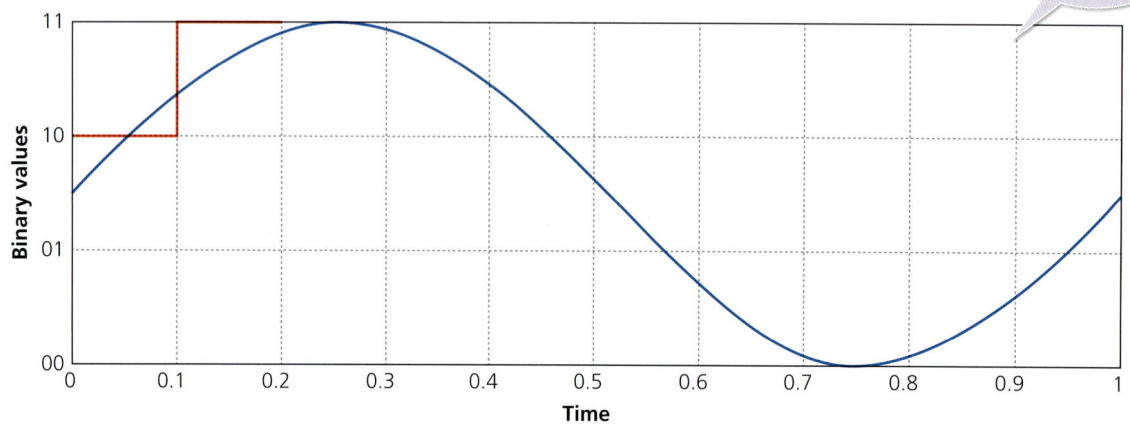

This sample is recorded using only two bits (a bit depth of 2). How accurate is the sound sample?

Now try sampling the same sound wave using 4 bits (1 nibble).

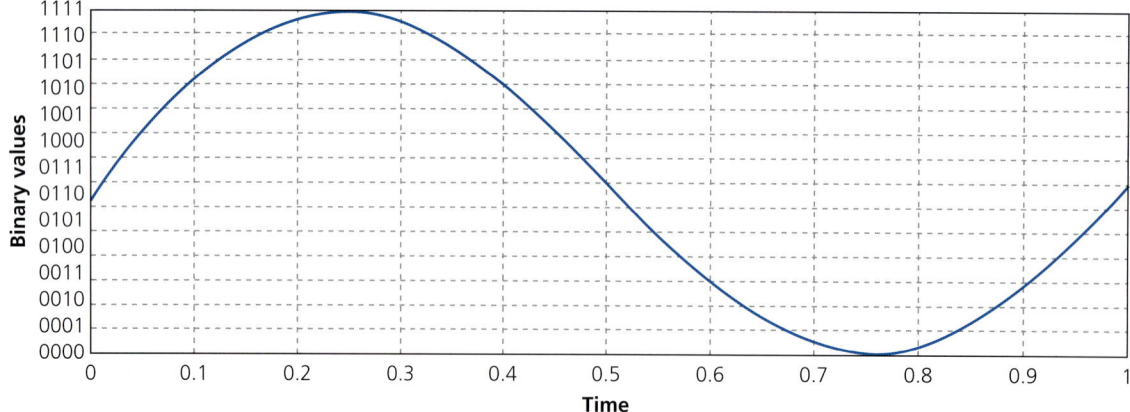

How does this 4-bit sample compare with the previous 2-bit sample? What happens to the quality of the samples taken? Discuss what you notice with your partner.

Which bit depth would you recommend and why?

Go further

We saw earlier how the robo-host may need to perform complex calculations where the result being calculated needs more than one bit to represent it; for example, 1 + 1 = 2 (which is 10_2 in binary).

To recap, add the following 8 bit binary numbers:

```
        (18 + 2)
            00010010
+           00000010
        (20 + 4)
            00010100
+           00000100
```

What happens when we try to add larger numbers? For example, a customer's bill for room service might include $193 for food and $93 for soft drinks.

How would the robo-host do the calculation 193 + 93?

Binary place values	126	64	32	16	8	4	2	1	Decimal calculation
	1	1	0	0	0	0	0	1	1 9 3
+ (1)	0(1)	1	0	1	1	1	0(1)	1	+ (1) 9 3
(1)	1	1	0	1	1	1	1	0	2 8 6

↑
Something called overflow now occurs, This is because the result needs more than 8 bits if it is to be stored correctly.

> We are able to use 8 bits to represent the answer produced from these calculations.

KEYWORD

overflow: when the number being represented is too large for the number of bits available

The largest 8 bit binary number is 11111111_2. In decimal this is $128 + 64 + 32 + 16 + 8 + 4 + 2 + 1 = 255_{10}$.

However when we add together the decimal numbers 193 + 93, the result is 286_{10}. We cannot represent this as an 8 bit number as it is too large and so the result of our binary addition is incorrect. This is known as an overflow error.

As we have seen, computers store data in groups of 8 bits. The additional 1 needed at the beginning when we add the final carry is a ninth bit which would need to be stored in another 8 bit memory space rather than in the original 8 bits used to store the two numbers being added.

> Use the layout shown above to help you add the 8 bit binary numbers provided in the scenarios below.

The robo-host is expected to perform calculations and output results for staff when they are producing bills for customers. Help the robo-host create bills for the following customers by adding up their bills using a pen and paper. Circle any overflow produced from the calculations.

◆ Mr Y has booked two rooms for his family who are staying for one night. The first room is charged at 00110011_2 and the second smaller room is charged at 00110001_2.
  ❏ What is the total cost of his stay? Show your answer in binary and decimal.
◆ Family A have a bill for 1011011_2 from the restaurant and 11100010_2 for their two night stay at the space station.
  ❏ What would their total bill be? Show your answer in binary and decimal.

Challenge Yourself

Arithmetic shifts

KEYWORD

arithmetic shift: a process of shifting binary digits left or right to help perform complex calculations

Earlier, we looked at how we can add binary numbers together to help us determine, for example, a customer's total bill for staying at the space station:

> Family A have a bill for $113 per night for a two night stay in the space station, plus a $91 stay for the restaurant.

To work out the total bill the robo-host would have to multiply the cost of 1 night by 2 to work out the cost of the hotel room first.

How would the robo-host work this out?

Think first about how we multiply numbers in our decimal number system. When we multiply by 10 in the decimal system we simply shift all of the numbers to the left and add a 0 as the least significant bit.

See page 18 to revise Least Significant Bits .

This is called carrying out an **arithmetic shift**.

Multiplying by 10

$$
\begin{array}{r}
2\ 0 \\
\times\ 1\ 0 \\
\hline
\end{array}
$$

shift '20' one place left → | 2 | 0 | 0   ← add 0 into blank position

Arithmetic shifts in binary operate in exactly the same way. The difference is that in binary, shifting one place to the left multiplies by 2, since binary uses two digits instead of ten.

So, if we want to multiply a binary number by 2 we simply shift the binary digits 1 place to the left and then fill the missing space on the right hand side with 0

For example, to multiply the binary number 101_2 by 2_{10}:

	128	64	32	16	8	4	2	1
	0	0	0	0	0	1	0	1

Now shift 101_2 (highlighted in yellow) one place to the left and add a zero in the right hand column:

	128	64	32	16	8	4	2	1
Shift left by 1	0	0	0	0	1	0	1	(0)

Fill blank under least significant bit with 0.

Shift left by one place the bit under the heading for 2 (this has the same effect as multiplying by 2).

The original number was 00000101_2, which is 5_{10} in decimal.

The new number is 00001010_2 which is 10_{10} in decimal. So, we have multiplied the original number by two: $5_{10} \times 2_{10} = 10_{10}$.

➤ Use this process of binary shifts and additions to carry out the following calculations in binary:

- $6_{10} \times 2_{10}$
- $12_{10} \times 2_{10}$
- $9_{10} \times 2_{10}$

Now use what you have learned to calculate the total bill for Family A.

> You will have to calculate the binary for each of the values in the calculation first.

> Family A have a bill for \$113 per night for a two night stay in the Space Hotel plus a \$91 stay for the restaurant.

Show your answer in decimal format.

> Convert 113_{10} into binary first of all and then use an arithmetic shift to calculate the cost of two nights. Add the results of the binary shift to the binary value for 91.

Final project

Part 1: Introducing the robo-host

Now that you understand how the robo-host will collect and process data from the space station customers, you can design the robo-host. Your first task is to consider what input and output devices the robo-host will need to allow it to interact with customers.

➤ Copy and complete the table below to show the input devices and the output devices that your robo-host will require and state what each will be used for.

List of input devices	List of output devices

➤ Draw a picture of your robo-host. You should label all of the input and output devices it will use. Include also a description of how your robo-host will move around the space station.

➤ With a friend, discuss how the introduction of the robo-host might:

- impact on jobs in the space station hotel
- positively and negatively affect the experiences of guests at the hotel.

➤ Copy and complete the following table to summarise your discussion.

Impact on jobs

Impact on guests	
Positive impact	Negative impact

Part 2: Abstraction and pattern recognition

When each guest arrives at the space station, they must record their voice pattern with the robo-host. The voice pattern is used to allow them to give instructions to the robo-host.

➤ Help the robo-host select the correct digital sound sample for guest X.

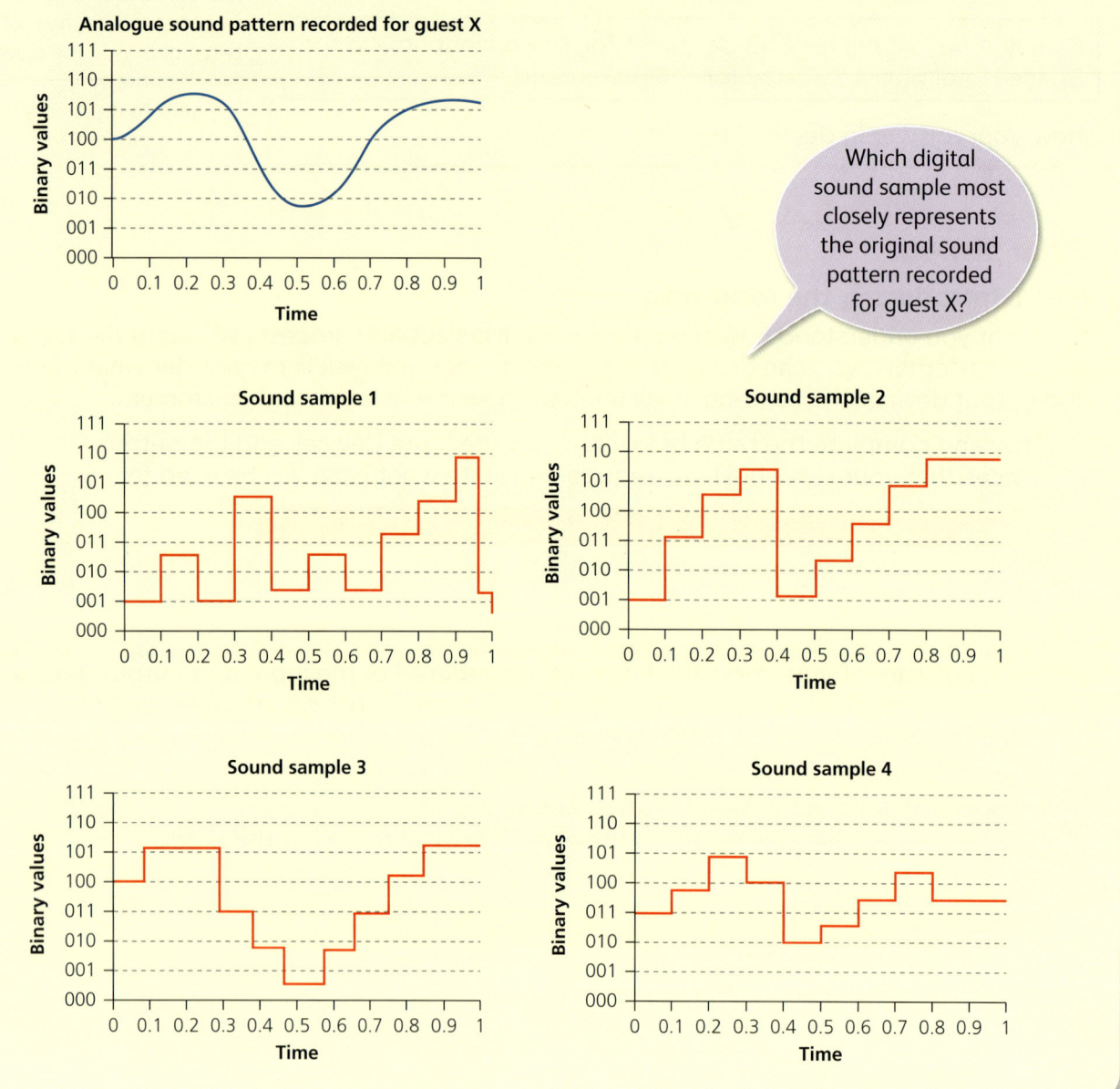

Which digital sound sample most closely represents the original sound pattern recorded for guest X?

Part 3: Decomposition and abstraction

Mr T has been staying at the space station hotel for three nights. The tariff is:

> Accommodation $50 per night × 3 = $150
>
> Food total: $98.00

Use what you have already learned about binary shifts and addition to help you with this task.

➤ Help the robo-host calculate his bill. You should do all calculations in binary and show your answer in binary. Show your working out as you go along.

➤ Show your answer in hexadecimal format.

Evaluation

➤ Examine your designs for your robo-host and ensure you have included:
- o input devices
- o output devices
- o information on how the robo-host can move around the hotel.

➤ Ask a partner for their thoughts on your robo-host design (Part 1). Based on the feedback what changes would you make to your design?

➤ Discuss your findings on the impact of the robo-host on jobs and guests with a partner with another table. Expand your table to include any new ideas you have learned from your discussion.

➤ Check your calculations with a friend to ensure you have produced the correct total for Mr T's stay at the space station. If your answers are different work through the calculations together and highlight any mistakes you made, making corrections if necessary.

e-communications: across the world in an instant

Businesses use many forms of digital communication to create an online business community.

In this unit you will learn about:

→ how businesses use emails, **emojis** and messaging applications
→ **VoIP** and **video conferencing**
→ using **social media** to help businesses
→ digital communication systems: **LANs** and **WANs**
→ using **web browsers** to view material online
→ using technology safely
→ threats to **cyber security**.

SCENARIO

You are the new e-communication manager for an online retailer called e-Shop. e-Shop is working to increase the number of customers it has across the world. It is making use of social media, email and video conferencing. In the recent past, e-Shop has decided to look at social influencers to improve sales. You have been asked to assess the many methods e-Shop plans to use to communicate with its world-wide customer base and between its many offices and staff. Your task is to build up a portfolio of information to:

• help staff understand what methods of communication they should use and when
• make sure staff understand the technology that allows them to communicate online
• make staff aware of the risks associated with online communication
• help staff to communicate respectfully and responsibly online.

Do you remember?

Before starting this unit you should be able to carry out the following:

✔ Use the internet to research.
✔ Use a word processor to create a report.
✔ Use email software to send, receive and forward emails.

KEYWORD

cyber security: the different ways in which we protect networks, programs and data from attack and unauthorised access

Name one type of cyber security.

Emails, emojis and messaging applications

> ### Learn
>
> Email or electronic mail allows users to send messages from a computer across the internet at any time. Emails can be read at any time by the recipient. To use email, users must have all of the technology required to connect to the internet.
>
> Email is one of the most important communication tools that e-Shop uses. Every staff member has their own email address made up of a **user identifier** followed by the @ symbol and the **domain name**, eshop.com.
>
> An example of an email address at the shop is:
>
> Jolong@eshop.com
>
> In this example, **Jolong** is the user identifier, and **eshop.com** is the domain name.
>
> Staff use email to contact customers, suppliers, each other, and other businesses. Staff receive about 100 emails every day and they must manage the communication.
>
> Staff use email to create and reply to messages. In addition, there are other features which are useful to the team at e-Shop.
>
> | Feature | Description |
> |---|---|
> | Forward | This feature is useful if a staff member receives an email which is really for someone else; they can forward the email to the correct person. |
> | Distribution List | Staff at e-Shop regularly have to send emails to certain groups of people. For example, as communications manager you will have to send emails to the managing directors. Instead of sending individual emails you can set up a distribution list and add all of the relevant people to the list. Then you only need to type the email once and add the distribution list in the To… section of the email. |
> | Attachment | e-Shop staff have to send documents such as bills or receipts to customers. The attachment feature allows staff to add these documents to an email. |
> | Read Receipt | If an important email is being sent, e-Shop staff must make sure that the recipient has read the email. When this is the case, the staff member will select an option which will request a read receipt. When the recipient opens the email, they will be asked to allow a read receipt to be sent. |
> | Delayed delivery | Staff can prepare emails in advance and schedule when the email should be sent. This is useful if the email is to be sent at a particular date or time, for example at night. The email can be prepared during the day and will automatically be sent at the correct time at night. |

KEYWORDS

user identifier: the part of the email address which uniquely identifies the user
domain name: the address of the server which holds the email

Here is a typical email window showing some of the features mentioned.

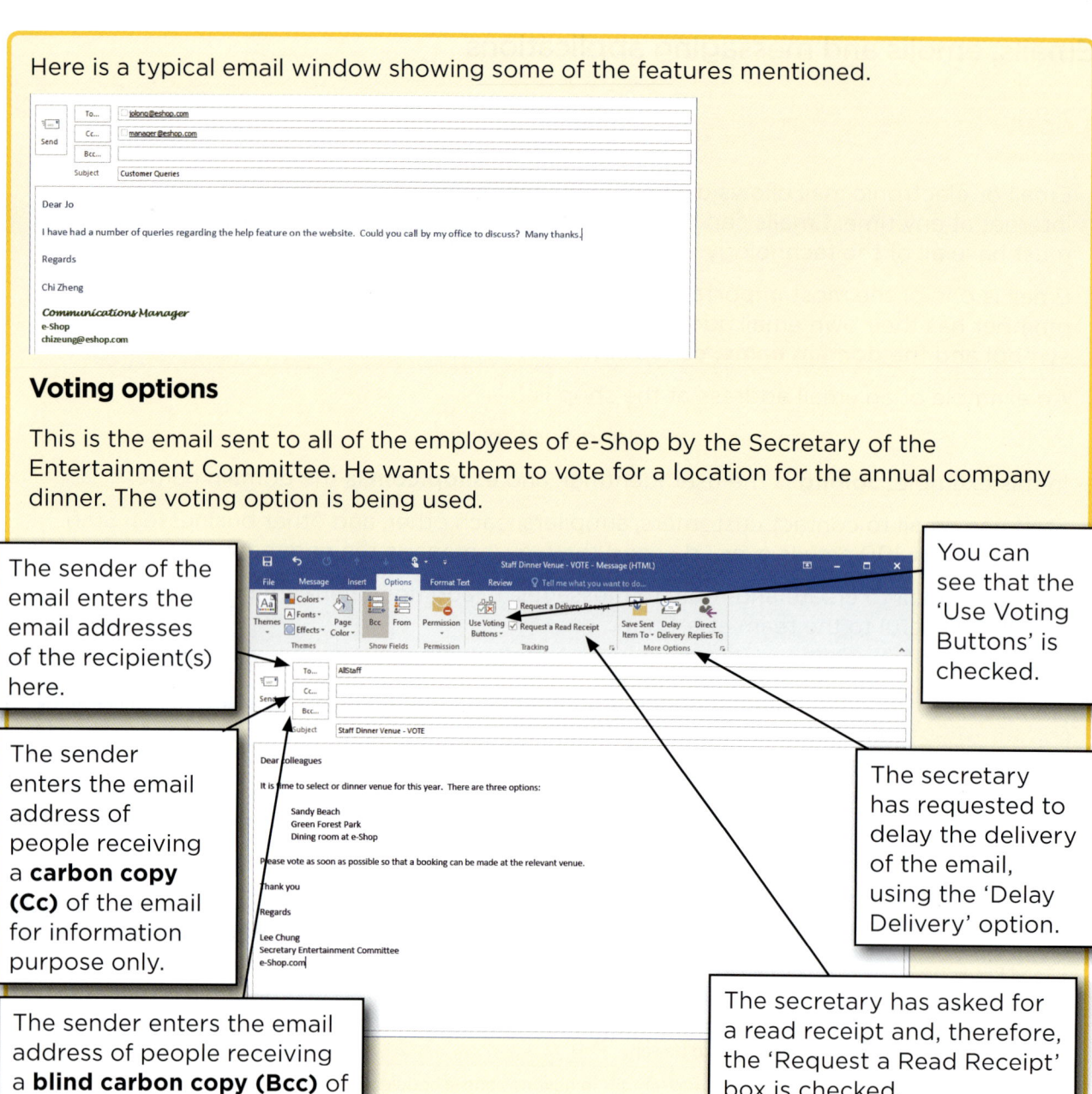

Voting options

This is the email sent to all of the employees of e-Shop by the Secretary of the Entertainment Committee. He wants them to vote for a location for the annual company dinner. The voting option is being used.

The sender of the email enters the email addresses of the recipient(s) here.

The sender enters the email address of people receiving a **carbon copy (Cc)** of the email for information purpose only.

The sender enters the email address of people receiving a **blind carbon copy (Bcc)** of the email. These recipients will not see any of the other recipients' email addresses.

You can see that the 'Use Voting Buttons' is checked.

The secretary has requested to delay the delivery of the email, using the 'Delay Delivery' option.

The secretary has asked for a read receipt and, therefore, the 'Request a Read Receipt' box is checked.

In *Microsoft Outlook*, when clicking 'Use Voting Buttons' the Properties dialog box opens.

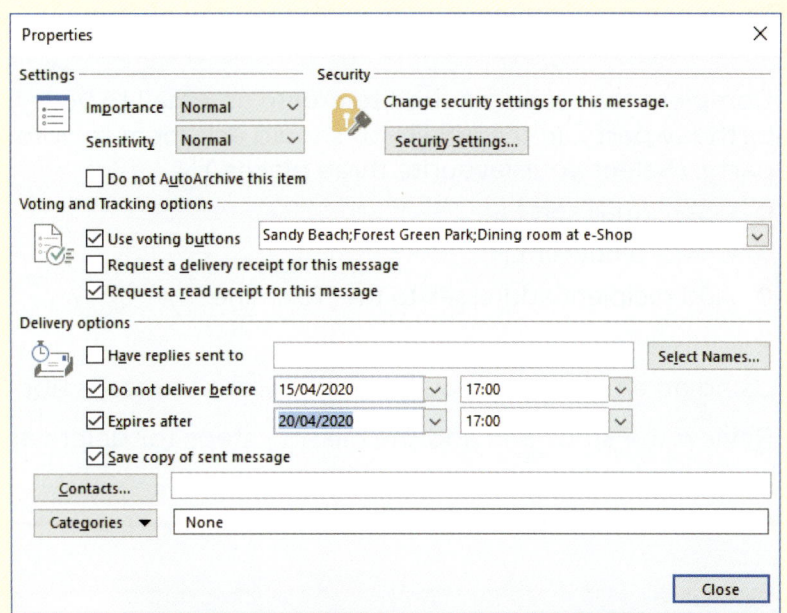

You can see that the options 'Sandy Beach, Forest Green Park, Dining Room at e-Shop' are entered in the 'Use voting buttons' box.

As the secretary has asked for a read receipt, when the email is opened, staff will be asked for a read receipt.

When you send an email you do not have to send it immediately. You can delay sending it. The secretary wants the email to be sent at 17:00 so that employees do not discuss it during the working day. So, the 'Do not deliver before' box has been ticked and a date and time have been entered.

On receiving this email, staff will be able to vote using a 'Vote' button. The Vote button will show the options and the staff member can make their choice. When they make a selection a message box confirming their selection is shown.

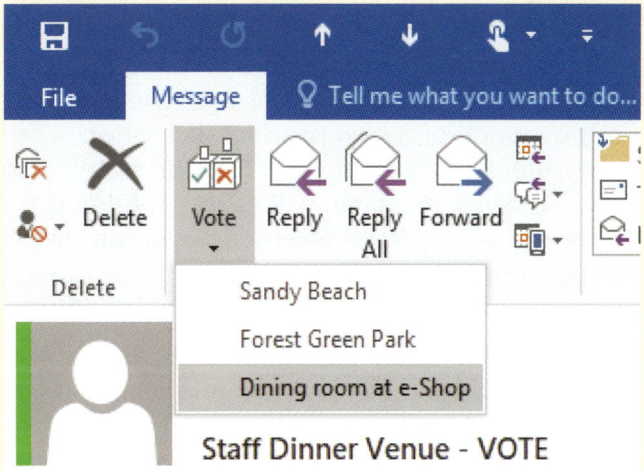

The secretary will also receive a read receipt.

Afterwards, the secretary can track responses using the tracking button. Votes are automatically counted.

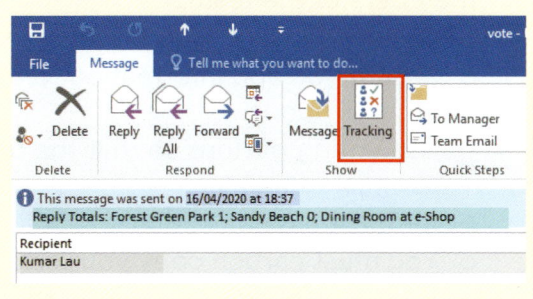

Decomposition and algorithmic thinking

Complete the steps required to create an email to your friends inviting them to your birthday party. In the email you should ask them to vote for one of three places for the party. (Select your favourite three places.)

✪ Open email software

✪ Create a new email

✪ Add recipient addresses to the 'To ...' line

✪ ....

Using an email tool of your choice, try out the steps above.

Review the steps and add the missing steps (or delete any unnecessary steps).

Make sure the steps are in the correct order.

Practice

Using an email application of your choice, complete the following tasks.

➤ Research how you create a distribution list in your email application. Then create a distribution list of three of your friends and draft an email which will inform them of the launch of a new product at e-Shop. The email should invite them to the launch which is going to be held at a top hotel. Guests should dress for dinner and a celebrity will attend. (You can select the hotel and the celebrity to include in your email.) Send the email to your three friends via the distribution list.

➤ As editor of your school's online magazine, you must email all of the team members about the front page story for this month's magazine. The suggested themes are:

o **successful sporting pupils**: an article about the three top athletes in the school.

o **musician of the year**: an article about the best musician in the school.

o **artists' corner**: an article about the new Art Club which has started in the school.

Using an email tool of your choice, create an email about the story and send it to the members of the team.

o Choose three of your friends as team members and set up a distribution list.

o Ensure you add information to the 'Subject' line which will tell the team what the email is about.

o Use voting buttons so that the team members can vote for one of the three suggested themes.

o Request a read receipt.

o You must carbon copy your class teacher into all emails about the magazine.

o You must blind carbon copy the web designer into the email because you cannot share the email addresses of pupils or teachers with other people.

Learn

Subject line

The subject line tells the recipient what the email is about. It is important to think about the subject line as you compose an email. People do not want to read a lengthy subject line and most email providers do not show the full subject line. It is important to keep it short to ensure that people want to open your email.

Watch your tone

The tone or mood of the email is important. You need to make sure that the correct message gets across to the recipient. Common mistakes include people writing an email in a hurry. The email can sound too abrupt. Remember you do not have gestures or your voice to support your message in an email.

Compare the following pairs of statements – in each case, both say the same thing but use different tones.

Please send me your monthly report immediately. ✗	Please send me your monthly report immediately – we've got a new boss and he has asked us to produce our papers on time this month! ✓
You promised to send me the final payment yesterday and you still haven't sent it. ✗	I need to sign-off the final payment. Can you please send it now. ✓

Always think carefully about the wording of an email. Read it aloud or print it and read it to ensure the tone is correct.

Know your audience

Emails should be audience-centered. That is, you should take time and think about the people for whom you are writing the email. The target audience should direct the content of the email. You need to think about the age, location and gender of the target audience. This is very important for e-Shop as they use email for marketing. They need to send relevant emails to people.

Email pros and cons

Advantages of using email	Disadvantages of using email
• Emails can be sent anytime. The recipient does not have to wait to receive them. Emails are stored in the inbox for reading at any time. • Emails are delivered instantly to any location in the world and to any number of people using distribution lists. • They are inexpensive and in most cases free. • Filtering of email can be carried out protecting users from junk mail and phishing emails. • The sender can attach any type of file to the email. Sound, graphics and text files can be easily distributed.	• Technology – the sender and recipient must have access to the internet. • It is easy to insert a wrong address into the 'To…' box. A confidential email could be sent to the wrong person. • Spam – unwanted emails selling or advertising products can be sent. This is like electronic junk mail. • Users are not notified of new emails unless they are logged on to the email system.

DID YOU KNOW?

There are more than 3.2 billion email accounts in existence. That's nearly half the population of Earth.

Practice

➤ As e-communications manager, you have received the following two emails from trainees. With a partner, review the emails with regard to tone and state which is most likely to be effective and why.

Email from Trainee 1	Email from Trainee 2
hey, i need help with my training manual, can i come by your office tomorrow thx	Hi Miss Zheng , I am in your trainee class on Wednesdays, and I have a question about the training manual that we have to create for next Tuesday. I'm not sure that I understand what is meant by the following sentence in the question: "Comment on how e-Shop use online communication to provide excellent help to customers." I am not sure what would count as "excellent" help. Can I call to your office tomorrow at 2:00 pm to discuss my question? Please let me know if that suits your schedule. If not, I could also call on Thursday after 3:00. Thank you, Anna Lau

➤ Here are two versions of an email from a supervisor, Jan More, to a group of her staff at e-Shop. With a partner review the emails. Which version do you think is most effective and why?

Version 1 of Jan More's Email	Version 2 of Jan More's Email
Subject: this evening As you know, this evening we'll be meeting to talk about the progress of each of our current projects. Coffee and biscuits will be provided. Please arrive on time and bring the documents you have been working on this week—bring a copy for everyone. Some of these material might include your calendars, reports, and any important emails you have sent. Also, I wanted to remind you that your building access requests are due on Friday; please send these to Ms Gray at reception or if she is not there when you call please email them to her.	**Subject: materials for Friday Project Meeting** Hi, everyone— For tomorrow's 6 p.m. project meeting in the lecture room, please bring 10 copies of the following materials: Your project calendar A one-page report describing your progress so far A list of goals for the next month Copies of any progress report messages you have sent to clients this past month See you tomorrow— Jan

➤ You should discuss the subject line, tone and how appropriate the text of the email is for the intended audience.

➤ Jan has asked to borrow your office for a team meeting. The last time she borrowed it she left the office in quite a mess. Write an email to Jan explaining that she can borrow the office but that she must ensure that she leaves it in a tidy state at the end.

➤ You have received a customer complaint about a product sold by e-Shop. The customer found the product to be broken on receipt. Write an email apologising to the customer and suggesting a way in which you will compensate them.

Learn

Interactive messaging systems

e-Shop also makes use of interactive messaging on its website. The company uses a chat facility to help customers make selections and complete the ordering process. It provides quick, immediate and relevant help using a text window. Customers type their questions and a member of staff at the other end is there to help. Live chat provides a different experience to email. There are no large sections of text and the answers are specific to the question.

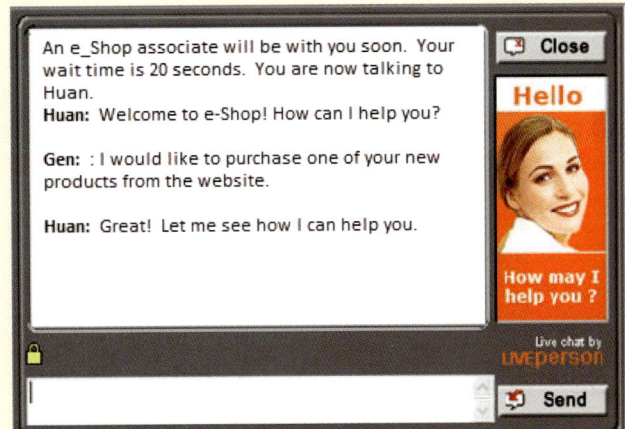

e-Shop uses a messaging app called ChatNow to send notifications to customers. This is cost effective and allows e-Shop to send interactive messages such as videos, products or reviews from customers.

ChatNow can be used to communicate with friends and family. You can do this by setting up a group of people who have joined the app. Text and voice messages can be sent easily to everybody in the group. Users can send stickers, videos or photographs and all members of the group can see them instantly. It is also possible to send any of these items to other users who are not in the group. ChatNow allows you to communicate and respond very quickly with your friends and family.

Pros and cons of messaging apps

Advantages of using messaging apps	Disadvantages of using messaging apps
• It is fast as communication is immediate and mobile phones are used by everybody. • Simple to use even for beginner users. Very little knowledge or experience is required. • More people read messages with notifications than will read email. • **Multimedia** messages containing video, sound, animation and text can be sent.	• Users have to be registered on the app to receive information and they must provide personal details . • Users need to remember to keep their profile private so that only people that they know can contact them. • Staff could use the application to talk to friends during work. • Staff need to be trained in the use of ChatNow, and e-Shop needs to make sure that it protects any details held about customers.

Using Emoji

Emoji is a tool to exhibit **nonverbal communication**. An emoji is a visual representation of an emotion. Emoji are commonly used in informal communications between friends. However, they can be included in more formal email communications to soften the tone. Emoji are useful for overcoming language barriers and expressing emotions. However, they should be used with care in business emails.

e-Shop uses emoji in the interactive chat on the website and on the messaging app, but the company has asked staff not to use them in business emails.

Practice

Recently, e-Shop has launched a new product aimed at 18–30 year old customers. There is a recommendation that the product should be launched using ChatNow. Prepare a report, using a word processor or presentation tool such as *Microsoft PowerPoint*, to present the arguments for and against using ChatNow. Your report should refer to:

➤ the target audience
➤ multimedia
➤ speed of communication.

Video conferencing and VoIP

Learn

Video conferencing (VC)

e-Shop has a number of offices across the world. Every month the senior managers from these offices 'meet' using **video conferencing**.

Video conferencing uses the internet to transmit pictures and sound between computers. Video conferencing can be done using a mobile personal device like a tablet or phone or on a desktop computer using a webcam, speakers and a microphone.

Mobile phone technology with software such as Skype and Facetime has made video conferencing accessible to anyone with a smartphone. e-Shop carries out interviews for new staff using this technology.

Video conferencing can also be carried out using purpose-built video conferencing systems. e-Shop has a video conferencing suite filled with equipment which helps reduce costs for the company.

Using video conferencing means that people based in different locations can 'meet' without travelling. This means that face to face meetings can be held with individuals from different places all over the world. The company saves money on travel and the workers can meet without the inconvenience of travelling.

e-Shop is also concerned about the pollution aspect of travel and so it wants to reduce its carbon footprint. The managing director sees video conferencing as one way to do this.

KEYWORDS

multimedia: a mixture of sound, video, animation and text
nonverbal communication: communication made without speaking such as gestures

Name one example of nonverbal communication.

KEYWORDS

high bandwidth: bandwidth refers to the amount of data that can be transferred on a communications line in a given time
telecommunications link: using technology like fibre optic cables, computers are linked to the internet; the link is the channel that allows communication between computers and the internet

Transmitting pictures and sound together requires a **high bandwidth telecommunications link** such as a fibre optic. Low bandwidth means that the images and sounds will not arrive together and the overall quality of the video will be poor.

Different types of connections provide different bandwidths. For example, a fibre optic connection can carry up to 10 gigabits per second.

> Think of bandwidth as a corridor in your school. The wider the corridor (bandwidth), the more pupils (data) can pass through without stopping.

Pattern recognition

One gigabit is equal to 1 000 000 000 bits. One character can be sent using 8 bits. How many characters could be contained in one gigabit?

Video conferencing requires the following equipment.

➤ A video camera or webcam to transmit pictures.
➤ Microphone and sound system to transmit and receive sound.
➤ A screen to view other participants.
➤ A high bandwidth telecommunications line.
➤ Video conferencing software.

Advantages of video conferencing	Disadvantages of video conferencing
• Allows collaboration with team members across the world. • Allows collaboration with people from other companies. • Visual and audio contact means that meetings are more like normal face-to-face meetings. • Full multimedia presentations can be shared during meetings (for example, someone can share their computer screen containing a presentation). • Meetings can be set up on-demand by connecting up to the videolink. • No travel costs for the company. • No travel time for the employees.	• High cost for initial setup. • Specialist training may be required to make use of a purpose-built VC system. • Network performance may be poor when VC is in operation. • A high bandwidth is required to ensure good performance.

Voice over Internet Protocol (VoIP)

VoIP enables you to use the internet to make telephone calls. A major advantage of this type of phone call is that charges are not incurred for individual calls.

All sales staff at e-Shop have company smartphones. The company has instructed them to use VoIP when calling clients. VoIP calls can be made on a wide range of devices, including a tablet, mobile phone and laptop. The device must be connected to the internet.

Using VoIP you can call anyone, anywhere on any type of telephone or network.

The call will sound the same as an ordinary telephone call. If you call someone on another VoIP device the call quality is much better than an ordinary call because voice signals are being transmitted digitally.

When a person is speaking into a **microphone** the sound that their voice makes is converted to electrical currents that are in analogue format. A computer can only accept data that is in digital format therefore the electrical signal must be converted. An analogue to digital converter (ADC) is used to do this. The ADC is normally a **sound card** inside the computer.

The ADC converts the electrical signals from the microphone into digital data that the computer can understand. For more information on how an ADC works see section 8.1.

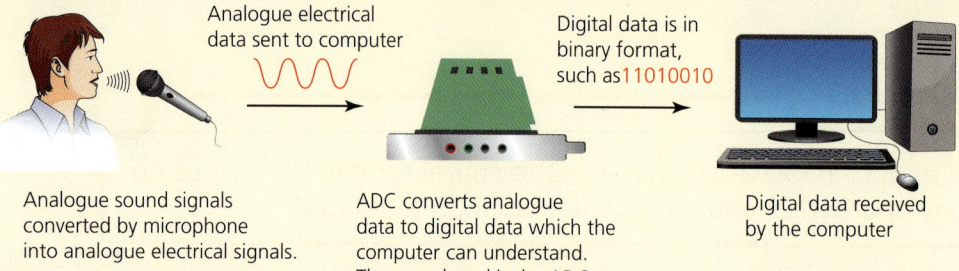

Analogue electrical data sent to computer

Digital data is in binary format, such as 11010010

Analogue sound signals converted by microphone into analogue electrical signals.

ADC converts analogue data to digital data which the computer can understand. The sound card is the ADC.

Digital data received by the computer

KEYWORDS

microphone: an input device used to enter sound into a computer

sound card: a hardware device inside a computer which can convert analogue sound signals to digital data

Practice

➤ As e-communications manager you have been asked to create a guidance document for staff about VoIP and video conferencing. Open the document called **VCVOIP.docx**, provided by your teacher, and complete the document using the information you have about VC and VoIP technologies.

➤ e-Shop wants to replace their current VC suite with a new HD VC system. Using the internet, research the new HD technology and provide a one page report which shows:
- o current prices for HD VC equipment
- o the features of HD VC equipment
- o the system that you would recommend for the company
- o a photograph of your recommended system.

Keeping it all social

Learn

Social media plays an important role in e-Shop's marketing strategy. The company uses Facebook, Twitter, Instagram and many of its employees are members of LinkedIn.

e-Shop has added a link back to the website and is hoping to achieve increased sales and increased traffic to the website. In turn, if the number of customers visiting the website increases they should see an improved **ranking** on search engines.

KEYWORDS

ranking: the position in which the company's website sits when an internet search is done. The higher the ranking the more popular the website is

Choose a topic and Google it. Which site is ranked number 1?

Multimedia and two-way conversation is possible within social media, leading to greater customer engagement.

This, in turn, will bring an opportunity to conduct market research about the customers and help improve products and services.

Social media helps e-Shop to reach a larger number of customers world-wide. This has led to greater access to international markets and improved networking opportunities with customers and other businesses. e-Shop wants to take advantage of this and is thinking about using **social influencers** to help market their products.

Successful social influencers spend a lot of time building trust with their followers. Followers become loyal and they believe in the person they are following. As a result they trust their recommendations and are likely to purchase the products they recommend.

Businesses collect data about our online activities as we move through social media applications. This data helps them to create a profile on our online or browsing habits. We create a **digital footprint**.

The data generated by all the users of a social network is vast and is described as **big data**. The 3Vs (**volume**, **variety** and **velocity**) are three defining properties of big data:

➤ volume refers to the amount of data

➤ variety refers to the number of types of data

➤ velocity refers to the speed of data processing.

KEYWORDS

social influencers: individuals who make use of social media and whose opinions and actions can influence other users of social media

Name a social influencer that you follow.

digital footprint: the digital data held about a person as a result of their online activity

big data: the large volume of data that is created by digital devices and websites every day; it is analysed using computer programs

volume: the amount of data generated

variety: the number of different types of data generated

velocity: the speed of data processing

Practice

As e-communications manager you have decided to use social influencers to improve e-Shop's marketing. These people are usually well known on social media and will help the company promote some of its products to particular groups of people. Many of the staff do not understand what you mean by 'social influencer'. So you have decided to find two examples of these people and present their stories to the staff.

➤ Using the internet, research and identify two young social influencers who are helping businesses to market their products. You should identify the companies they work with and how they have helped the company. Prepare a poster about the two young influencers which you can display in the marketing department. The poster should explain their role in marketing e-Shop's products.

➤ Produce a questionnaire for adults to complete to collect information on the ways they make use of each of the social media applications (at home and at work, for their social and working lives).

➤ Social media has impacted most businesses. They use it to advertise their products and build customer loyalty.

Companies also use it to organise contests and give away prizes. Use the internet to research and find two companies who target young people in this way.

➤ Use your research findings to complete the document **socialmedia.docx**, provided by your teacher.

➤ Technology has changed the way in which we live and work. Digital media, such as photographs and videos, can be sent around the world in seconds and can be easily copied for free. Research each of the following music recording devices. Then create a timeline, showing how the recording of music has evolved. Include: 4-Track (Stereo-Pak), 8 Track, MP3, Blu-ray disc, Compact cassette, Compact disc, and DVD.

➤ Here is an example of a timeline template. You would need to replace the text and dates with your own.

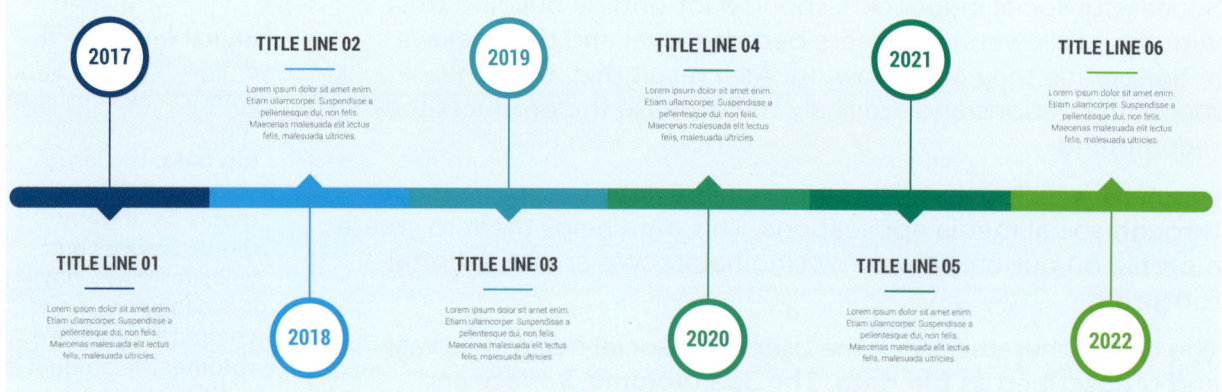

➤ You could use a graphics package, such as *Adobe Photoshop*, or a word processor to create your timeline. Your timeline should include a picture of each device, the year in which it was created and a description of how it works. Identify clearly the different digital music formats.

➤ Discuss with a friend whether, due to social media, the musician's work is better protected now or in the past.

➤ Using social media generates big data. Data, such as a person's location, age and gender, can be collected when they use social media.

o Suggest **two** other pieces of data that might be collected.

o How could the company use these data items to help sell its products?

How does it all happen?

Learn

Staff within an organisation need to know how to use the technology safely and how to protect the data on the networks from cyber attack.

Networks: LANs and WANs

Networks are collections of computers and other hardware connected together. Organisations use networks to share information and resources. Networks are supported by a variety of hardware and software without which they could not function.

e-Shop's communication is supported by different types of networks. A network is made up of a number of computers linked together using wireless or wired connections. Computers which are linked together like this are able to share devices like printers and scanners. They can also communicate with each other.

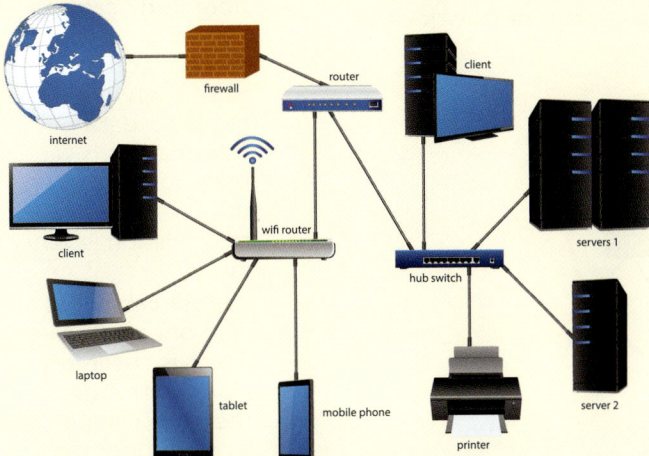

There are different types of networks. Some are made up of just a few computers linked together. Others have many computers linked together in one building or school. These are called **local area networks (LANs)** because they are linked together on a single site or small geographic area.

Data is transmitted from one computer to another along the network cables or wireless connections.

e-Shop uses computers connected to a LAN rather than **standalone computers**. It is more convenient for the company to organise its computers like this because:

➤ expensive **peripherals** (such as printers) can be shared between computers; for example, one printer or scanner can be used by several computers on the network

➤ software is stored on the **file server** and this is shared by all the computers on the network; the file server is the most powerful computer on the network – it is used to communicate with and manage all of the other computers

➤ a network allows users to communicate with each other via email or video conferencing

➤ users can share files and work on joint projects using shared resources and folders on the network; these files and folders are stored on the file server

➤ users can log on to any computer on the network and access their files.

DID YOU KNOW?

The internet allows communication between any device on any continent regardless of oceans or mountains. This is possible because the data can travel over long distances using fibre optic cables underground and under the ocean. Cables have been laid as deep as 8000 metres under the ocean. These cables are coated in layers of metal tubing, plastic, rubber and other substances to protect them.

KEYWORDS

standalone computers: computers which are not connected to a network

peripherals: hardware connected to a network such as printers and scanners.

Which peripherals do you use at home?

file server: the main computer on the network; it is more powerful than all of the other computers with a large amount of RAM and hard disk space

A wired connection uses a physical link, like copper cables or fibre optic cables, to connect computers. A wireless connection uses Wi-Fi, Bluetooth or satellite to connect computers.

A **wide area network (WAN)** is a network of networks which extends over a large geographic area. A WAN is connected using a cabled or wireless link. Since they cover a large area, **satellite links** or **fibre optic cable** are more likely to be used because of their capacity to carry data over longer distances.

The internet itself is a WAN, consisting of a global network of computers.

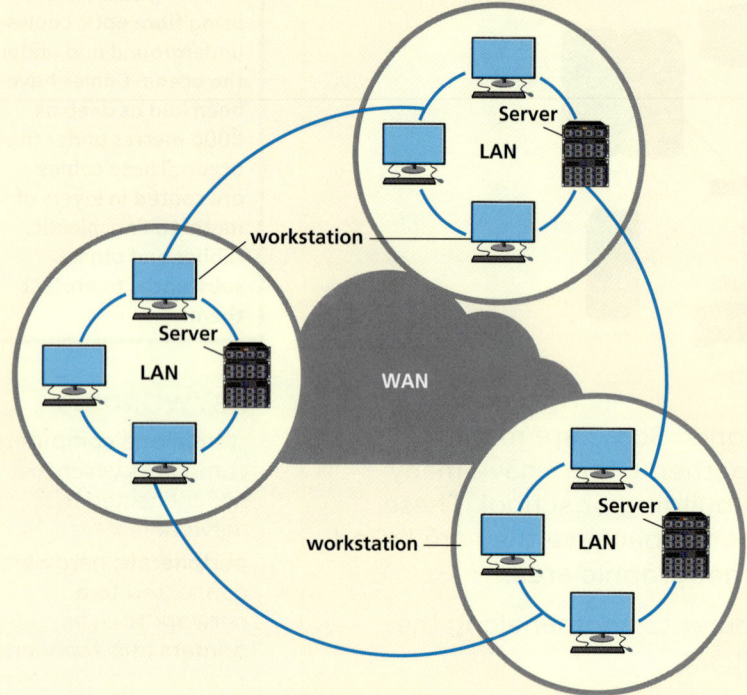

e-Shop needs to be connected to the internet, which is a WAN. This is because e-Shop has customers all over the world who need to be able to order online and communicate with them. They could not use email, video conferencing, VoIP or other communication technology without the internet. e-Shop's website is also available via the internet.

Main differences between LANs and WANs

A LAN is spread over a small geographic area, usually one or two buildings.	A WAN is spread over a vast geographic area over countries or the world.
Computers on a LAN are normally linked together using **copper cabling** or wireless technology.	A WAN is a network of networks – these networks are often linked together using fibre optic cable or satellite links.

How do WANs and LANs talk to each other?

Computers and networks which communicate with each other must 'speak the same language'. A **communications protocol** is an agreed standard (or set of rules) for sending and receiving data on a network. If a computer receives data on a network, it must support the communications protocol of the sending computer.

KEYWORDS

satellite link: a radio link between one station transmitting on Earth and another through a satellite

fibre optic cable: a cable with a glass or Perspex core used to link networks together; data transmission is via light signals and the speed of data transmission is very fast

copper cable: has a core of copper wires which is covered in plastic or rubber; the wires can be twisted together; data transmission is through the use of electrical signals; copper cable is cheaper than fibre optic cabling but the speed of data transmission is much slower

communications protocol: an agreed standard or set of rules for sending or receiving data on a network

router: a piece of networking equipment that shares a network connection between devices; it can be wired or wireless and allows a LAN to connect to the internet

Practice

You have been promoted within e-Shop and are now responsible for global training in the area of digital communication and networks. e-Shop has asked you to travel across the world to provide specialist training in a range of new areas.

As part of your new job, e-Shop has asked you to talk to two new trainee technicians. The technicians are new to the job and do not know much about networks. Create a presentation for them which will answer each of the following questions.

➤ What is a LAN?
➤ What are the advantages of having a LAN?
➤ What devices does e-Shop have connected to the LAN?
➤ Why does e-Shop need to be connected to a WAN?
➤ The importance of communications protocols for e-Shop's business.

> This section should mention the use of communications technology, its importance to e-Shop and the impact on the company if there is no WAN connection. You should also mention the website and online selling.

Your presentation must include pictures, sound and text to explain each of the above.

You can use a presentation tool, such as *Microsoft PowerPoint* or *Google Slides*, or you could create a movie with software such as *Windows Movie Maker*, with pictures and a voiceover.

Checking it out online

Learn

To connect to the internet you need both hardware and software. As well as a computer, e-Shop needs to have:

➤ web browser software
➤ an **internet service provider (ISP)**
➤ a wired or wireless connection
➤ a hub or router.

KEYWORD

internet service provider (ISP): a company who provides users with an internet connection for a subscription fee

DID YOU KNOW?

The protocol used on the internet is called Transmission Control Protocol / Internet Protocol (TCP/IP). The protocol used to transmit data around a LAN may be different. A router connects the LAN to the internet and allows these two networks, which may use different protocols, to communicate.

HTTP means Hypertext Transfer Protocol. This is the protocol used for data transfer on the world wide web.

HTTPS means Hypertext Transfer Protocol Secure. This is the protocol used for secure communication on the world wide web, for example, when credit card details are being entered. We can usually tell when a website uses https as there is usually a padlock symbol beside the website address.

DID YOU KNOW?

ISPs can see all of the data you generate when you browse the internet. They can see the websites that you visit and the material that you view. Over time they could build up a profile of your browsing habits.

What is the name of the ISP you use?

A website address or URL is made up of several different parts.

https://www.amazon.com/gp/help/customer/display.html

| Protocol | The domain name stored on a domain name server (DNS) | The folder where the web page is located | The web page requested |

When a website address is typed into the browser:

➤ The computer sends the request for the web page to the router.

➤ The router passes the request to the ISP which looks up the domain name on a domain name server (DNS). The DNS converts the text-based URL (such as www.amazon.com) to a numeric IP address (such as 108.174.10.10). The IP address describes the location of the server for the website that has been requested.

➤ The IP address is returned to the browser which sends a request via the ISP to the particular server identified in the IP address for the web page.

➤ The server containing the web page has a folder and file structure just like on your own computer. The final part of the URL contains the details of this folder structure and exactly where on the server to find the web page.

An internet service provider (ISP) is a company which provides internet access to businesses or individuals for a fee. This access is normally provided by connecting a router to the internet via a copper or fibre optic cable. The ISP can provide a range of services such as:

➤ a variety of **bandwidth** options – which means different download and upload speeds

➤ an email service

➤ a security package; this can include protection against hacking, viruses, spyware and identity theft

➤ **cloud storage** facility

➤ a **domain hosting service** which allows users to upload their own web pages

➤ online and telephone assistance

➤ **website filtering** and **parental controls**.

When a user selects an ISP they may need to install the software for that ISP onto their computer. This allows the computer to communicate through a hub or router to an internet file server, enabling the user to browse different websites.

Internet Service Providers include: CMC Telecom, FPT, Expereo and Hanoi Telecom.

DID YOU KNOW?

IPv4 and IPv6 are used to create IP addresses. IPv4 is displayed in decimal whereas IPv6 is displayed in hexadecimal. IPv6 was introduced because IPv4 could not provide addresses for all the new devices connecting to the internet. IPv4 is limited in the number of addresses it can represent whereas IPv6 has an almost unlimited number of addresses available.

IPv4 sample address: 13.243.232.166

Each dot separates an 8 bit binary number which is displayed in decimal. So IPv4 is made of four 8 bit numbers.

IPv6 sample address: 2003:0bd7:0000:0000:0 000:ff00:0043:6879

Each semicolon separates a 16 bit binary number which is displayed in hexadecimal. So IPv6 is made of eight 16 bit numbers.

For more on binary and hexadecimal, see unit 8.1.

KEYWORDS

cloud storage: online storage space for files and documents

Which types of cloud storage do you use?

domain hosting service: a service where users can upload their own website and make it available on the internet

Practice

- ➤ Find the IP address of a computer.
  - o Use a Windows computer.
  - o Press the Windows Start key to open the start menu.
  - o Type cmd and press Enter.
  - o Type ipconfig/all (this will provide the network card settings on your computer).
  - o The MAC address and the IPv4 address will be listed.
  - o Take a photograph or screenshot and compare your result with another pupil in class.
- ➤ Using the internet, find out what a MAC address is.
- ➤ Use your photograph or screen shot and create an electronic poster which explains what the IPv4 and MAC addresses are.
- ➤ Email your poster to a friend and ask them to review it to ensure it is accurate and error free.

Web browsers

Learn

e-Shop's business is supported by the internet and a website. The website design needs to be updated every year. When the website is updated, e-Shop must test the new version in different browsers to make sure it works well.

A web browser is software which allows users to view and use the web pages on the internet. The web pages are usually in **Hypertext Markup Language (HTML)** format.

HTML is a programming language used to create web pages. Web pages can contain **hypertext** which provides the user with clickable links to other pages on the web. Sound, video, animation and graphics can also be embedded in the HTML web page.

There are many different web browsers available. Some of the most widely used include Firefox, Google Chrome, Safari and Opera.

Features of a typical web browser:

- ➤ **Address bar** – the user can enter the web address or URL of the website they want to visit. Smart address bars will suggest sites already visited if the user types the first few letters of the URL. The URL is converted to an IP address as described above.

You can find more about HTML in unit 8.3.

KEYWORDS

website filtering: software which enables websites to be allowed or blocked based on their content

parental controls: rules, set by parents, which govern the websites that are allowed to be viewed on a device

Give an example of a parental control.

Hypertext Markup Language (HTML): the language used to create web pages

hypertext: clickable links on a web page

meta tags: a coding statement that describes some of the content on the web page; this can be used by search engines to help identify if the page should be returned in a search

➤ **Search engine** – the user can enter text into the search engine box and the search engine will search the internet for other web pages containing that text. If a match is found, links to the web pages are displayed. The user can click on these links to visit the relevant websites.

Meta tags allow people who create web pages to specify special words in the heading of the HTML page. These words will help the search engine categorise the page and decide whether or not to include it in the results for a particular search.

Using a search engine to search for information can return many links. You can reduce the number of search results by thinking carefully about keywords to include in your search. This will refine your search and return the most relevant websites.

➤ **Navigation bar** – allows the user to move between the web pages visited. For example, the user should be able to:
- go back and forward to previous web pages
- refresh a web page
- set a homepage (this is the page that will automatically load when the browser is opened; the user can return to this web page at any time by pressing the home button or icon).

➤ **Bookmark option** – where the user can keep a list of their favourite websites by adding the URL to a list. The user can open a list of bookmarks and go directly to the website.

➤ **History button** – the user can click on the history button to see a list of web pages visited; normally, the user can set the number of days that web addresses are stored in the history list.

➤ **Customisation** – most browsers will allow you to change the appearance of the browser. For example, the theme or colour, font size and page zoom can all be changed.

This is a simple browser showing a search engine page. The browser can be customised using the setting feature shown.

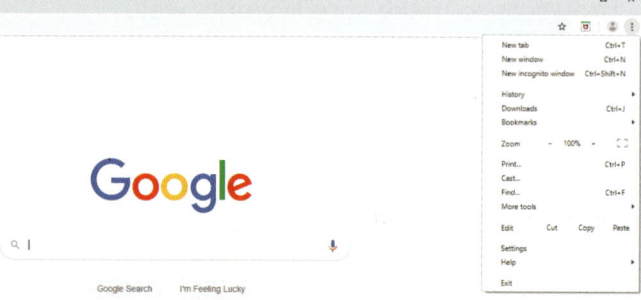

- Browser software can also allow content to be filtered. For example, content, language and whole websites can be filtered.
- Users can decide if they wish to have certain buttons showing on the browser, for example, a link to their email, bookmarks or homepage.
- Privacy settings are very important and these can be customised. For instance, users can turn on private browsing. This means that any websites visited are not stored in the history list. You may want to stop cookies

DID YOU KNOW?
Web browsers can be used to view HTML pages whether they are online or offline.
In 2020, around 65% of users used Google Chrome.

from being installed on the home computer used by children so that online advertisers can't track their browsing habits. The privacy settings on your web browser can be changed so that cookies are not installed. This setting can usually be found in the Tools section of a browser.

- Users can add toolbars to the browser, for example, the Google Toolbar and manage security settings.

Practice

As e-communications manager you want to create a resource for colleagues to help them understand the key features of a web browser.

Review two different browsers such as Google Chrome and Safari.

List the features that each browser provides and note any differences.

Create a dictionary showing the features of a browser. The dictionary should have images demonstrating the main features and hyperlinks to sample browsers.

Using technology safely

Learn

Staff at e-Shop spend a lot of time at a computer. Some staff deal with customer orders and spend a lot of time looking at orders online. Other staff are responsible for updating the website, for example, changing prices, adding new products and removing old ones. Without the right advice on using computers safely, employees in these roles could develop health problems. It is important that employers make sure employees are safe at work.

e-Shop has created a Health and Safety at Work team. The function of the team is to make staff aware of how to avoid health problems and injuries that can arise because of prolonged use of computer technology.

The team are meeting with a number of employees who have developed some health problems. The team intend to observe the employees at work to try to help resolve the problems. The company doctor, Dr Kecheng, will give advice on how these problems can be avoided and a leaflet will be created from the information collected.

Here are some of the problems the team and Dr Kecheng have seen:

John, a web designer

Symptoms: Sore arms, shoulders and neck. His wrists are also sore.

Diagnosis: RSI – repetitive strain injury, caused when an employee has been using the same muscle group to perform the same actions over and over again, such as working at a keyboard all day.

Treatment: Take regular breaks, use an ergonomically designed keyboard and mouse, Use a wrist rest underneath the keyboard and a foot rest.

Joy, a sales executive

Symptoms: Headaches, blurred vision and worsening eyesight.

It was observed that Joy's work rate decreased as the day went on.

Diagnosis: Eyestrain.

Treatment: Use on anti-glare screen; make sure the screen has a swivel base to deflect light; use screens that have adjustable brightness and contrast; have good lighting in the office; Have regular eye tests.

Min the receptionist

Symptoms: Occasionally she appears to have mobility problems.

Min has been observed to have poor posture while sitting at the computer for prolonged periods.

Diagnosis: Back pain

Treatment: Use adjustable chairs that allow height adjustment and backrest tilting.

Take regular breaks and regularly exercise affected muscles.

Take training for improving desk posture.

Practice

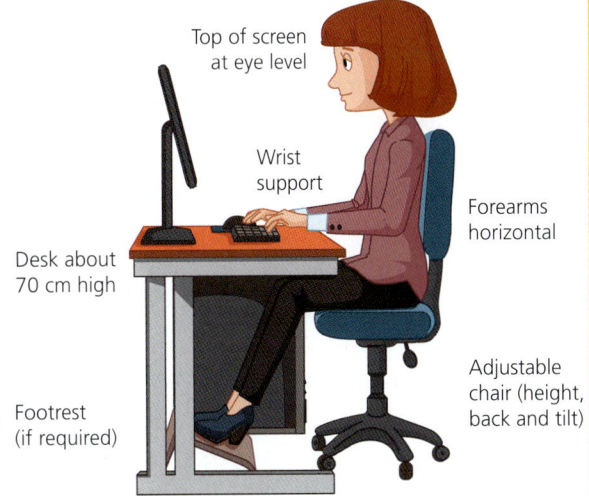

- ➤ The team have created this graphic to help staff understand the way in which they should use their computers to avoid health problems. This will be used on social media and the staff area of the website.

- ➤ Work in a team of four. e-Shop is going to tweet the graphic with a message for employees about their health and safety. Compose:
  - o a message for Twitter (less than 280 characters) that will accompany the graphic to help ensure employees are safe at work
  - o an email to the Managing Director which asks him to review the staff workstations to make sure they are safe for staff to use; your email should explain some of the problems that can be caused if workstation design is not right.

Labels on graphic: Top of screen at eye level; Wrist support; Forearms horizontal; Desk about 70 cm high; Adjustable chair (height, back and tilt); Footrest (if required)

Cyber security

Learn

Cyber crime

Cyber crime is the use computers to commit an act which is against the law. e-Shop has a global business which would be badly affected if it was a victim of cyber crime. So, it has strict rules relating to the protection of its systems and data.

Despite these rules, on a number of occasions there have been cyber attacks on the company. The network managers (responsible for all the devices and software on the network and ensuring that it runs without problems) across a number of countries met via video conference to discuss the issues. The following problems were identified.

Malware

A number of customers reported that **malware** had been downloaded from emails received from e-Shop. Malware is malicious software which is unintentionally downloaded onto a computer via an email or portable storage device like a USB drive. Malware is a generic term for different types of

KEYWORDS

cyber crime: a malicious attack on a computer system

malware: software designed to damage a computer system or its data

malicious software which includes **viruses**, **worms**, **spyware** and **keyloggers**.

➤ A virus is a program which has been designed to damage a computer when executed.

➤ A worm is a virus which replicates itself so that it can spread to other computers. A worm can arrive as a spam email message. The process of replicating itself will use system resources and slow the computer or network down.

➤ Spyware is software designed to take information from a computer without the knowledge of the user. The spyware software will pass the information on.

➤ A keylogger is a program which logs every keystroke made on a computer. In the hands of a hacker, it could be used to steal passwords and PINs.

Phishing

Customers also reported receiving **phishing** emails asking them to update their personal details using a hyperlink. Phishing emails look to be from a reliable source but when users click on the links they are taken to fake websites. If they enter their details on the fake website (such as a password) then the criminals gain access to their real accounts and all their personal details.

Pharming

Customers have also been subjected to **pharming** where their web browsers have been redirected to fraudulent websites instead of the real e-Shop website.

Spyware

Staff at a number of locations have detected spyware on their computer. The spyware was downloaded without their knowledge and used an internet connection to collect information about their online activity. Staff were concerned that the spyware could have collected data such as credit card numbers.

DDoS

Network managers at two locations have reported disrupted connections to their web servers. They believe this to be a **distributed denial of service (DDoS)** which is a malicious attack on a network that can prevent users from logging on to access their data. When you hear about a website being 'brought down' it is usually because it has suffered a DDoS attack. Hackers use malware to generate millions of bogus requests for access to the website. The aim of the attack is to stop the website from working by flooding it with more network traffic than it can handle. The website will eventually crash.

KEYWORDS

virus: a program which gains access to a computer and seeks to damage the computer system or collect data

Tell a partner about a time when one of your devices got a virus.

worm: a malicious software application which spreads across computer networks; typically used when an email attachment is opened and the program is activated

spyware: software that gathers information about a person or organisation without their permission. The software is usually downloaded without the user's knowledge

keylogger: a malicious software application which collects the keystrokes that a person is typing typically used to find out peoples' passwords

phishing: sending fake emails to capture personal details

pharming: redirecting users to fake websites to capture personal details

distributed denial of service (DDoS): an attack on a network that can prevent users from logging on to access their data

Data security

The network managers have identified three areas where the company could improve in terms of **data security**.

Encryption

Data which is being transmitted across a WAN or a LAN could be intercepted and read by unauthorised users. To prevent this, data can be **encrypted**. Encryption is the process of encoding data which is to be sent across a network, making that data unreadable to anyone who intercepts it. Only a user with the **encryption key** software can read the data when it arrives at its destination.

Encrypting data whilst it is travelling on the network is one way of keeping data secure. Data can also be stored in encrypted form. This means that users can only read the data if they have access to the special software which will decrypt or decode the data.

Algorithmic thinking

An encryption key is needed to decode messages received. Using the key below, decode this message:

GPETARVKPI FCVC KU HWP

LETTER	A	B	C	D	E	F	G	H	I	J	K	L	M
CODE	C	D	E	F	G	H	I	J	K	L	M	N	O

LETTER	N	O	P	Q	R	S	T	U	V	W	X	Y	Z
CODE	P	Q	R	S	T	U	V	W	X	Y	Z	A	B

Create your own encryption key and use it to create a message. Ask a friend to decode the message using the key you have created.

Firewalls

A **firewall** can be a hardware device or a software program. It monitors and filters data entering and leaving a network. It uses security settings or rules which block data which does not comply with the organisation's security policy. It can prevent:

➤ **hackers** from entering the network via the internet

➤ viruses and **spam** from entering the network via the internet

Give an example of some spam you have recently received.

➤ users/computers within the network from uploading data onto the internet.

Levels of access

Another way of keeping the network secure is to limit the activities different users can perform by allocating **levels of access**. For example sales staff, managers and network managers have different levels of access.

A sales person can:
➤ access software and the internet
➤ change their password, and the content and location of their user files
➤ connect and use printers portable storage devices.

A manager can do everything that a sales person can and also:
➤ give users printer credits
➤ reset user passwords
➤ monitor user activity using special software
➤ set up shared folders for staff to use.

The system manager can do everything a sales person and manager can do and also:
➤ set up new users and delete or disable existing users
➤ change the amount of disk storage that each user is allocated
➤ copy files between users
➤ allocate network resources such as printers
➤ connect new devices to the network
➤ install software.

KEYWORD

levels of access: limiting the activities different users can perform on the computer system, based on their role in the organisation

Practice

Produce an infographic which illustrates the main threats to online users and the methods available to help secure online communications.

Go further

e-Shop staff need to know about the problems that could arise if email is not used properly. You have been asked by the Managing Director to try to find out how much staff know about email.

◆ Create a phishing email which you will send to all staff.
 ❏ The email should have a suitable subject which will trick staff into thinking it is a genuine email.
 ❏ The email should have an attachment containing incorrect information about the company.
◆ Create a pharming email which you will send to all staff.
 ❏ The email should contain a message which redirects all staff to www.hoddereducation.com – however the staff must not realise that they are being redirected there.

◆ Create a final email explaining to staff what pharming and phishing emails are, and why they should not respond to emails that ask for personal details.

Create a table of information for a photo that you have stored. Use these headings:

File name	File type	File size	Additional data provided by the photo, such as location data	Description of the image

◆ How could your friend make use of the data above?
◆ How could a business like e-Shop make use of the data above?
◆ How does this picture contribute to your digital footprint?

Open the document called **networkdata.docx**, provided by your teacher. Complete the table so that you have information on the hardware and software components in your school's computer system and how they communicate with each other. Include an image of the device.

Give your table to a friend to review.

You have been called to an interview for the Network Manager's job at your school. Your friend will interview you.

The interview will last five minutes and your friend must ask you five questions about the information you have collected in your table.

At the end of the interview discuss whether or not you should get the job and why.

Digital data

Challenge yourself

Data in a computer is represented in binary format. As you know, a bit is a single binary digit which can have a value of 1 or 0. Since there are only two values, the binary system counts using base 2. (We normally count using base 10 as there are ten digits 0–9.)

Counting using base 2 means that we use powers of two. For example:

	2^{10}	2^9	2^8	2^7	2^6	2^5	2^4	2^3	2^2	2^1	2^0
Base 10 value	1024	512	256	128	64	32	16	8	4	2	0

Use a calculator to verify that the decimal values above are correct.

A byte is made up of 8 bits.

8 bits = 1 byte

1	0	0	1	1	0	1	1

A byte can represent a single character such as the letter 'H'.

1 kilobyte (kB) = 10^3 bytes = 1000 bytes.

1 megabyte (MB) = 1000 kB

1 gigabyte (GB) = 1000 MB

Computer storage and memory is measured in MB and GB.

➤ Calculate the amount of storage needed to store a file with 1 million characters in it. Give your answer in kB.

➤ How much space will be left on a 1GB disk if a user stores files which take up 20 000 kB?

➤ How many bits are there in 10 kilobytes?

➤ 1 terabyte is the next largest unit after gigabyte. Can you guess how many gigabytes are in a terabyte? Create a graphic in the shape of a triangle which shows the units of storage starting with 1 bit at the top of the triangle moving down to 1 terabyte.

➤ Examine a file which you have stored on your computer system. Calculate the number of bits stored in the file.

Data transfer speeds

The names and abbreviations for numbers of bytes can be confused with those used for bits.

➤ When referring to bits we use a lower-case 'b'

➤ When referring to bytes we use an upper-case 'B'

As one byte is made up of eight bits, the difference can be significant.

For example, if a broadband internet connection is advertised with a download speed of 5.0 Mbps, its speed is 5.0 megabits per second.

To convert the value to megabytes per second we must divide by 8.

So the internet connection speed is 0.625 megabytes per second (which would be abbreviated as 0.625 MBps).

You need to look carefully at these values when comparing internet connection speeds.

Pattern recognition

Data transfer speeds are normally measured in bits per second not bytes per second but the same prefixes are used; for example,

1 kilobit (kbps) = 1000 bits per second

1 megabit (Mbps) = 1 000 000 bits per second or 1000 kbps

1 gigabit (Gbps) = 1 000 000 000 bits per second or 1000 Mbps

✪ If an internet connection is advertised as having a speed of 1.5 MBps what is its speed in Mbps?

✪ Create a poster entitled 'Gigabit or Gigabyte?' and explain the difference between the two units. Your poster should include an explanation of:
  o the terms bit and byte and how they relate to each other
  o the difference between gigabit and gigabyte using the correct abbreviations
  o what gigabit and gigabyte are used for in computer systems.

Final project

WonderLife Cruises is a new luxury cruise company. The company has six ships which rank among the largest in the world. The company intends to make extensive use of digital communications systems for business purposes. Before the company opened, the owner had a state of the art website constructed. The website will be used to sell cruises and there will be a section where staff can log on to find out information.

Your challenge, as an e-communications expert, is to provide advice about the use of communication tools within the company.

➤ Create a report or presentation with three sections. Each section should contain the following information.

- **Section 1: The use of email in the workplace**
  This section should:
  - state how professional emails should be written
  - explain phishing and pharming
  - explain why employees should be vigilant when reading emails containing attachments or requests for personal information.

- **Section 2: The advantages of using social media in business**
  This section should:
  - explain about the data that is captured about customers on social media
  - suggest how the company could use this data
  - recommend two social media apps that would be suitable for the company to use.

- **Section 3: The equipment required for video conferencing**
  This section should:
  - list the equipment required for video conferencing
  - explain how bandwidth can affect video conferencing
  - explain how the company could use the technology
  - explain the benefits of video conferencing to the company and to the environment.

Your presentation or report could make use of hyperlinks from a main page to each of the sections above.

➤ You have been asked to speak to the staff on board the cruise ships about cyber security. In groups of four, discuss the cyber security issues that may occur for the company. You should include information about:

- attack from malware
- attack from hackers
- how encryption could help protect customer data
- how encryption could be used, using a simple example.

At the end of your discussion, create a list of potential cyber security threats to WonderLife Cruises if they make use of digital communications.

➤ Use the list of threats created in the discussion above to make a list of measures that the company can take to prevent breaches of security. For each threat you have mentioned you must include a measure which will protect the company.

➤ Add this new section to your report or presentation.

➤ WonderLife Cruises wants to design a healthy work space for the captain of the cruise ship. Draw a simple block diagram showing how his desk should be arranged. Include instructions to help the company organise his work space.

Evaluation

➤ Read your report and ensure that it is complete by ensuring that you have included all of the detail required above.

➤ The purpose of your report or presentation was to provide advice on the use of digital communications to the company. The members of staff must understand the challenges associated with using things like email and social media.

➤ Prepare a typed set of questions that you would ask someone to ensure they understood the messages in your report or presentation. Your questions should be made up of:

  o one question about Section 1

  o two questions about Section 2

  o one question about Section 3

  o two questions about cyber security threats and measures.

➤ Give a verbal summary of your report to a group of four classmates.

➤ Ask your classmates to complete the six questions.

➤ Review the answers to the questions. Do you think your classmates understood the summary? Look at their answers and comment on:

  o the technical information they have include

  o the accuracy of the information they have provided.

➤ Was your report effective in delivering the message?

About HTML and CSS

HTML and **CSS** are used to build websites and web-based applications such as online games, movie streaming applications or online document editing tools. **Website developers** create professional, **interactive web pages** using a HTML and CSS. Once an HTML document is developed it can be viewed using a **web browser application** such as Internet Explorer or Opera. Developers use HTML to add content to their documents and CSS to add style and consistency to a website using templates and master documents. CSS also helps developers change the look and feel of an HTML document so that it can be tailored to different audiences and cultures around the world.

Documents and web pages on the internet are made up from **HTML elements** created using **tags**. Most HTML tags have an opening and closing tag with content placed in between. The tags tell the web browser how to display the content on the screen. For example:

\<h1\>will display text in the browser window like this\</h1\>

`<h6>`will display text in the browser window like this`</h6>`

HTML tags can be used to add text, images, video and sound to web pages.

CSS can be used to change the colour, font and position of text and images on a web page. It is the language used by developers to make sure their applications can be viewed on various screen sizes, such as laptops, mobile phones or tablets.

In this unit you will learn:
- → how to use storyboarding and structure diagrams to plan website content
- → the importance of using templates
- → how to present text in list and table format using HTML
- → the importance of incorporating **accessibility** elements into website design and development
- → how to use CSS to amend the presentation of content on an HTML document
- → that CSS can be part of an HTML document or its own separate file and the advantages/disadvantages of each of these approaches.

> The website www.csszengarden.com lets you see the impact changing CSS can have on the look and feel of an HTML document. With your class examine the CSS designs available on CSS Zen Garden.

KEYWORDS

CSS (Cascading Stylesheets): the language used to describe how content on a web page should be displayed in the browser window

website developers: individuals or groups of individuals responsible for the end-to-end coding of websites

interactive web page: a web page containing content the user can engage with, for example through the use of buttons to make selections, including videos and sounds for the user to play, or games for the user to play

web browser application: a software package used to view website content

HTML elements: the opening tag, closing tag and content to be added to an HTML document; for example, \<p\>This is a paragraph\</p\> is an HTML element

tags: hidden key words in a web page which describe the content to be displayed in the browser window; for example, \<p\> is an opening tag which is used to describe a paragraph, \</p\> is the closing tag for the paragraph

KEYWORD

accessibility: providing support for the individual needs of all users, for example by including audio output of content for users with visual difficulties

SCENARIO

Alex, the founder of a new local charity called Getting Your Head Straight has asked you to create a new website for the charity. Alex wants to use the website to help raise awareness among young people and adults about the importance of maintaining good mental health. The site should include advice on taking care of yourself and some tips on managing stress.

Alex has said the website should include the following.

- A homepage which includes some information about what is meant by mental health.
- Two additional pages related to:
  - taking care of yourself
  - coping with stress.
- At least one podcast which offers advice on mental health.
- Links to additional websites which can offer help to users.
- A direct email link to the organisation's email address, alex@gettingyourheadstraight.com
- A form which can be used to input details to sign up for a newsletter which is sent out regularly by the organisation.
- The website should be easy to use (user friendly) and should include special features to provide accessibility for users with visual impairments.
- The website should be professional and all web pages should look the same.

> This address is fictional. If you do need advice on mindfulness or any of the other issues brought up in this unit of work, please speak to a trusted staff member, parent or other adult.

Alex has also asked for two versions of the website, one aimed at young people and one aimed at adults.

Before you agree to develop the web page for Alex, you have told him that you would like to spend some time developing new skills in a language called CSS which will help you give him the professional and consistent web page he wants for the charity.

KEYWORDS

homepage: the start-up page of a website, the page that loads first when the website is displayed in a web browser

Describe to a partner a homepage you like.

podcast: a digital audio file that is made available on the internet and can be listened to online or downloaded to a computer

Describe a podcast you have recently listened to.

DID YOU KNOW?

Different browsers have different ways of handling CSS styles. A web page using CSS might look slightly different when opened using the web browser Internet Explorer than it would if opened using the Opera web browser.

Do you remember?

Before starting this unit, you should be able to:

✔ use a text editor to create a HTML documents

✔ edit and preview HTML documents

✔ use paragraph and break tags to break up the displayed text in an HTML document

✔ use the style tag to incorporate basic CSS into HTML tags (inline CSS) to amend the colour of text displayed in an HTML document

✔ insert images into HTML documents and amend the size of an image to be displayed in a browser window

✔ insert sound and video files into HTML documents

✔ create internal and external hyperlinks in HTML documents.

KEYWORDS

navigational structure: the pathway the user can follow when visiting the various web pages on a website

structure diagram: a diagram illustrating the pathway through the pages of a website

storyboard: a set of line drawings which provide a basic outline of the content of pages of an application

Draw a storyboard of the steps it takes for you to do a common function on a social media application you frequently use.

Planning websites

Learn

Before developing a website such as this one it is important that you consider the **navigational structure** and the content of the application.

Structure diagrams can be used to plan how users can navigate between different pages of a website and **storyboards** can be used to plan the content of individual pages.

Practice

After some discussion with Alex you have agreed on the following design for the website's structure and index page.

The homepage of a website (the first page which is to be loaded into the browser window) should be saved as index.html.

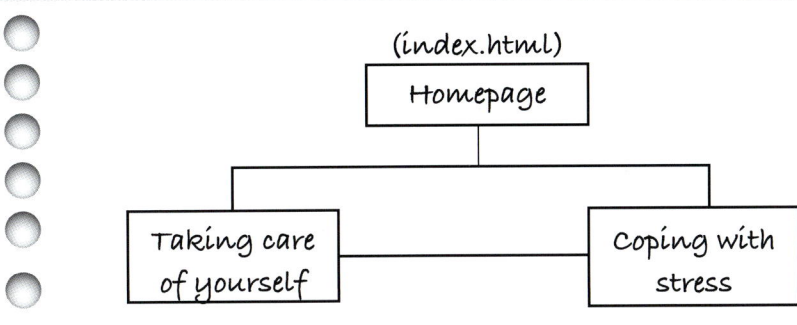

Storyboard for index.html			
Getting Your Head Straight Logo			
Hyperlink to Home	Hyperlink to Taking care of yourself	Hyperlink to Coping with stress	Hyperlink to Contact us

Mental Health (heading)

Mental health includes our emotional, psychological and social well-being. It can affect how we think and feel and how we get on with others.

Mental health is just as important as physical health.

It is tough to talk about sometimes, but talking helps you to cope with problems.

Help yourself, stay healthy with:

- Exercise
- Balanced diet
- The right amount of sleep
- Talking about problems
- Learning to say no (don't be pressurised into doing anything you don't want to do)

Click below for more information on:

Taking care of yourself	Coping with stress
Image of young person using mobile device	Image of young person working at a desk

You must now produce a storyboard for two more pages of the website: Taking care of yourself, and Coping with stress.

The storyboard for each web page should include:

➤ the organisation's logo
➤ a page title
➤ links to all other web pages in the website
➤ an indication of where the images will be located, and a description of the images
➤ an indication of where the text will be located, and what the text will say.

You should also:

➤ add a table to the bottom of the Taking care of yourself page use the table to display hyperlinks to websites of at least two organisations that are local to you and which support mental health
➤ include a video at the bottom of the Coping with stress page (the video can be downloaded from the internet and saved in your asset folder or it may be included as a link to another website).

Think carefully about where the logo, hyperlinks, headings, text and images are placed.

Use the same layout on the storyboard for each of your two new web pages. Consistent layout keeps web pages professional looking and easier to use.

Once the storyboards are complete you will need to:

➤ search for relevant websites on taking care of yourself and coping with stress
➤ use the information you have found to help you write two short paragraphs on each topic.

Generalisation

You can use the layout for the homepage as the basis for the layout of the two additional pages. This is an example of generalisation.

Decomposition

When searching for websites on taking care of yourself and coping with stress, break each topic down and decide on the keywords for internet searches. You need to search for the following assets and information for each of your web pages.

✪ Information that you can rewrite in your own words.
  (You will need to write one paragraph for each page/topic.)

✪ Relevant images for each web page.

✪ Hyperlinks to the websites of at least two organisations which support mental health.

✪ A short video about coping with stress. You should source the video from the internet; we will look later at alternative ways of linking the video into your website.

Always remember to attribute credit to data, images or videos created by someone else when you are using them. You can do this by including the address of the originating website or the original author's name.

Save any images and or videos you wish to use on your assets folder inside the MyWeb folder. This folder will be provided by your teacher. You will use these later.

HTML: paragraphs and lists

Learn

Web pages do not only contain text and images. They will often contain content displayed in lists and tables.

Lists can be shown in **ordered** or **unordered** format on web pages using HTML. Styles can also be applied to lists.

> In HTML you use the `<p>` `</p>` tag to insert paragraphs of text and use `<br>` to add a line break without starting a new paragraph.

> Style can be applied to ordered and unordered lists. For example, unordered lists can be displayed using circle, square or disc markers. Ordered lists can be displayed as numbers, letters or **Roman numerals**. These are known as Type '1', 'a', 'A', 'i' or Type 'I'.

Example of an unordered list:

```
<ul>
 <li>Exercise</li>
 <li>Balanced diet</li>
 <li>Talking about
problems</li>
 <li>Learn to say no</li>
</ul>
```

- Exercise
- Balanced diet
- Talking about problems
- Learn to say no

Example of an ordered list:

```
<ol>
 <li>Exercise</li>
 <li>Balanced diet</li>
 <li>Talking about
problems</li>
 <li>Learn to say no</li>
</ol>
```

1. Exercise
2. Balanced diet
3. Talking about problems
4. Learn to say no

Example of a styled unordered list:

```
<ul style = "list-style-
type: square">
 <li>Exercise</li>
 <li>Balanced diet</li>
 <li>Talking about
problems</li>
 <li>Learn to say no</li>
</ul>
```

❑ Exercise
❑ Balanced diet
❑ Talking about problems
❑ Learn to say no

Example of a styled unordered list:

```
<ol type="i">
 <li>Exercise</li>
 <li>Balanced diet</li>
 <li>Talking about problems</li>
 <li>Learn to say no</li>
</ol>
```

i. Exercise
ii. Balanced diet
iii. Talking about problems
iv. Learn to say no

KEYWORDS

ordered list: a list where each item on the list is given a place value such as '1', 'a', 'A', 'i' or 'I'

unordered list: a list of text appearing on a web page with no special order or sequence

Roman numerals: for example, i, ii, iii, iv

Practice

Now that you are familiar with adding lists using HTML, Alex would like to see a first draft of the index.html page. He has asked you to put this together for him based on the Home Page storyboard in the *practice* panel on page 70.

Your teacher will provide you with a folder called **MyWeb**.

This folder contains a file called **index.html**. This file will contain some basic HTML which can then be used to build the index page for the Getting Your Head Straight website. You will also be provided

> All work completed throughout this chapter should be saved to the **MyWeb** folder.

with a folder called **assets**. This folder will contain some images you may find useful when creating your website.

You will use an application called Notepad++ to produce the HTML needed in the production of the website for this project. Using the file **index.html** and what you know already about HTML and lists, edit the HTML in the file **index.html** provided by your teacher so that it contains all of the text and images described in the storyboard for index.html.

➤ Open the folder called **MyWeb**.
➤ Right click on the file called **index.html**.
➤ Select Edit with Notepad++.
➤ Edit the HTML provided to ensure that when it is displayed as a web page the **index.html** page contains all of the information shown by the storyboard.

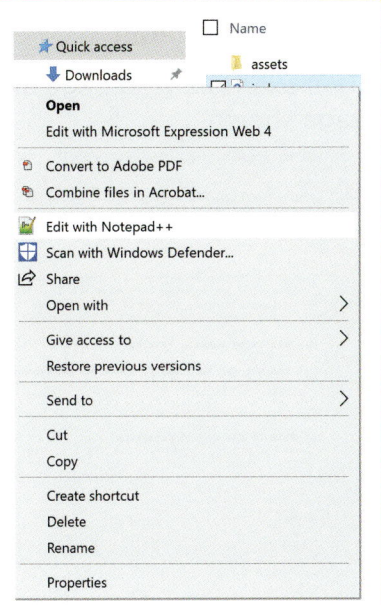

Abstraction and generalisation

The illustration and example shown below provides some hints.

✪ Use abstraction to identify the tags you will not need.

✪ Using generalisation and your previous experience of HTML, select the correct tags from those provided below to add the rest of the content to the web page.

Throughout this chapter you will use an application called Notepad++ to create HTML pages. This application can be downloaded from https://notepad-plus-plus.org/downloads

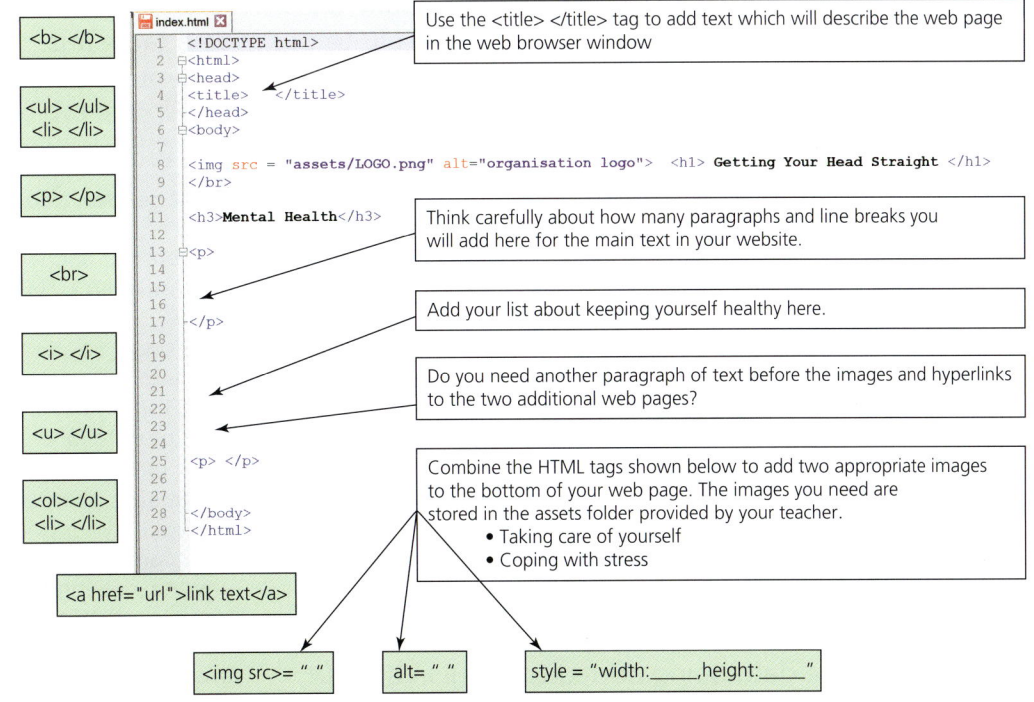

✪ Save **index.html**

This example web page and HTML code will also help you remember HTML syntax for the tags shown.

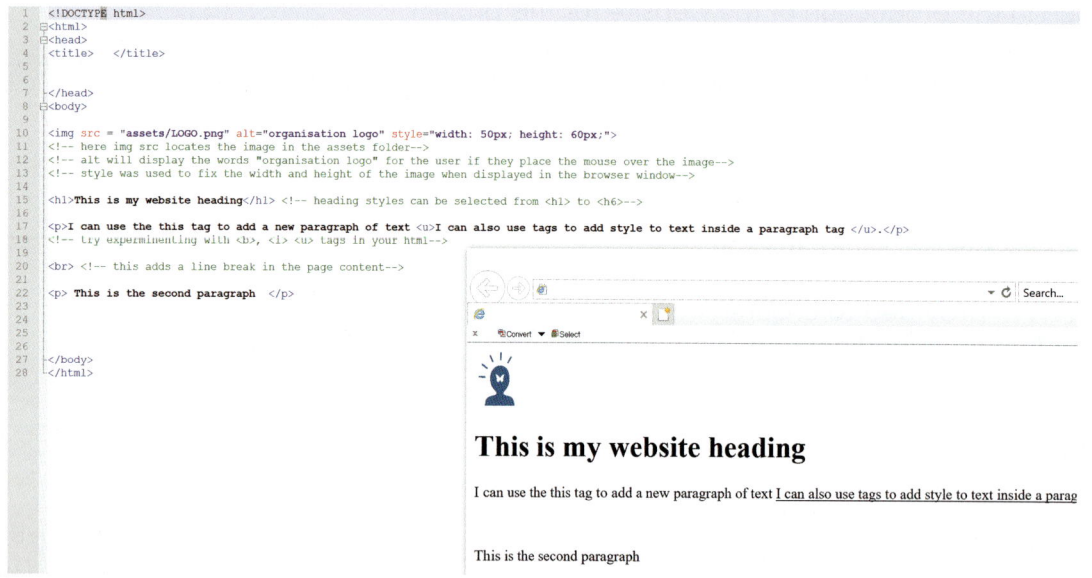

> Look also at the examples shown on page 72 on creating lists using HTML.

HTML: tables and comments

Learn

Tables are an excellent way of providing information in an easy to read and organised way. They normally contain **table headers** and **cells** that make up rows and columns. We can use HTML to add tables to web pages. When using HTML to describe a table it is important to plan ahead and think carefully about how many rows and columns the table will have, the headers for each column and the data that will be in each cell in the table.

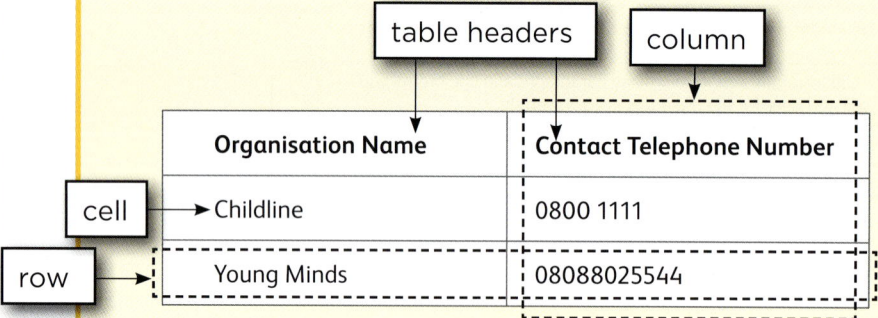

KEYWORDS

table header: data used to describe the contents of each column in an HTML table

cell: single square or rectangle in a table used to contain an item of data or a table header

comments: text used to explain your code; they can be seen by anyone viewing the HTML code but are not displayed in the browser window

HTML uses the following tags to describe a table which is being added to a web page.

➤ `<table> </table>` tag defines the start and end of the table

➤ `<tr> </tr>` defines the start and end of a table row

➤ `<th> </th>` identifies a table header

➤ `<td> </td>` describes the data being added to a cell in a table

The code used to create the table shown on the previous page would be:

```
<!DOCTYPE html>
<html>
<head>

</head>
<body>

<table>
    <tr>
        <th>Organisation Name </th>
        <th>Contact Telephone Number </th>
    </tr>
    <tr>
        <td>Childline </td>
        <th>0800 1111</th>
    </tr>
    <tr>
        <td>Young Minds </td>
        <th>08088025544 </th>
    </tr>
</table>



</body>
</html>
```

HTML code produced to create tables and other website content can become very long and difficult to understand.

You may have noticed that some of the text shown in the HTML example on page 74 was coloured green. These lines of text represented **comments**. Coders use comments to help explain what their code is doing. This can help other people to understand it. It is also helpful if they need to make changes to the code in the future. Comments in HTML are written in between the **<!-- -->** tags

<!--this is how a comment might look in HTML -->

Practice

Before you can create the last two web pages of the Getting Your Head Straight website, we should check that you understand tables.

Your teacher will provide you with a file called **tabletest.html** to allow you to complete this task.

➤ Open Notepad++.
➤ Open the file called **index.html**.
➤ Edit the HTML in **index.html** to include the table definition shown (below left). This will create the table shown (below right) in a browser.

```
<!DOCTYPE html>
<html>
<head>

</head>
<body>

<table>
    <tr>
        <th>Organisation Name </th>
        <th>Contact Telephone Number </th>
    </tr>
    <tr>
        <td>Childline </td>
        <th>0800 1111</th>
    </tr>
    <tr>
        <td>Young Minds </td>
        <th>08088025544 </th>
    </tr>
</table>


</body>
</html>
```

Organisation Name	Contact Telephone Number
Childline	0800 1111
Young Minds	08088025544

➤ Save **index.html** and preview it in a browser window to ensure you have entered your code correctly.

➤ Add comments to show where the table definition starts and ends in the HTML file.

➤ Add comments to show where each row in the table begins and ends.

➤ Add comments next to the row headers and the data in the tables.

➤ Add another row to the table to include the name and telephone number of a local organisation which provides mental health support to young people.

➤ Save **index.html** and close Notepad++.

The table produced by the HTML does not look professional. With a friend, discuss how you might improve the appearance of this table.

HTML: CSS style tags

Learn

Developers can add **style information** to an HTML document by adding a **style tag** (`<style>` `</style>`) and **CSS style rules** to the HTML document.

Some of the CSS styles which can be added to a table in an HTML document include border, padding, text-align, border-spacing and border-collapse.

➤ **Border:** if you do not define a border for your table it is displayed without borders. The border can be specified in terms of pixels; for example, the border in the example shown on the next page is 1 pixel wide, it is a solid line and coloured black.

➤ **Padding:** provides spacing between the contents of the cell and the cell border. Cell padding is defined in pixels. In the example shown there is a space of at least 15 pixels between the borders and any content appearing in each table cell.

KEYWORDS

style information: information relating to how an item will be presented on an HTML document when it is opened in a browser window

style tag: used to contain information or rules which will define how items described using HTML will be displayed in the browser window

CSS style rules: the actual rules used to define how items described using HTML will be displayed in the browser window

➤ **Text-align:** defines where in the cell the text will be placed. Table headings will automatically display as bold and centred and data will automatically be left aligned. You can alter the way text is displayed in each cell by using the text-align style. The text-align style allows you to align text to the left, right, centre, or justify (the cell content will be stretched so the lines are equal in width).

➤ **Border-spacing:** provides a space between the cells in the table.

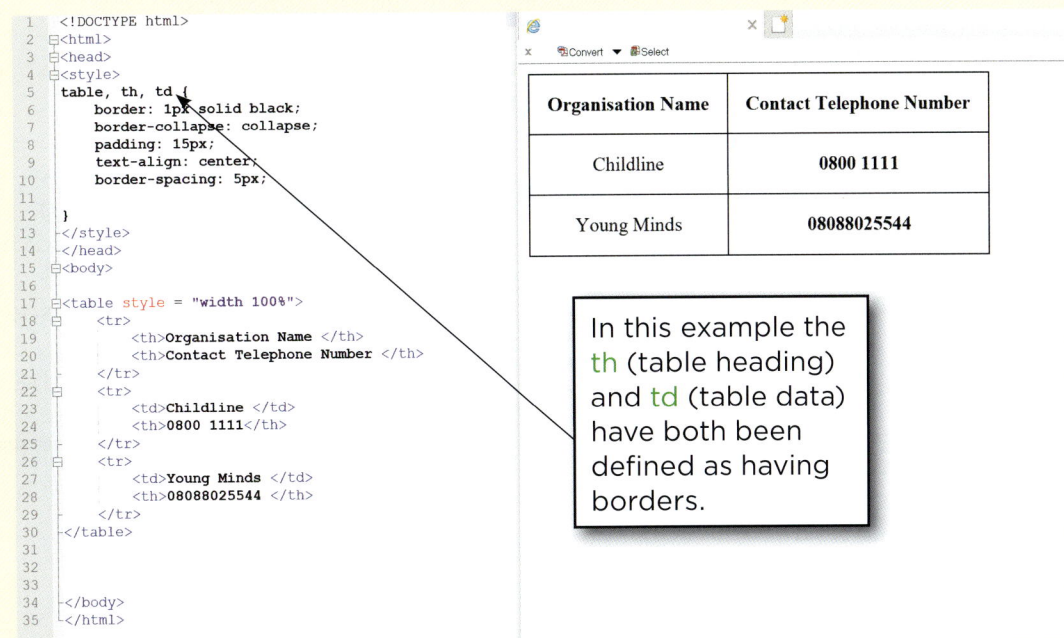

In this example the th (table heading) and td (table data) have both been defined as having borders.

➤ **Border-collapse:** collapse reduces multiple borders to a single border. You can try adding and removing border-collapse to your table when you complete the practice task that follows.

Practice

Add some CSS to your HTML to improve how the table appears.

➤ Open Notepad++.
➤ Open **index.html**.
➤ Add the style tag in between the opening and closing head tag as shown below.

The head tag in an HTML document can be used to store metadata (data about data). Adding the style tag to the **<head>** tag at the start of an HTML document is an example of metadata: the data placed in the style tag is used to describe how the content defined by the HTML tags on this web page will appear in when it is displayed in a browser window.

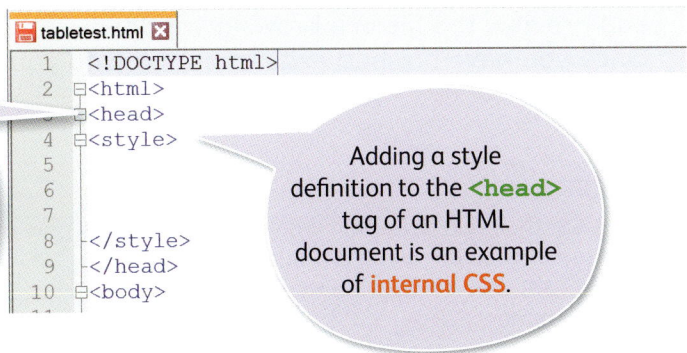

Adding a style definition to the **<head>** tag of an HTML document is an example of internal CSS.

> Edit the content of the style tags as shown below.

```
1   <!DOCTYPE html>
2   <html>
3   <head>
4   <style>
5   table, th, td {
6       border: 1px solid black;
7
8
9   }
10  </style>
11  </head>
12  <body>
```

You can experiment with: alternative pixel widths for your table borders; different border styles (for example, instead of 'solid', use 'dotted' or 'double' to see how this changes the appearance of the table); change the colour of the border (for example, try red or blue instead of black).

> Save **index.html** file and preview the file in a browser window. With a friend, discuss how this has changed the appearance of your table.

> Try expanding the style tag as shown on the right.

Try removing **border-collapse** to see how this alters the way the table looks.

```
1   <!DOCTYPE html>
2   <html>
3   <head>
4   <style>
5   table, th, td {
6       border: 1px solid black;
7       border-collapse: collapse;
8       padding: 15px;
9       text-align: center;
10      border-spacing: 5px;
11
12  }
13  </style>
14  </head>
15  <body>
```

Try changing **border**, **padding** and **border-spacing** to see how this impacts on the way the table looks.

Add each style one at a time, save **index.html** and preview your change in the browser window before moving on to add and experiment with each new style.

CSS can also be used to specify how much of the web page you would like your table to take up when it is displayed in the browser.

To specify the width of a table using CSS, use the width property.

> change your table tag in the main body of your HTML so it now reads **<table width="100%">**.
> Save your HTML document and then preview it in the browser window.
> How has the table display changed?
> When you use percentages to determine the size of an element you are telling the browser how much of the screen you want that element of the screen to fill. If you change the size of your browser window the element will change size also.
> Once you are happy with how your table looks, save **index.html** and preview the file in a browser window.
> Once you have finished experimenting with your style definitions save **index.html**.

Adding CSS to the HTML tags in the **<body>** section of an HTML document is an example of **inline CSS**.

KEYWORDS

internal CSS: the style definition would be included as part of the <head> </head> tag at the start of an HTML document
inline CSS: CSS which is applied to a single element in the <body> section of an HTML document

DID YOU KNOW?

HTML is used to define the content and structure of a web page; CSS defines how that content is presented.

HTML and CSS: divs and styles

Learn

When you add content to your web pages using HTML it is important that you think about the layout of the page and the sections it is divided into.

Website developers often use formatting or colour to distinguish different sections of a web page.

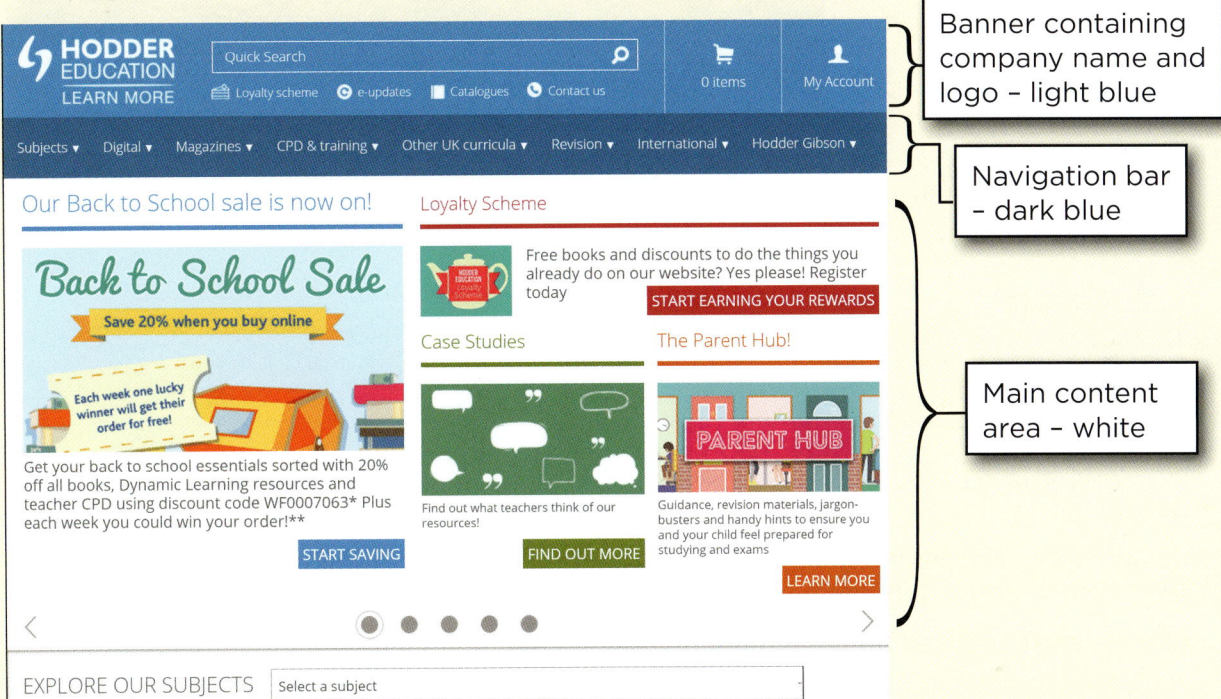

Banner containing company name and logo – light blue

Navigation bar – dark blue

Main content area – white

Website developers use a tag called the **division tag** (or **div tag**) `<div>` `</div>` to split their web page into sections. You can then use HTML and CSS to make changes to any content contained inside a set of div tags. Any content or elements which are outside that set of div tags will not be changed.

CSS allows you to use style **attributes** to change how an HTML element will display on the screen. A CSS style can be applied to all of those elements inside a `<div>` tag at the same time.

In the example below you can see how index.html has been broken into sections or `<divs>`. There are four `<divs>`.

➤ The first `<div>` will contain the page header.
➤ The second `<div>` contains the navigation section for the page.
➤ The third `<div>` contains the main page content (text and images).
➤ The fourth `<div>` contains a table of information.

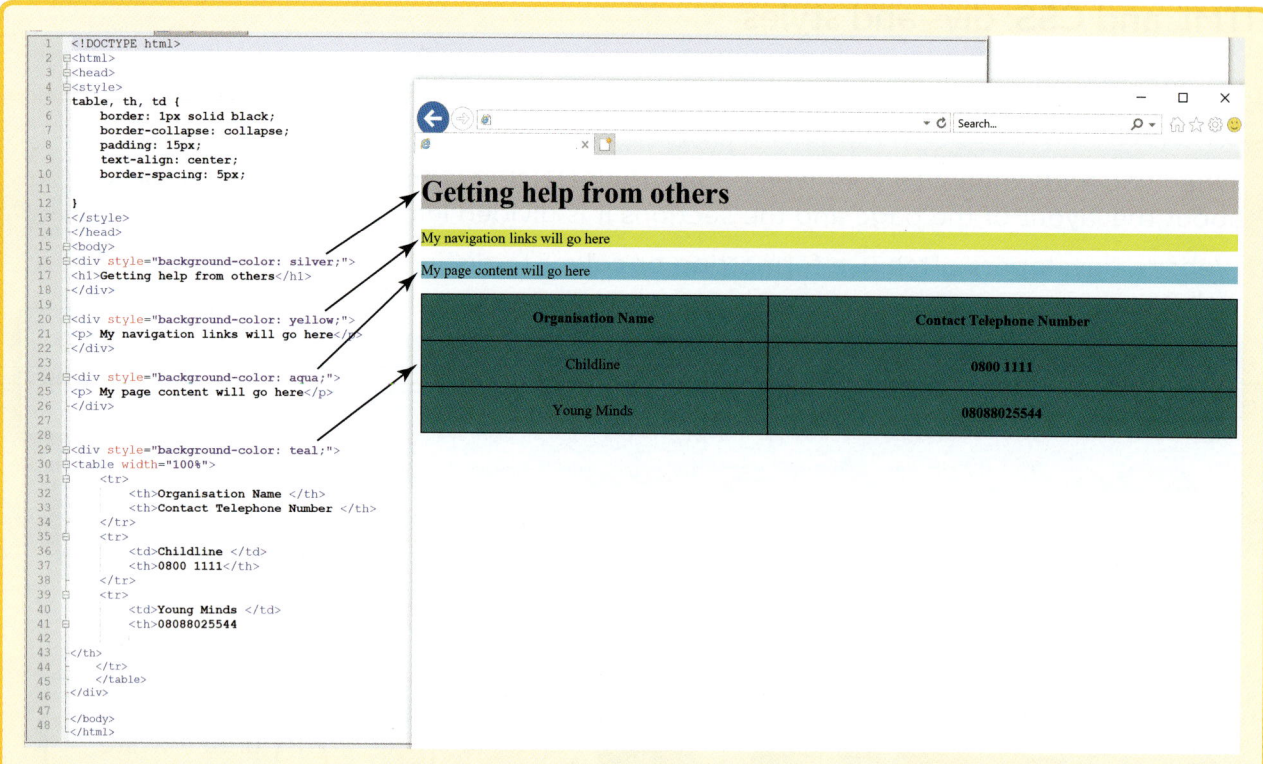

The example above also shows how different style attributes were applied to each of the **<divs>**.

You can apply CSS styles to any HTML tag as long as you remember the **syntax rules**: all CSS elements need to have the following.

<[html tag] style="background-color: red;">

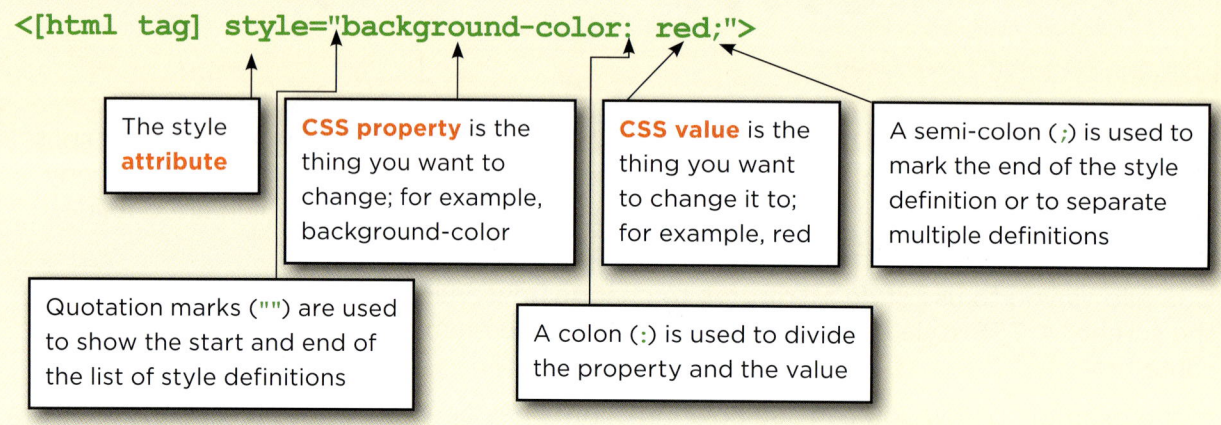

The style **attribute**

CSS property is the thing you want to change; for example, background-color

CSS value is the thing you want to change it to; for example, red

A semi-colon (**;**) is used to mark the end of the style definition or to separate multiple definitions

Quotation marks (**""**) are used to show the start and end of the list of style definitions

A colon (**:**) is used to divide the property and the value

KEYWORDS

div tag: a tag <div> </div> used to group sections of HTML elements together for further formatting, for example, using CSS

attribute: used to define how the text, images and other content is to be displayed on a web page, normally added to the opening tag of an element; for example, <p align = 'left'>This is left aligned</p>

syntax rules: the rules of a programming language which determine how its instructions are written

CSS property: the attribute you want to change using CSS

CSS value: the new value you wish to assign to the property identified in a CSS style tag

Practice

Style tags can be used to contain more than one style attribute. Let us look at how you can add multiple style attributes to a single style tag.

Your teacher will give you a copy of a file called **usingdivs.html** to allow you to complete this task.

➤ Open Notepad++.
➤ Open the file called **usingdivs.html**.
➤ Amend the code in **usingdivs.html**, adding the property and value "`display: inline-block`", so that it reads:

```
<div style="background-color: silver; height: 100px; width:
100%; display: inline-block">
<h1>Getting help from others</h1>
</div>
```

➤ Save **usingdivs.html** and preview the file in a browser window. Do you notice anything different now that you have added the "`display: inline-block`" style?
➤ Amend the style definition for the paragraph which reads 'My navigation links will go here' to include "`display: inline-block`".
➤ Save **usingdivs.html** again and preview the file in a browser window.

> Do you notice now how the gap has been removed between the first and second colour blocks?

Generalisation

Use your knowledge of HTML to describe how the CSS property values shown below would amend the display of **usingdivs.html**. Complete the table below to describe what each CSS property does. Your teacher will give you a file called **Describing CSS Properties**. It contains a copy of this table for you to complete.

CSS Property	Description	Example values
background-color		red; yellow; green;
color		red; yellow; green;
height		120px; 120%
width		120px; 120%
border		2px solid black;
float		left; right; none
font-size		12px; 12pt;
text-align		left; right; centre;
margin		5px;

Algorithmic thinking

Once you are confident using and applying multiple styles to each **<div>** section you can now amend your **index.html** file to apply additional styles to each div.

Use what you have learned about combining HTML and CSS to experiment with applying some of the CSS properties above to the content of the file called **usingdivs.html**; for example:

```
<div style="background-color: yellow;">
<p> My navigation links will go here</p>
</div>
```

```
<div style="background-color: silver;">
<p> My page content will go here</p>
</div>
```

Here we have used the property **background-color:** to separate the navigation section of this web page from the section which will be used to display the main web page content.

Getting help from others

My navigation links will go here

My page content will go here

- Try adding multiple CSS properties to the same div.
- Remember to save and preview the file in the browser window each time you add a new CSS property.
- When you are happy with the way your index.html page looks when you preview it in a browser window, close **index.html** and close Notepad++.

This lets you see the changes made by each new CSS property you have added but also makes it easier to debug your code if you have made an error. If you have only added one new property you only need to look at it to check for errors!

CSS: classes and styles

Learn

CSS provides developers with some very effective ways of changing the presentation of an HTML document. In the previous task you saw how the CSS style attribute can be used to contain more than one CSS property.

The HTML needed to produce even the simplest of web pages can become very long and complicated, especially if it contains inline CSS code. This can make the code very difficult to interpret, especially if you need to make changes to it at a later stage.

```
1   <!DOCTYPE html>
2   <html>
3   <head>
4   <style>
5   table, th, td {
6       border: 1px solid black;
7       border-collapse: collapse;
8       padding: 15px;
9       text-align: center;
10      border-spacing: 5px;
11  }
12
13  .header {
14  background-color:silver;
15
16
17  }
18  </style>
19  </head>
20  <body>
21  <div style="background-color: silver; height: 100px; width:100%; display:inline-block">
22  <h1>Getting help from others</h1>
23  </div>
24
25  <div style="background-color: yellow; height: 100px; width:100%; display:inline-block">
26  <p> My navigation links will go here</p>
27  </div>
28
29  <div style="background-color: aqua; height: 50px; width:100%; display:inline-block">
30  <p> My page content will go here</p>
31  </div>
32
33
34  <div style="background-color: teal; height: 200px; width:100%; display:inline-block">
35  <table width="100%">
36      <tr>
37          <th>Organisation Name </th>
38          <th>Contact Telephone Number </th>
39      </tr>
40      <tr>
41          <td>Childline </td>
42          <th>0800 1111</th>
43      </tr>
44      <tr>
45          <td>Young Minds </td>
46          <th>08088025544
47
48  </th>
49      </tr>
50      </table>
51  </div>
52
53  </body>
54  </html>
```

One of the ways developers can help make the code easier to understand is by using the **class attribute**.

Earlier in this chapter you looked at adding a style definition to the **<head>** section of a web page.

KEYWORD

class attribute: an attribute which can be used to define styles for other elements with the same name so they all have the same style

For example, you used the border: attribute to add a solid black line border around the table. This was an example of what is known as an **internal style**. By adding the style to the **<head>** tag of the web page you were also adding **metadata** to the HTML document.

When we first added style definitions to our table we created an internal style definition as shown on lines 5-12 in the example below.

The example creates a new class called **.header**. The **.header** class now includes all of the style definitions for the page header in the HTML document.

KEYWORDS

internal style: CSS definitions which have been included in the <head> tags of an HTML document

metadata: data about other data; for example, the use of style definitions in an HTML document used to describe how web page content is to be displayed

```
1    <!DOCTYPE html>
2    <html>
3    <head>
4    <style>
5    table, th, td {
6        border: 1px solid black;
7        border-collapse: collapse;
8        padding: 15px;
9        text-align: center;
10       border-spacing: 5px;
11
12   }
13
14   .header {
15   background-color:silver;
16   height:100px;
17   width:100%;
18   display:inline-block;
19   }
20
21   </style>
22   </head>
23   <body>
24   <div class="header">
25   <h1>Getting help from others</h1>
26   </div>
27
28   <div style="background-color: yellow;h
29   <p> My navigation links will go here</
```

The CSS properties and values for headers have been moved from being inline with the HTML and are now listed under the class selector instead.

Give the class a name and add a full stop (.) before it so the browser knows you are defining a class.

Instead of using " " to group the properties, use { }.

The class can now be used inside the HTML code when it is needed.

Generalisation and algorithmic thinking

Use the example shown below to help you create and then use a class definition for the page header section of your **index.html** file.

Practice

➤ Underneath your existing table CSS definition create a class definition called **.header** and add style definitions for the background-color, height and width and display features as shown.

```
1    <!DOCTYPE html>
2    <html>
3    <head>
4    <style>
5    table, th, td {
6        border: 1px solid black;
7        border-collapse: collapse;
8        padding: 15px;
9        text-align: center;
10       border-spacing: 5px;
11
12   }
13
14   .header {
15   background-color:silver;
16   height:100px;
17   width:100%;
18   display:inline-block;
19   }
20
21   </style>
22   </head>
23   <body>
24   <div class="header">
25   <h1>Getting help from others</h1>
26   </div>
```

> Amend the colour and height of the header section if you wish but keep width set to 100 %

> See line 24 in the example shown.

➤ Save the file called **index.html**.
➤ You can call this .header class inside the opening **<div>** tag by writing **<div class = "header">**.
➤ Preview the web page in the browser.
➤ When you are happy with the display of your web page create your own class definitions for the following sections of the web page.
  o Navigation area (**.nav**)
  o Main content (**.maincontent**)
  o Table (**.tablesection**).
  o Use **class="nav"**, **class="maincontent"**, and so on to call each class from inside the opening **<div>** tag for each section in your index.html page.
  o Save **index.html**.
➤ One of the main advantages about setting up class definitions is the fact that classes can be reused.
➤ New content can easily be added and the same styles reapplied. This is possible as the styles have already been defined.
  o Open **index.html**.
  o Underneath the last **</div>** tag in your HTML code (the **.tablesection**) we can add some additional text to remind the user if they ever need help. We will use the **.maincontent** class to style these elements.

o Use **<h1> </h1>** and **<p></p>** tags to add the text shown below; an example of how this might look can be seen on page 86.

Here to help!

Contact any of the above organisations anytime if you need help

---

o Place a **<div>** and **</div>** tag at the start and end of this section of text and use the **.maincontent** class to format the paragraph display.

```
65
66
67  □<div class= "tablesection">
68  □<table width="100%">
69  □    <tr>
70          <th>Organisation Name </th>
71          <th>Contact Telephone Number </th>
72  └    </tr>
73  □    <tr>
74          <td>Childline </td>
75          <th>0800 1111</th>
76  └    </tr>
77  □    <tr>
78          <td>Young Minds </td>
79  □        <th>08088025544
80
81  └</th>
82      </tr>
83      </table>
84  └</div>
85
86
87  □<div class= "maincontent">
88  <h1> Here to help!</h1>
89  <p> Contact any of the above organisations anytime if you need help</p>
90  └</div>
91
92
93  └</body>
94  └</html>
```

Organisation Name	
Childline	
Young Minds	

Here to help!

Contact any of the above organisations anytime if you need help

o Save **index.html** and preview your web page in a browser window.

➤ For additional practice creating and applying new styles, complete the following task.

o Create a new class definition called **.contactdeveloper**. This style will be used for a small section (about 100 pixels in height) which will appear at the bottom of your web page.

o Your new style should contain appropriate definitions for
   • **background-color**
   • **height**
   • **width**
   • **display**.

o Create a new **<div>** at the end of your HTML and apply the style called **.contactdeveloper** to this div.

o Add the following HTML to your new **<div>** section at the end of your HTML document:

```
<p>Last updated (add date here), To contact the web
designer <a href="mailto:webdesigner@my _ email.
com">Click Here</a></p>
```

> Notice how there is a small space between the table and the new content. Think about adding **display: inline-block** to the table class definition in the **<head>** section to help with this.

> **DID YOU KNOW?**
> The **<a>** tag can be used to create a hyperlink which will automatically allow the user to send emails to a pre-defined address.

> Change the email address to your own (or your school's email address, if you would prefer to keep yours private).

CSS: external stylesheets

Learn

CSS allows web developers to quickly and easily change how web pages look. Using classes speeds up the editing and coding process for when amending the presentation of a website. Previously, we saw how a class can be used more than once in an HTML document.

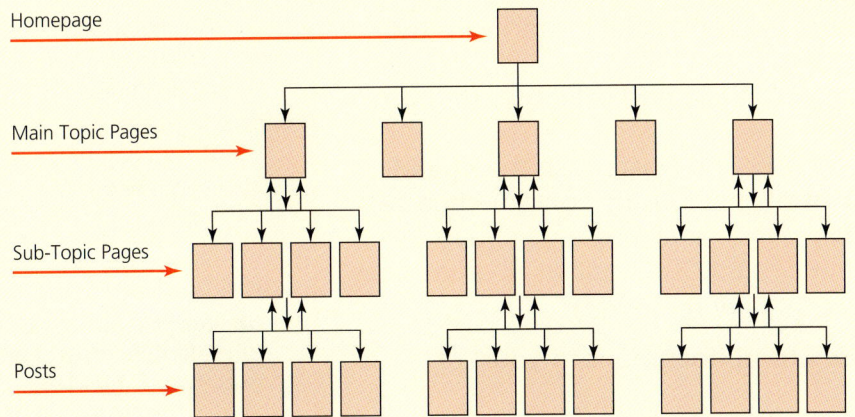

Homepage

Main Topic Pages

Sub-Topic Pages

Posts

This website has 30 pages. If the website is to look professional each page should have a similar look and feel.

Discuss with a friend the difficulties of coding and editing classes used over and over again on each of the 30 pages.

Developers use external stylesheets to store details of the CSS and classes they wish to use on multiple pages on their website.

External stylesheets, internal styles and inline styles can all be applied to an HTML document. An HTML document that contains all three will apply the styles in the following priority order.

Each page would need all of the classes setting up again within the `<header>` tags.

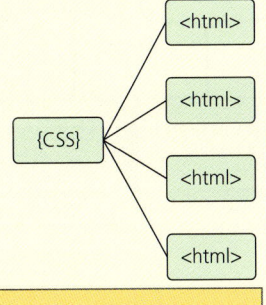

Priority order (highest priority at top)	Explanation
Inline style	CSS which has been incorporated into the body of an HTML document has the highest priority. It will be applied in place of CSS included in internal styles or external stylesheets
Internal style	Internal stylesheets or CSS which has been included in the `<head>` tags of an HTML document have the next highest priority. They will be applied in place of CSS found in external stylesheets. Internal styles must be defined for every page they are used in.
External stylesheet	External stylesheets have the lowest priority. External stylesheets are saved separately from the main HTML document but are called from within the `<head>` tag. Any inline CSS and internal CSS will override the external stylesheet.

DID YOU KNOW?

Using an external stylesheet saves you a lot of work – you can update a whole website by amending that one file.

KEYWORD

external CSS: A separate document is written containing the CSS for a website. Each page in the website contains a link to that file inside the <head> </head> tags at the start of an HTML document

Practice

Let's practise creating and using our own external CSS file before we create our 'Getting Our Head Straight' website. First, we need to make a copy of **index.html**.

➤ Open Notepad++.
➤ Open **index.html**.
➤ Click on 'File' and then 'New' to create a new blank HTML page.
➤ Highlight the CSS in **index.html**.
➤ Right click on the highlighted text and select 'Cut' from the drop down menu that appears.
➤ Right click in the new blank HTML file and select 'Paste' from the drop down menu.
➤ Once you have complete the Cut and Paste task the `<head>` tag in the file called **index.html** should only contain `<head>` `<style>` `</style><head>`
➤ Save the file containing your copied CSS code as **mystyles.css**.
➤ Save **index.html** (with the CSS now removed).

You now need to link the **index.html** document to your **mystyles.css** file.

➤ Edit the `<head>` `</head>` in **index.html** as shown:

```
1  <!DOCTYPE html>
2  <html>
3  <head>
4      <link rel="stylesheet" href="mystyles.css">
5  </head>
6  <body>
```

Tells the browser that the linked document is a stylesheet.

This is the stylesheet you have just created.

Specifies there is a relationship between the current file and the linked file. It allows the web browser to fetch the stylesheet from memory before it is used. This helps speed up the load time for a web page.

Specifies where the linked document is stored.

DID YOU KNOW?

Most developers will make regular copies of their work, especially if they are making a lot of changes to their code. This is called making a backup.

This file should now contain CSS style definitions for each `<div>` section of your practice web page.

KEYWORD

backup: the process of making a copy of a program or file. This allows the developer to restore work if the original file becomes damaged

When was the last time you backed up a file? What was it?

Go further

Now that you have expanded you knowledge of HTML and are able to use CSS you are ready to create the remaining two web pages for the 'Getting Your Head Straight' website.

Your web pages should have the following sections (at least). They will be used to display the following.

◆ The header (displaying the charity logo and name).
◆ Navigation (hyperlinks to the other web pages).
  ❏ Here's the syntax for HTML to add hyperlinks to a document:
    ```
    <a href="add your web address here">add your
    hyperlink text here</a>
    ```
◆ Content (the main content of your web pages).
◆ Images and the location of any images on your web pages.
  ❏ Here's the syntax for HTML to add images to a document:
    ```
    <img src="filename.filetype" alt="any rollover
    text should appear here">
    ```

You are already familiar with the structure of an HTML document and the various tags required to add content to an HTML document.

Use the storyboards you created and the information you collected to create two additional HTML pages for the website.

Make sure that both new pages are saved to the **MyWeb** folder, provided by your teacher

◆ Open Notepad++.
◆ Create a new HTML file called **selfcare.html**.
◆ Add the following HTML tags you need before adding content to your web page:

```
<!DOCTYPE html>
<html>
<head>
<title> </title>
</head>
<body>
</body>
</html>
```

> This will help you later when you are ready to add an external stylesheet with class attributes to your website.

> Remember using the div tag on page 85.

> The logo is in the assets folder provided by your teacher when you completed the HTML for **index.html**.

- ◆ Decide on the appropriate HTML tags needed to add:
  - ❏ the charity logo and name
  - ❏ text you can use as hyperlinks to the other two web pages
  - ❏ a title for the main body of text on the web page
  - ❏ the text you included in your storyboard for the 'Taking care of yourself' web page created during the practice task on page 69.
  - ❏ any images you located to help you illustrate the content of this page.
  - ❏ add comments to explain your code.

- ◆ Create a link in the `<head>` section between **selfcare.html** and **mystyles.css**.

- ◆ Save **selfcare.html** and preview the file in a browser window to ensure the styles in **mystyles.css** have been applied correctly.

Now repeat this process and create a second web page on Coping with Stress. You should call this file **copingwithstress. html**.

- ◆ Save **copingwithstress.html** and preview the file in a browser window to ensure the styles in **mystyles.css** have been applied correctly.

- ◆ Remember to make sure you have:
  - ❏ added hyperlinks between each of the pages in the website
  - ❏ included a table in your web page about Taking Care of Yourself
  - ❏ included a video on your web page about coping with stress.

For a reminder of how to use any of the tags used previously, visit www.w3schools.com.

You should add comments using `<!-- -->`.

See page 69 to help you with this.

Remember to create a link in the `<head>` section between copingwithstress.html and mystyles.css

If you are unable to download an appropriate video about coping with stress, add a hyperlink to a website containing an appropriate video.

Challenge yourself

Alex is running an online workshop on looking after yourself. He has asked you to add a small input form to the bottom of the page called **selfcare.html**.

The form is to be used to collect the name and email address of anyone interested in joining the online workshop.

➤ Open Notepad++.

➤ Open **selfcare.html**.

➤ Open and close a new **<div>** tag at the very bottom of the HTML on this page.

➤ Add a suitable heading tag and instructions to the user about the purpose of the form.

> The signup form for the workshop will be added inside these tags.

```
<div> <!-- add signup form -->
<h3>Sign up for our online self-care workshop </h3>
</div>
```

➤ In HTML the **<form></form>** tag is used to indicate that a part of the HTML document contains a form for collecting information from the user.

➤ Edit the HTML to include **<form></form>** inside the **<div>** tags.

```
<div> <!-- add signup form -->
<h3>Sign up for our online self-care workshop </h3>
<form>
</form>
</div>
```

➤ You can add text boxes and labels to the data form using the **<input type = "text">** element.

➤ Edit the **<form>** tags to now read:

```
<form>
First name: <input type="text"
name="firstname"> <br>
</form>
```

> This adds an input field to the form. The user can add text to the input field. The data entered is stored in a **variable** called **"firstname"**.

KEYWORD

variable: a named memory location used to store data of a given type during the program execution; a variable can change value as the program runs

➤ Add similar input text fields for second name and email address.

➤ Save **selfcare.html** and preview the form in a browser window.

At the moment the form does not do anything. It simply displays the heading and text boxes created using HTML tags.

If the user is to be able to send their details to Alex, a Submit button is needed on the form. Another input type element can be added to the form to allow this to happen.

➤ Underneath the HTML for the **"Email address:"** add the **<input type = submit>** as shown below:

```
<input type="submit"
value="Submit">
```

This adds a button to the form. The button displays the word 'Submit'. When the user clicks on the button the web page can carry out some kind of action.

Before an action can be performed when the user clicks on the Submit button we need to tell the browser what that action will be.

➤ Edit the opening **<form>** tag to read:

```
<form action="mailto:alex@gettingyourheadstraight.com" name="submit">
```

This tells the browser to send the contents of the form to alex@gettingyourheadstraight.com, when the user clicks on the **<input type = "submit">** button.

➤ Save **selfcare.html**.

➤ Preview the web page in a browser window to ensure the form displays correctly.

When the user clicks on the Submit button the following message appears.

➤ Use what you have learned about CSS and HTML to improve the layout of the form. You could do this by adding styles to the **<div>**, or by adding additional spacing between the form elements.

Final project and evaluation

Alex had asked for two versions of the website.
The version of the website you have been working on should have a look and feel which is more suitable for an adult audience. However, Alex would now like you to design a second version which is better suited to a younger audience.
Use the information provided in the table below to help you think about how an adult website might differ from a website produced for children.

Websites for children	Websites for older users
Larger text (font size)	Smaller text (font size)
Brighter colours (children prefer secondary colours such as red, blue, green)	More subdued colours (more professional or subdued colours)
Simple, easy to understand text	Complex sentences

Create a new CSS file which contains a new set of style properties which will make the website more suitable for children.

Carry out the following tasks before creating your new CSS file.

➤ With a friend discuss how you might make the website suitable for children. What colours, font or style of writing might a younger audience prefer?

➤ Think about the tags you would use to change: **background-color**, **text-color**, **text-align**, the div height for example. Remember, if you want your div sections to display without spaces between them, use **display: inline-block**.

➤ Experiment with **font-size** and **font-style** tags

➤ Save your new stylesheet as **mystyles2.css** into the folder called **MyWeb** which contains your **index.html** file and the HTML files for the two additional pages in your website.

> You can find out more about these tags on www.w3schools.com/html/html_styles.asp.

➤ Link this stylesheet to **index.html**.
```
<link href="mystyles2.css" rel="stylesheet">
```
➤ Open **index.html** to test your stylesheet.

➤ If you are happy with how your web page looks, link the stylesheet to the remaining two pages.

Alex also wanted a version of the website that would help improve accessibility for users with visual impairments.
Website accessibility can be improved in a number of ways, including the following:

➤ Ensure you have included Alt text for all images.

➤ Use external CSS for styling.

➤ Use simple language on your website.

➤ Use contrasting colours on your website for backgrounds and text.

For users with visual impairments you can improve accessibility by:

1 creating a version of your web page with increased text size

2 including voice recordings of some of the text so that users who are unable to read the text can have it played back to him.

DID YOU KNOW?

Alt text added to images can also improve website accessibility. Alt tags can be added in the form: `<img src="filename.filetype" alt="any rollover text should appear here">`. Alt text is used by assistive screen readers to describe the image.

- ➤ Make a copy of your **MyWeb** folder and rename the copy **MyAccessibleWeb**.
- ➤ Edit the **mystyles.css** file to ensure the font displayed on each web page is larger in size than the previous version of your website.
- ➤ Create a voice podcast of some of the text on your **index.html** file.
  - Go to www.naturalreaders.com/online
  - Copy some of the text from your file called **index.html** and paste it into the text box as shown. Experiment with languages and voices until you find one that you like.
- ➤ Download the mp3 version of the voice to text file and save it in **MyAccessibleWeb/assets**.

- ➤ Beside the text recorded in the mp3 file, create a text-based hyperlink which reads 'Click here to read this text'.
- ➤ The website storyboard also showed a Contact Us hyperlink in the navigation bar. Alex wanted users to be able to email the organisation if they needed more information.
- ➤ Use www.w3schools.com to find out more about how you can combine the following tags to convert this text into an email hyperlink.

```
</a>
<a href=mailto:alex@keepingyourheadstraight.com>
Contact Us
```

The online workshop on taking care of yourself was so successful that Alex has decided to run another workshop for coping with stress.

- ➤ Edit **copingwithstress.html** to include a data input form which can collect the first name, surname and telephone number from anyone interested in taking part.
- ➤ The form should be added to a new **<div>** section at the bottom of the existing page and users should be able to email Alex at alex@gettingyourheadstraight.com.

Now that the Getting Your Head Straight website is complete it is important that you test and evaluate all parts of the website before Alex takes ownership of it.

Your teacher will provide you with a copy of an evaluation table which can be used to allow you to evaluate your own website.

- ➤ Open your completed **index.html** and use the Web evaluation table to help you evaluate your website.
- ➤ When you have completed the grid write a short paragraph describing any changes you made to your website. Say why you made these changes.
- ➤ Ask a friend to evaluate your website. Your teacher will provide them with a copy of the same evaluation table. When your friend has finished evaluating your website, discuss their scores and ask them what additional changes they would make to the website and why.
- ➤ If time is available make any appropriate changes to your website and say why you agreed with the comments your friend made.

About Python

Python is a programming language created by Guido van Rossum in 1991. It is widely used in education to teach programming, and in business and industry to create programs. YouTube, Google, Instagram and Spotify all use Python. The language was created so that the code could be read and understood easily.

Python's Integrated Development and Learning Environment (IDLE) provides features for creating, editing and running programs.

In this unit you will learn to:

→ use features of the Python programming language to create a solution to a problem

→ use the **IDLE interface** to code in script mode

→ create and edit code in Python which

- sequences input, process and output

- uses different **data types**

- uses **arithmetic operators** and **assignment statements** to perform calculations

- uses **built-in** Python functions

- is easy to read and understand

→ use **selection** in Python

→ use **repetition** in Python

→ use simple **validation** to ensure user input is correct

→ test and evaluate a Python program.

KEYWORDS

IDLE interface: Python's Integrated Development and Learning Environment which provides features for creating, editing and running programs

data types: the different ways in which data can be stored; for example, number, string, date

arithmetic operators: +, − , *, / and other symbols which can be used for arithmetic

assignment statements: a statement which assigns a variable a value; for example, x=3

built-in functions: functions that can be used in the Python language without adding any additional code

KEYWORDS

selection: selecting statements based on a decision

repetition: repeating sections of code in a loop

validation: ensuring that the data entered by the user is acceptable

SCENARIO

Younger children need to understand the importance of secure passwords. Your company wishes to promote online safety and as a programmer you have been asked to create an electronic solo adventure game for young children aged 8–10 years old. The adventure game should provide the children with some different pathways to follow as they progress through a story.

The child will play the main character in the game. They will meet a robot and sweet shop owner on their journey. They need to find the Chocolate Room in a digital sweet shop.

When they find and enter it there will be two questions. If the child answers the questions correctly they will be given three of the letters from a four letter password. They then go on to guess the password after being given a clue. If they guess the password they open a digital treasure chest and win the game.

Your challenge is to examine existing program code and find out what it does, correct errors in the code and complete the game.

You will need to use the different programs provided by your teacher.

You will add new code, edit code and test any changes made to the code to make sure that it works correctly.

KEYWORDS

solo adventure game: a game in which the player assumes the role of the main character

program code: the Python code created in the IDLE

DID YOU KNOW?

Do you know that Python is one of the official programming languages that is used at *Google*?

Do you remember?

Before starting this unit, you should be able to:

✔ create sequences of code to form algorithms

✔ be able to break down a problem into smaller, more manageable tasks (decomposition)

✔ understand the terms 'target audience' and 'user requirements'

✔ select an appropriate data type for a data item

✔ make use of selection with IF statements

✔ create a simple flowchart which represents a solution to a problem

✔ identify when loops can be used to increase the efficiency of an algorithm

✔ evaluate an application based on the way in which the user requirements have been met.

Using Python

Learn

Python is normally installed on a computer with an Integrated Development Environment (IDLE). The IDLE provides lots of functions that are useful when writing Python code. Click on the IDLE (Python) icon on your computer to launch.

Python can operate in two modes: the first is **interactive mode**.

When you launch the Python IDLE, the prompt >>>, on the last line, shows that you are in the **Python shell**. This is the interactive mode which allows individual Python commands to be typed directly and carried out.

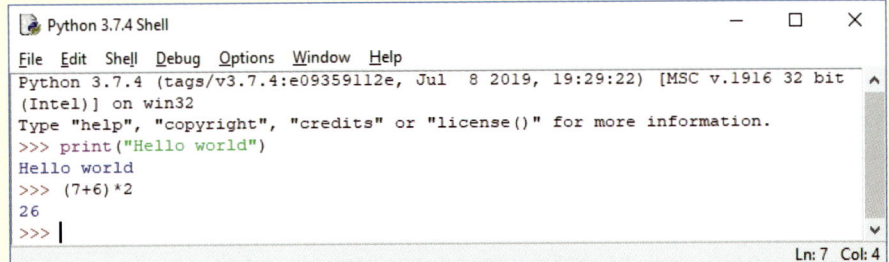

In the example above you can see a **print statement**. The print statement is a Python command which outputs information onto the screen. This print statement will output the words Hello world onto the screen.

The next line (7+6)*2 will output the result of the calculation. Notice you do not need to use the print command when performing calculations.

When using Python code you need to ensure that you type commands using lower case letters.

Python can tell the difference between upper-case (capital) letters and lower-case (small) letters (it is **case-sensitive**).

For example, if you enter `Print("Hello world")` an error should occur because 'Print' (with a capital 'P') is not the same as 'print' (with a small 'p'). You should always type Python commands in lower case.

Python also provides help at the command prompt. You can type `help()` and find out how to use commands in a Python program. You can also type `help(print)` to find out how to use the print command, such as how you can use it to display different data types on screen.

KEYWORDS

interactive mode: the Python shell allows commands to be entered and run immediately

Python shell: the Python interactive mode, where commands can be typed directly

print statement: a Python statement used to output text or values onto the screen

case-sensitive: can distinguish between capital and small letters

Python can use arithmetic symbols such as '+' for adding, '/' for dividing and '*' for multiplying. Remember the example above: **(7+6) *2** gives 26.

To close Python type **exit()**.

When a command is typed it must be 'translated' so that the computer can understand it. The IDLE has an **interpreter** which does this. Each command is changed into a form of **machine code** so that the computer can carry out or execute the command.

Typing commands directly into the Python shell is called programming in interactive mode. One disadvantage of using interactive mode is that the code cannot be saved when using Python in this way.

KEYWORDS

interpreter: the feature of Python which translates the Python code into language that the computer can understand, line by line

machine code: the language that a computer uses to carry out instructions

Practice

➤ Open the Python IDLE. (Your teacher will tell you where on the computer you can access Python.) The Python Shell will open as shown here:

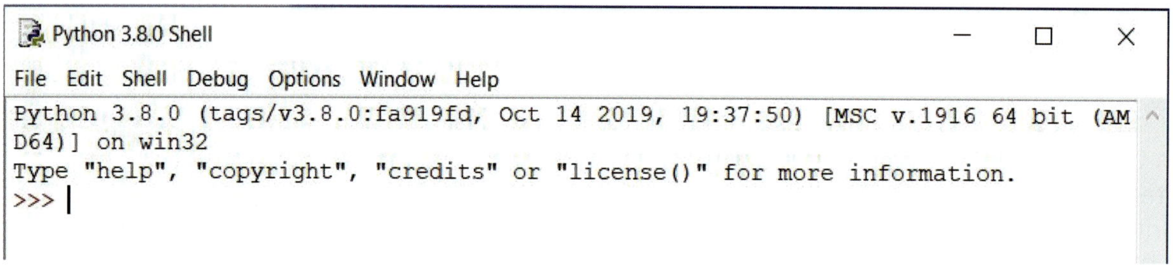

```
Python 3.8.0 Shell                                          —    □    ✕

File  Edit  Shell  Debug  Options  Window  Help
Python 3.8.0 (tags/v3.8.0:fa919fd, Oct 14 2019, 19:37:50) [MSC v.1916 64 bit (AM
D64)] on win32
Type "help", "copyright", "credits" or "license()" for more information.
>>> |
```

➤ Enter this command at the interactive prompt (>>>), and press ENTER:

`print ("Welcome to the Python Shell")`

➤ Now enter a command to print your name onto the screen and press ENTER:

`print ("add your name")`

➤ Now try this command:

`print ("Hello World)`

An error should occur because you have left out a set of quotation marks. Correct the error and execute the command again.

➤ Try entering this calculation:

`(7 + 3 * 2`

Look at what has happened this time. Why do you think this is? Correct the error and execute the command again. The answer should be 20.

➤ Try entering three or four of your own maths commands. Remember that the '*' (star symbol) is used for multiplying.

➤ Get Python to add 150 and 23 together, and then multiply the result by 3.

Using the Python IDLE in Script mode

Learn

On the previous pages you used the Python Shell to enter single lines of Python code. These are translated and executed one at a time and they cannot be saved.

Most of the time people write programs with many lines of code which they want to save.

Python can operate in two modes. The first was interactive mode using the Python shell. To create and save a program, Python's IDLE is used in the second mode: this is called **Script Mode**.

You use a text editor (a bit like Notepad) which allows you to enter and save lines of code.

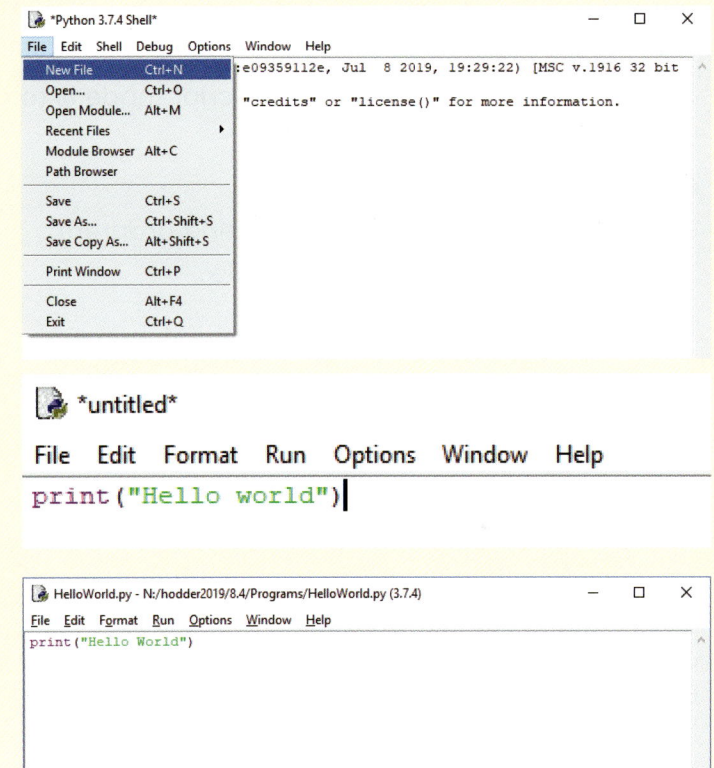

Create a program

Follow these steps to create a new program.

➤ From the Python Shell select 'File'.

➤ Then select 'New File'.

➤ A new window will open and you can enter lines of code into this text editor.

Type the command shown on the right into the new file.

Save a program

Follow these steps to save the program.

➤ From the text editor menu select 'File'.

➤ Then select 'Save as'.

➤ Call the program 'HelloWorld' and save it. (Note: all Python programs will have .py at the end to show that they are Python files.)

Run a program

Once you have completed the code you can run the program.

➤ From the text editor menu select 'Run'.

➤ Then select 'Run module' (or Press F5). This will cause the Python interpreter to **execute** the program.

> The output from the program will appear in the window of the Shell. In this case you should see the words 'Hello world' in the Shell window.

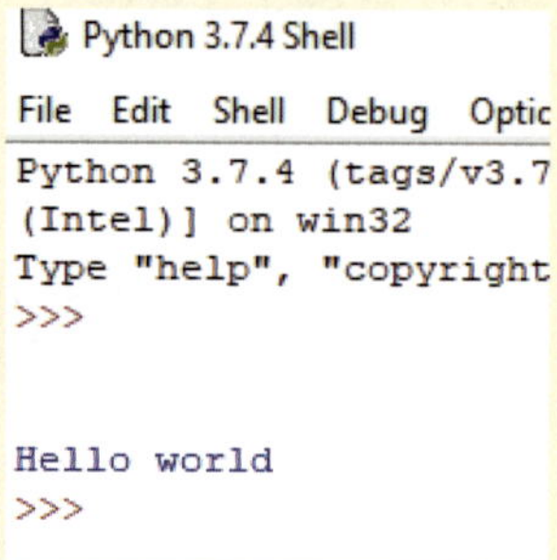

Correct errors

Here's how to correct errors in Script mode.

Look at the code in the screenshot below. There is an error (remember that Python can tell the difference between capital and small letters).

Can you see the error?

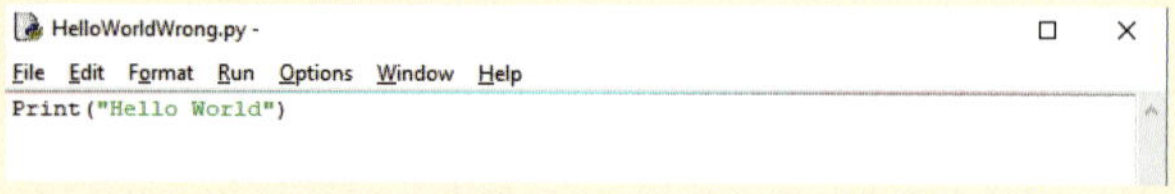

If there are errors in the code, they will be highlighted in red after you Run or execute the program:

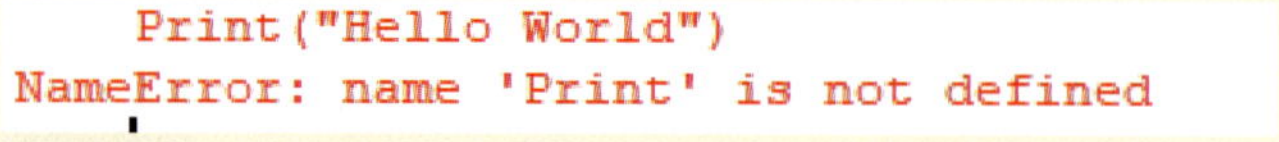

```
Print("Hello World")
NameError: name 'Print' is not defined
```

The only way to correct errors in Script mode is to open the program and correct the mistake in the code.

Open a program

Follow these steps to open an existing program.
> From the Python Shell select 'File'.
> Then select 'Open'.
> Select the name of the file you wish to open.
> Edit or correct the code.
> Save the program.

Add comments

Here's how to add comments to a Python program.

Adding **comments** to code allows you to explain what the code does or to provide extra information about the code. In Python you can do this by starting the comment with a hash (#) symbol. Any text on a line after a # symbol will be ignored by the interpreter.

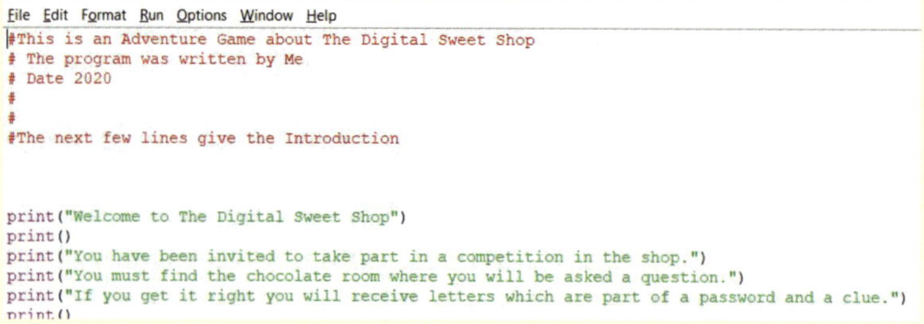

```
#This is an Adventure Game about The Digital Sweet Shop
# The program was written by Me
# Date 2020
#
#
#The next few lines give the Introduction


print("Welcome to The Digital Sweet Shop")
print()
print("You have been invited to take part in a competition in the shop.")
print("You must find the chocolate room where you will be asked a question.")
print("If you get it right you will receive letters which are part of a password and a clue.")
print()
```

KEYWORDS

script mode: Python's text editor which allows programmers to enter a list of commands and they are executed together

execute: another word for running a program

comments: text entered by the programmer to improve the readability of the code. They start with the # symbol in Python

Practice

➤ Open the file called **ad1.py** provided by your teacher.

➤ This file shows some of the introduction screen for the game. As the programmer you must add two comments to the code (remember to use the # to start a comment):

1 Add your name as a comment.

2 Add today's date.

➤ Run the program and look at the layout of the story on the screen. Discuss with a friend how you could improve the layout of the story on the screen. Ask these questions:

o Do you need to split any of the lines because they are too long? You can split the code by separating one print statement into two statements. For example, this is quite a long print statement:

```python
print("You will meet two people - one is
the sweet shop owner who wants to steal the
password so he can keep the sweets.")
```

o Why not split it into two statements like this?

```python
print("You will meet two people - one is the
sweet shop owner who wants to")
print("steal the password so he can keep the
sweets.")
```

o Do you need to add extra print statements to improve the layout and readability of the story? For example, you can add a blank line between statements by adding a blank **print()** statement, like this :

```python
print("You will meet two people - one is the
sweet shop owner who wants to")
print()
print("steal the password so he can keep
the sweets.")
```

➤ Add in some code for blank lines to space the text out on the screen. Do this by inserting **print()** on a line on its own.

➤ Edit the code to improve the layout of the story on the screen based on your discussions.

➤ Run the program and make sure the text in the story is laid out as you expect.

➤ Ask a friend to look at it and tell you if it is easy to read and understand.

If there are errors in your program, go to the line identified in the error message and check the spelling of the word print.

Check that you have two brackets around the text and check that there are two sets of quotation marks around the text.

Capturing user input

Learn

You have already seen how to output information onto the screen using the print statement. A computer program should also be able to accept input data from a user (for example the user should be able to answer questions or enter values on the screen).

Variables are used to store data in a program.

A variable is a named location in the computer's memory which stores data of a particular type. Data is entered by the user whilst the program is running.

Variables can hold data of different types. In order to store data you must decide on a name and a data type for the variable first. For example, to store the player's age you will need to name a variable which can hold a whole number (also known as an **integer**):

Variable Name	Data Type
playerage	integer

To store the player's name you will need a variable which can hold letters – this is called a **string**.

Variable Name	Data Type
playername	string

The variable names have been chosen as **playerage** and **playername** but they could have been called anything we wanted.

Variables can hold different data types. The table shows some examples of each data type.

Data Type	Example
String	Any textual characters, such as 'Hello World' or 'WWW1234'
Integer	Any whole number, such as 1 or 345 or 1000
Real	Any number with a decimal point, such as 1.2 or 56.8
Boolean	True or False; used when evaluating conditions in an IF statement

To capture data from the user you use the **input function**.

The input function captures user input as a string data type. This contains numbers, letters and symbols. For example 'Robot', 'Password123' and '**WWW777' are all examples of string data type.

Input is a built-in function in Python – it is part of the Python language.

KEYWORDS

variable: a named memory location used to store data of a given type during the program execution; a variable can change value as the program runs

integer: whole number

string data type: data which is made up of letters, numbers or any characters on the keyboard

input: a function which Python uses to capture string data from users

Notice that the string data type can include numbers. You may wonder why there is a separate data type for integers and real numbers. If numbers are stored as a string data type then Python does not know they are numbers and cannot use them in calculations.

The input statement prints a question onto the screen and captures the user's answer to the question in a variable called **playername**.

```
playername=input("What is your name? ")
print("Welcome " + playername)
```

playername is then used in the next line of code and printed onto the screen as part of a welcome message. Can you guess what will be printed onto the screen?

Practice

You are going to practise using string data types.

➤ Look at the code shown below. Running the code has produced an error in red text. Try to identify the error in the code.

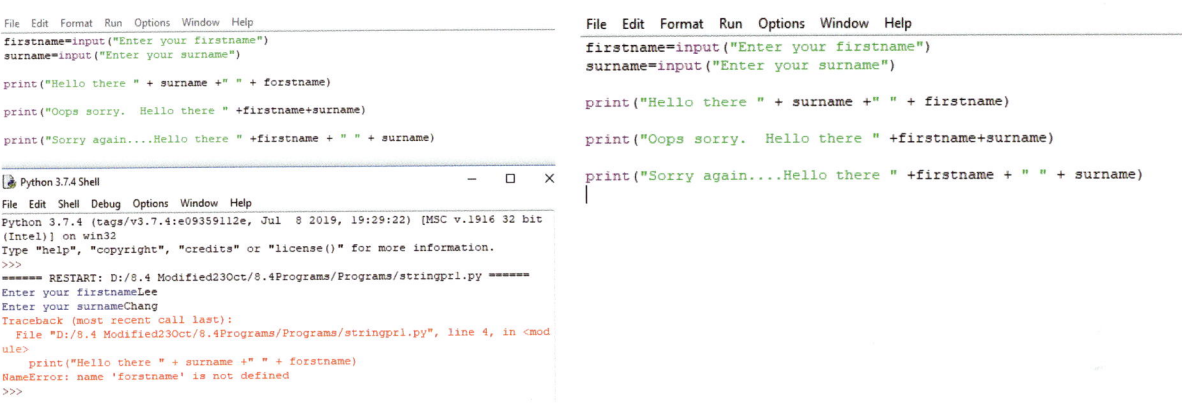

```
File Edit Format Run Options Window Help
firstname=input("Enter your firstname")
surname=input("Enter your surname")

print("Hello there " + surname +" " + forstname)

print("Oops sorry.  Hello there " +firstname+surname)

print("Sorry again....Hello there " +firstname + " " + surname)
```

```
Python 3.7.4 Shell                                    —   □   ×
File Edit Shell Debug Options Window Help
Python 3.7.4 (tags/v3.7.4:e09359112e, Jul  8 2019, 19:29:22) [MSC v.1916 32 bit
(Intel)] on win32
Type "help", "copyright", "credits" or "license()" for more information.
>>>
====== RESTART: D:/8.4 Modified23Oct/8.4Programs/Programs/stringpr1.py ======
Enter your firstnameLee
Enter your surnameChang
Traceback (most recent call last):
  File "D:/8.4 Modified23Oct/8.4Programs/Programs/stringpr1.py", line 4, in <mod
ule>
    print("Hello there " + surname +" " + forstname)
NameError: name 'forstname' is not defined
>>>
```

```
File Edit Format Run Options Window Help
firstname=input("Enter your firstname")
surname=input("Enter your surname")

print("Hello there " + surname +" " + firstname)

print("Oops sorry.  Hello there " +firstname+surname)

print("Sorry again....Hello there " +firstname + " " + surname)
```

➤ The error has now been corrected. Look at the code below:
➤ Write down what you think the outputs will be on a piece of paper. You should include everything that is being printed out onto the screen.
➤ Exchange your drawing with a friend.
➤ Open the file called **stringpr2.py** provided by your teacher, run it and check your drawing to see if you are right.

A robot called Botty in the Digital Sweet Shop game is going to create some directions so that you can get to the sweet shop. He has emailed the following directions to you:

> Greetings my friend. If you want to go to the Digital Sweet Shop you must walk across the long street and turn left at the traffic lights. There is a large shopping centre on the corner. Turn left here and you will see the Digital Sweet Shop beside the flower shop. The flowershop owner has a dog called Biscuit who barks all the time. Be careful he can bite!

> ➤ Open the file **robot.py**, provided by your teacher. It contains the program which Botty is using to send your email.
> ➤ Unfortunately his motherboard has become damaged. Run the program and look at the output. You will see that the strings are all mixed up.
> ➤ Edit the code so that the message Botty sends matches the one above.

Learn

The input function can only capture data as a string data type, so if you need a number from a user that you want to use in a calculation, you will need to convert the string data type to a number data type.

Your adventure game will ask the age of the players to ensure they are allowed to play the game. We can ask them to input their age using a statement such as:

```
input("What age are you? ")
```

We want to store their answer as a whole number (or integer) because we want to perform a calculation with it. However, as we know, this input statement only stores string values. Python uses the **int()** function to change the string value from the input statement into an integer (or whole number).

If we use a variable called **playerage** to hold the player's age as a whole number, then we can add the following statement to convert the input string to an integer (or whole number):

```
playerage = int(input("What age are you? "))
```

Integer	String
playerage	input("What age are you? ")

A single **print statement** can only display data of the same type. You cannot combine string data types with integer data types in one single print statement. So, if you want to print the player's age together with some words you must convert their age back to a string value.

The **str()** function will change an integer value to a string value.

For example let's say the player enters an age of 8, and the program has converted their input to an integer data type called **playerage**. To display some words along with their age you would write:

```
print ("You are aged " + str
(playerage))
```

Integer	String
playerage	str(playerage)
8	"8"

```
playerage=int(input("What age are you? "))
print("You are aged " + str(playerage))
```

The **int()** function is added to the input statement and this converts the data to an integer value and stores it in a variable called **playerage**.

playerage is then used in the next line of code and printed onto the screen as part a message. The print statement can only print data of type string; therefore, the **playerage** must be converted to a string for printing. The **str()** function is applied to the **playerage** to convert it to a string.

Practice

➤ Botty the robot has to be able to calculate the average score for the pupils who play the game. He has managed to program himself to do it for two players but needs help to do it for all five.

➤ Open the file called **robot2.py**, provided by your teacher.

➤ It contains Botty's code but he needs it to work for five values.
  o Add three more input statements so that you can enter five scores.
  o Change the total score calculation so that it calculates the total for five scores.
  o Change the average formula so that the average for five values is calculated.

➤ Change the **print** statement so that the program outputs the following message before printing the average: "The average of the five scores is".

```
File  Edit  Format  Run  Options  Window  Help
print("Hi I'm Botty the robot.  Please enter the five scores that you")
print("need me to find the average of")

score1=int(input("Enter score 1"))
score2=int(input("Enter score 2"))
#add more input statements here for score3, score4, score5


#change the total score calculation to include score3, score4, score5
totalscore=score1+score2

#change the formula for average to find the average of 5 values
average= totalscore/2

print(average)
```

Learn

The value of a variable can also be set by using an **assignment statement**. This gives the variable a value.

In your adventure game the player will start with three lives and two bars of chocolate. Two variables are needed to hold this data: one variable for the lives and one variable for the chocolate.

In the game these variables are called **playerlives** and **chocolate**.

A player can lose a life or eat a bar of chocolate during the game to get help with certain challenges. This means the value of these variables can change during the game. Assignment statements use the equals sign to do this.

For example, if a player loses a life, then we need to remove '1' from the **playerlives** variable:

playerlives=playerlives–1

Or, if a player eats a bar of chocolate, then we need to remove '1' from the **chocolate** variable:

chocolate=chocolate–1

When you use a variable it is sensible to give it a starting value at the start of the program. This is known as **initialising** the variable.

Below are two initialising assignment statements for the adventure game:

playerlives is assigned a value of 3 and **chocolate** is assigned a value of 2.

```
#Set player lives and chocolate
playerlives=3
chocolate=2
```

An assignment statement includes an equals symbol and takes the form:

name of variable=value
for example:
playerlives=3
total=score1+score2
playername="George"

Notice that, when assigning a string to a variable, you need to use quotation marks.

KEYWORD

initialise: setting a variable to a starting value. For example, x=0

Practice

➤ You have already used assignment statements in Botty's average calculation program in the last section.

➤ Open the file called **robot3.py**, provided by your teacher. Add assignment statements to carry out the tasks shown in the screenshot on the right. The first one has been done for you.

➤ Add a print statement to carry out the task in number 6.

```
print("Look at the assignment statements")

#1.  set a variable called playerlives equal to 3
playerlives=3

#Write assignment statements for 2 to 5 below

#2.  set a variable called chocolate equal to 2

#3.  set a variable called scorevalue equal to 4

#4.  set a variable called totalscore equal to scorevalue * 3

#5.  set a variable called robotname equal to "Botty"

#6.  write print statements to output all of the variables above
```

Practice

Now try these tasks using some code from the adventure game:

➤ Look at the code below.

```
File  Edit  Format  Run  Options  Window  Help
#This is an Adventure Game about The Digital Sweet Shop
# The program was written by Me
# Date 2020
#
#
#The next few lines give the Introduction
print("Welcome to The Digital Sweet Shop")
Print()
# Hint : fix the print statement above
print("You have been invited to take part in a competition in the shop.")
print("You must find the chocolate room where you will be asked a question.")
print("If you get it right you will receive letters which are part of a password and a clue.")
print()
# Hint : fix the print statement above - should Print have a capital 'P'???
print("You have been invited to take part in a competition in the shop.")
print("You must find the chocolate room where you will be asked two questions.")
print("If you get it right you will receive letters which are part of a password, and a clue.")
print()
print("At the end you must figure out the password and use it to open the")
print("treasure chest which contains a year's supply of all your favourite sweets.")
print("You will meet two people - one is the sweet shop owner who wants to steal the password so he can keep the sweets.")
print("the other person is a robot who will help you.")
print("W E L C O M E    T O    T H E    D I G I T A L    S W E E T    S H O P")
print()
print()

#Set player lives and chocolate
playerlives=3
chocolate=2


#Enter player details
playername=input("What is your name? ")
print("Welcome " + playername)
print()
playerage=int(input("What age are you? "))
print("You are aged " + str(playerage))
print()

print("You can give the two people in the story names")
ownername=input("What name do you want to give the sweet shop owner? ")
print("You have named the owner"+ownername+"that's a good name!!!")
print()
print()
```

➤ There are some errors in the code. Look at the hints in the code and write down how you would fix these two errors.

➤ With a partner, write down what the code will do when the errors are fixed. Explain the code using information about the:
  o print statements
  o assignment statements
  o input statements.

- Now open the file **ad2.py**, provided by your teacher.

```
Print()
# Hint : fix the print statement above
```

- Run the program. You will find that there are two errors and some repetition in the code. Use your previous analysis above to help you:
  - o fix the error on line 9 which is stopping the program from running
  - o fix the error on line 12 which is stopping the program from running

```
Print("Each clue will give you letters which is part of a password.")
print()
# Hint : fix the print statement above – should Print have a capital 'P'???
```

  - o run the program and ensure that the errors have been fixed
  - o save the program.
- Edit the code so that the user can enter a name for the robot they will meet into a variable called **robotname**. Save the program.

> Look at page 102 to remind yourself how to get an input from the user, then save the program.

- Edit the code so that the program outputs a suitable message to the user about their choice of name for the robot. Save the program.
- Look at the output created by the line below. There is a small problem here. Hint: when you run the program check to see how the output from this line looks on the screen.

```
print("You have named the owner"+ownername+"that's a good name!!!")
```

- Edit the program so that the output on the screen is correctly presented. Save the program.
- Edit the code so that the user is asked to enter the number of times that they have already played this game. This question should appear after they are asked to enter their age.

> You should think about how to convert an input from a string to a number – see page 104.

- Store the data in a variable called **gamesplayed**.
- The rules of the game have changed and players now only have one bar of chocolate. Edit the code so that this is the case.
- Edit the code to so that the user details are output onto the screen together after both questions have been asked, instead of after each value has been input.

```
What is your name? Linh

What age are you? 13
Welcome Linh
You are aged 13
```

> Remember that the print function can only output data of the same type. Therefore, **gamesplayed** needs to be converted to a string using the **str()** function. Look at the previous code and the *Learn* box on page 104 to remind you how to input a numeric value.

- Save the program.
- Run the program.
- Fix any errors that have arisen.
- Ask a friend to review your program and discuss other changes you could make to improve how the program appears to the user.

Adventure choices

Learn

Selection

Sometimes decisions have to be made in a program. This is usually because the program has reached a point where there is more than one option or choice. For instance, in the adventure game players must enter their name and age and then (if over 8 years old) they will enter a name for the sweet shop owner. Then there are a number of possible pathways for the program to follow depending on how the player answers certain questions.

Selection occurs when a question is asked. It is important in programming because the programmer can offer the user choices about the way in which they move through the program. Selection is achieved by using IF statements. You should already have some experience of IF statements.

The structure of an IF statement

Here are two simple IF statements:

`if playerage>10:` `print("You are too old to play this game")`	Condition 1 is that **playerage** is greater than 10.
`if playerage<8:` `print("You are too young to play this game")`	Condition 2 is that **playerage** is less than 8.
This statement uses two conditions and two IF statements.	

Remember logical operators:	
Equal to	==
Not equal to	!>
Less than	<
Greater than	>
Less than or equal to	<=
Greater than or equal to	>=

Remember: A **condition** contains a logical operator. The logical operator combines the parts of a condition together. For example **playerage>10** is a condition. The condition can evaluate to true or false.

IF statements can be extended to IF–ELSE statements which allow for more than one outcome.

`if` condition statements are be carried out when the condition is true.

`else` statements are carried out when the condition is false.

When a condition in an IF statement evaluates to true, the indented statements following IF are executed (but the statements following ELSE are *not* executed).

When a condition in an IF statement evaluates to false, the indented statements following ELSE are executed (but the statements following IF are *not* executed).

For example, this IF–ELSE statement allows for two different outcomes:

```
if (playerage>=8:
    print("You can play this game")
else:
    print("You cannot play this game")
```

Here is a flowchart representing the solution. You can see the two possible paths:

1   one for 'Yes', when the condition is true and the statements following IF are carried out

2   one for 'No', when the condition is false and the statements following ELSE are carried out.

The exact way of writing IF–ELSE statements in Python is as follows:

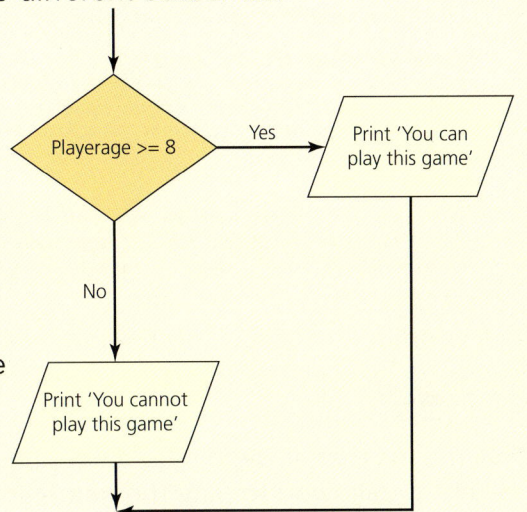

```
if condition:
    #statements to be
    carried out when the
    condition is true
else:
    #statements to be
    carried out when the
    condition is false
```

Note the indentation used in the lines following **if** and **else**. This is achieved by typing four spaces or pressing the tab key. Python uses indentation so that it knows which statements belong with **if** and which belong with **else**. Review the flowchart above: in Python code, the print statements would need to be indented.

You must include the colons in an IF–ELSE statement.

As you develop the adventure game you will have to use IF–ELSE statements. For example, as the game is for children aged between eight and ten, no child under the age of eight should be allowed to play. In this section of code, the IF–ELSE statement has been used to select which code will be carried out based on the age entered by the player. For example, what happens if a player is under eight, and what happens if they are eight or over?

The following code and section of flowchart represents a solution to the problem:

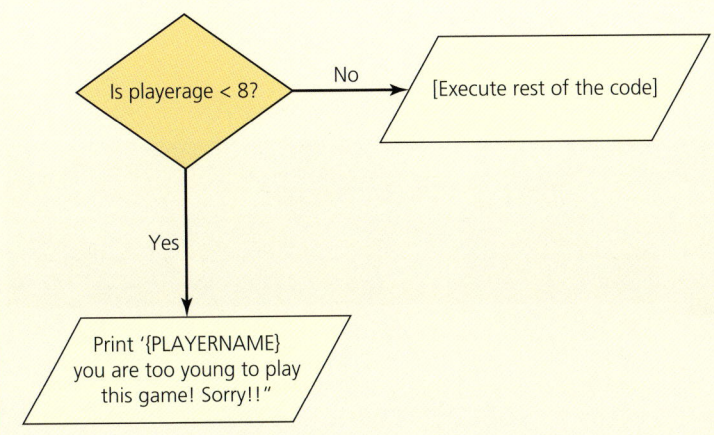

KEYWORDS

condition: an expression which evaluates to true or false; for example, X<10?

suite: a section of code which has been indented at the same level

indent: move the Python code in by four spaces

dedent: move the Python code out by four spaces

```
if playerage < 8:
    print(playername + " you are too young to play this game!  Sorry !!")
else:
    #Enter owner and robot's details
    print("You can give the two people in the story names")
    ownername=input("What name do you want to give the sweet shop owner? ")
    print("You have named the owner "+ownername+" that's a good name!!!")
    print()
    print()
    print(".......................................................")
    robotname=input("What name do you want to give the robot? ")
    print("You have named the robot "+robotname+" that's a good name!!!")
    print("Let's start the game.......good luck " + playername +"!!!!")
```

The condition for checking the player's age is:

```
if playerage<8
```

This means that, if the player enters an age less than eight, they will not be allowed to play the game and the message 'You are too young to play this game! Sorry!!' appears on the screen.

If the player enters an age of eight or more, the statements following the ELSE statement are executed.

From the code above, you can see that the next stage is to give the sweet shop owner a name.

Note that the indentation (spaces before statements) is very important because this is how Python decides to group statements together. The statements with the same indentation belong to a group and are called a **suite**. Python will indent the statements automatically after you type the ':' symbol.

If indentation is not correct you will get an error because Python needs to know which statements to group together.

DID YOU KNOW?

Indentation (adding spaces before program statements) is used in Python. This refers to the spaces that are used at the beginning of a statement.

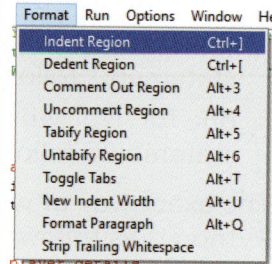

You can use the indent function on Python's menu to highlight code and indent it all together.

If you want to remove the indent, you can highlight the code and use the **dedent** feature. This will move all highlighted code out by four spaces.

Practice

- ➤ Open the file **indentfile.py** provided by your teacher.
- ➤ The file has errors because the indentation of the print statements is incorrect.
- ➤ Select the print statements as shown.
- ➤ Use the dedent option to bring the print statements back to the correct position.
- ➤ Save the program.
- ➤ Run the program.

```
File  Edit  Format  Run  Options  Window  Help
#This is an Adventure Game about The Digital Sweet Shop
# The program was written by Me
# Date 2020
#
#
#The next few lines give the Introduction


        print("Welcome to The Digital Sweet Shop")
        print()
        print("You have been invited to take part in a competition in the shop.")
        print("You must find the chocolate room where you will be asked two questions.")
        print("If you get them right you will receive letters which are part of a password, and a clue.")
        print()
        print("At the end you must figure out the password and use it to open the")
        print("treasure chest which contains a year's supply of all your favourite sweets.")
        print("You will meet two people one is a hacker who wants to steal the password so he can have the sweets.")
        print("the other person is a robot who will help you.")
        print("W E L C O M E    T O    T H E    D I G I T A L    S W E E T    S H O P")
        print()
        print()
```

Learn

Combining conditions

Decisions sometimes need to be made based on two or more conditions.

Example 1: if you help Botty with directions to the Digital Sweet Shop OR help with his calculations, then you can have some sweets.

> Remember:
>
> AND and OR are called Boolean operators.
>
> AND needs all of the conditions to be true to execute the statement that follows
>
> OR needs only one of the conditions to be true to execute the statement that follows.

Example 2: if you help Botty with directions to the Digital Sweet Shop AND help with his calculations, then you can have some sweets.

What is the difference between the way in which conditions are combined in Examples 1 and 2? Does using AND and OR make any difference?

The answer is yes. In Example 1, you only need to do one of the two tasks. In Example 2, you must do both.

IF statements can be combined using logical operators, such as AND and OR.

Look at the following IF statement. It is more efficient than the previous examples as two conditions have been combined into one:

``python
if (playerage>=8 and playerage<=10):
    print("You can play this game")
``
	Condition 3 is made up of two conditions; this statement is to be carried out *only* when both condition 1 **(playerage>=8)** AND condition 2 **(playerage<=10)** are true.
	
	When a condition in an IF statement evaluates to true, the statements following IF are executed.

Remember: Using the AND operator will give an overall outcome of true if *both* condition 1 and condition 2 are true; otherwise it gives an overall outcome of false. Using the OR operator will give an outcome of true if *either* condition 1 *or* condition 2 is true; otherwise it gives an overall outcome of false.

Here is another version of an IF statement which uses two conditions combined with the OR operator.

```python
if playerage < 8 or playerage >10:
    print(playername + " you are not the correct age to play this game!  Sorry !!")
```

What are the rules for evaluating conditions combined using an OR operator?

Condition 1: **playerage<8**

Condition 2: **playerage>10**

Boolean operator: **OR**

This table shows what will be printed by the program for a few different ages.

Player age entered	Print statement executed
10	
7	You are not the correct age to play this game! Sorry!!
9	
20	You are not the correct age to play this game! Sorry!!
6	You are not the correct age to play this game! Sorry!!
12	You are not the correct age to play this game! Sorry!!:

Multiple conditions can also be used within IF–ELSE statements.
For example, this IF–ELSE statement allows for two different outcomes:

```
if (playerage>=8 and playerage<=10):
  print("You can play this game")
else:
  print("You cannot play this game")
```

if condition 3:
    statements to be carried out when condition 3 is true (and condition 3 is only true when conditions 1 and 2 are true).
else:
    statements to be carried out when condition 3 is false, where condition 3 = `playerage>=8` AND `playerage<=10`

When a condition in an IF statement evaluates to true, the statements following IF are executed. Otherwise, the statements following ELSE are executed.

Practice

➤ Look at these IF statements relating to the **playerage**:

```
if playerage>10 or playerage <6:
  print("You can play the game")
else:
  print("You cannot play the game")
```

Player age entered	Print statement executed
10	You cannot play the game
7	
9	
20	
6	
12	

➤ Using the IF statements above, copy and complete the table by writing which print statement will be executed for each of the player ages entered. The first one has been completed for you.

➤ Discuss with a friend, how this IF statement will change the age rules for playing the game.

➤ Create a new IF statement which will ensure that players aged 7 to 11 can play the game. Use the following partially completed IF statement to help you.

```
if playerage >=7 AND _____:
  print _____
else:
  print _____
```

Algorithmic thinking

Draw a flow diagram for a program that does the following:

- A player enters their age.
- If the player is aged between 13 and 19, the program prints the words: "You are a teenager!"
- If the player is any other age the program prints the words: "You are not a teenager."

Learn

The player has now entered data for:

playername, **playerage**, **gamesplayed**, **ownername** and **robotname**.

Now they must decide whether or not to enter the Digital Sweet Shop.

The program should ask the user if they want to enter the shop. The user will have to answer this question. If they enter 'Y' that means 'Yes'. If they enter 'N' that means 'No'.

We must store the user's response in a variable. Let's call the variable **entershop**.

An IF statement is used to check the value of **entershop**.

Look at the code below and discuss what happens if the player enters 'Y' (for yes) or 'N' (for no).

```
#Enter the shop??
print("You walk up the steps to the shop......you open the door.  There is nobody there")
print("and the shop looks to be in bad repair.  ")
entershop=input("Do you enter the shop? Enter Y for yes and N for no ")
if entershop== "Y":
    print("Lets go.....up the stairs")
else:
    print("You are a coward!!!...Goodbye")
```

Note the condition in this case:

```
if entershop== "Y"
```

Why do you think we use '==' instead of '='? Look at the table below.

Assignment statement	entershop="Y"	Sets the value of the variable **entershop** equal to 'Y'
Comparison	entershop=="Y"	Checks the value of **entershop** to see if it is equal to 'Y'

When checking the value of a variable in a condition, you should use the **==** symbol.

When you want to assign a value to a variable, you should use the **=** symbol.

Practice

➤ Copy and complete the following table by inserting either **=** or **==**.

Task		= or ==	
set the player age equal to 9	**playerage**		9
check to see if the player age equals 11	**playerage**		11
set the games played equal to 0	**gamesplayed**		0
check to see if the **gamesplayed** equals 3	**gamesplayed**		3

➤ Look at the code shown below. A syntax error has occurred. Python has rules for spelling and grammar. These are called syntax rules.

A syntax error occurs when a statement is written incorrectly. For example, a misspelt word or variable name or missing brackets. A program cannot run if there are syntax errors, they must be corrected first.

Can you tell what the problem is here?

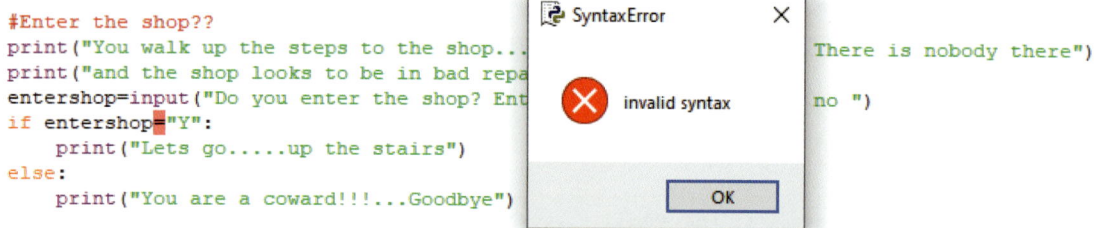

```
#Enter the shop??
print("You walk up the steps to the shop...                There is nobody there")
print("and the shop looks to be in bad repa
entershop=input("Do you enter the shop? Ent                 no ")
if entershop="Y":
    print("Lets go.....up the stairs")
else:
    print("You are a coward!!!...Goodbye")
```

SyntaxError   ×

✗ invalid syntax

OK

➤ Now try these tasks using some code from the adventure game:
  o Open the copy of **ad5a.py**, provided by your teacher.
  o Run the program and see what the output is from the program when you enter different values for the player's age.
  o Edit the code so that the message for a player under eight reads:

> Sorry [NAME OF PLAYER], you are only [AGE] years of age and are too young to play the game.

So, for instance, if the player was called Yang and was aged seven, the message would read:

> Sorry Yang, you are only 7 years of age and are too young to play the game.

You can do this by editing the print statement following the IF statement. You will need to change the order of the things in the print statement. For example, the **playername** will have to come after the word 'Sorry'.

> Look at the print statements used to output the **ownername** and the **robotname** on to the screen.

Decomposition

- Use the file **flowchartIF.docx**, provided by your teacher. Complete the flowchart which represents a solution to the following problem.

  In the adventure, when the player goes upstairs in the shop, they are presented with a choice. The player can go left or right at the top of the stairs. Different things will happen based on their choice. Unfortunately, there is a hole in the floor to the right and so the player will lose a life if they choose right. So, the game will take one life away and place the player at the top of the stairs at a door. If the player goes to the left, they go straight to the door at the top of the stairs without losing a life.

  You need to add these steps to the flowchart.

  o The program outputs this first message onscreen: 'You have reached the top of the stairs and you can go right or left'.

  o The program asks the user to enter 'R' for right and 'L' for left, and stores the user's response in a variable called **direction**.

  o If the player enters 'R' the program outputs the message 'You have fallen through the hole in the floor and lost a life – you must start again'.

  o If the player enters any letter other than 'R' the program outputs the message 'You are standing at the door of the Chocolate Room'. This is not what we want - we only want this message to appear when they enter 'L'. We will however resolve this issue a little later on.

- Ask a friend to review your flowchart to ensure that the solution is correct.
- Modify the flowchart if necessary.

Algorithmic thinking

- Turn the flowchart into Python code on a piece of paper using a pencil. Use the code in the file **ad5a.py** to help you create the new section of code.
- Write a print statement to output the first message to the player: 'You have reached the top of the stairs and you can go right or left'.
- Write an input statement with a message to capture the user's response in a variable called **direction**.

  Hint:
  ```
  direction=
      input
  (_____)
  ```

- Write an IF–ELSE statement and conditions to check the value of the variable **direction** and to output the correct message for R and L.

  Hint: start with **if** **direction==**

- Write a few comments to explain the code. Start each comment with the # symbol.
- Review the code with a friend and look out for any syntax errors such as:
  o missing quotation marks
  o too many brackets or missing brackets
  o misspelling of variable names or keywords like print and input
  o incorrect use of capital letters.
- Correct any visible errors.

Practice

➤ Add the code you have written to the program **ad5a.py**, following the line:

print("Let's go.....up the stairs")

Note that the program will show you where to put your newly written code. Look for the line:

"#continue your code here at this level of indent"

around line 64.

➤ Save and Run the program.

➤ Correct any errors that have occurred. You have seen syntax errors but programs can also contain **logic errors**. These occur when there is an error in the logic of the program. For example, parts of the program may be missing, in the wrong order or could be using the wrong data. The program will run but may not produce the correct output.

➤ The section of code below contains a logic error. Look at the code and discuss what is wrong with it, with a friend.

> Hint: look at the IF statement.

```
#Enter the shop??
print("You walk up the steps to the shop......you open the door.  There is nobody there")
print("and the shop looks to be in bad repair.  ")
entershop=input("Do you enter the shop? Enter Y for yes and N for no ")
if entershop=="N":
    print("Lets go.....up the stairs")
else:
    print("You are a coward!!!...Goodbye")
```

➤ Testing is an important part of creating a program. You need to know that the program works correctly. A test plan will help identify errors that could occur. A test plan can be created using a table with columns as follows.

Test	Variable to test	Reason for test	Value to be used	Expected Outcome	Actual Outcome	Does Expected Outcome match the Actual Outcome? (Y/N)	Type of error (Syntax or Logic)
1	playerage	player too young	7	too young message	too young message	Y	None
2	playerage	player correct age	9	player can proceed and play game	player can proceed and play game	Y	None
3							

➤ Create a **test plan** for your solution using different values for the variables **playerage**, **entershop** and **direction**. You can do this by creating a table with the headings shown above.

➤ Test your program using the test plan you have created and correct any errors in the code.

KEYWORDS

logic error: when the program does not do what the programmer wanted it to
test plan: a document containing information about how the program will be tested and the data used to test it

Adventures with lots of choices: going upstairs in the house

Learn

What if the player had more than two directions to take at the top of the stairs? Let's add another direction – 'S' for straight ahead.

Python uses the **ELIF** statement to allow you to check multiple conditions for TRUE. This means that if a condition evaluates to true, the block of code following that particular ELIF statement will be executed.

Using IF–ELSE statement with three directions:

```
if direction=="R":
    print("You have fallen through the hole in the floor and lost a life.")
if direction=="L":
    print("You are standing at the door of the Chocolate Room.")
if direction=="S":
    print("You reach a dead end. You turn around and this time turn left
    at the stairs.")
else:
    print("You were meant to enter R, L or S! Never mind - you decide to go left
    and reach the Chocolate Room.")
```

All of the IF statements are executed one after the other even if the correct one is found.

Using ELIF statement with three directions:

```
if direction=="R":
   print("You have fallen through the hole in the floor and lost a life.")
elif direction=="L":
        print("You are standing at the door of the Chocolate Room.")
elif direction=="S":
        print("You reach a dead end. You turn around and this time turn left at
        the stairs")
        print("You are now standing at the door of the Chocolate Room.")
else:
        print("You were meant to enter R, L or S!  Never mind - you decide to go
        left and reach the Chocolate Room.")
```

- We can add as many choices as necessary using ELIF.
- ELIF is more efficient because, once the correct IF statement is found, the program will stop checking.
- We can add a statement which is executed if none of the IF or ELIF statements are true.

We would like the player to enter 'R', 'L' or 'S'. However, they could enter any other letter too. If they did we would like to display the message: 'You were meant to Enter R, L or S! Never mind – you decide to go left and reach the Chocolate Room.' We can write either of the following to do this:

ELIF makes writing code easier when we have to think about a lot of options.

➤ Like the ELSE statement, the ELIF statement is optional. That is, you do not need to have one in an IF statement.

➤ However, whereas the ELSE statement can only be used once in an IF statement, the ELIF statement can be used as many times as needed.

The structure of a statement containing ELIF is shown below.

```
if condition1:
    statements to be carried out when condition1 is true
elif condition2:
    statements to be carried out when condition2 is true
elif condition3:
    statements to be carried out when condition3  is true
```

The else statements are to be carried out when none of the above conditions is true.

The flow chart below shows how the different Python statements in the example above are selected when using ELIF.

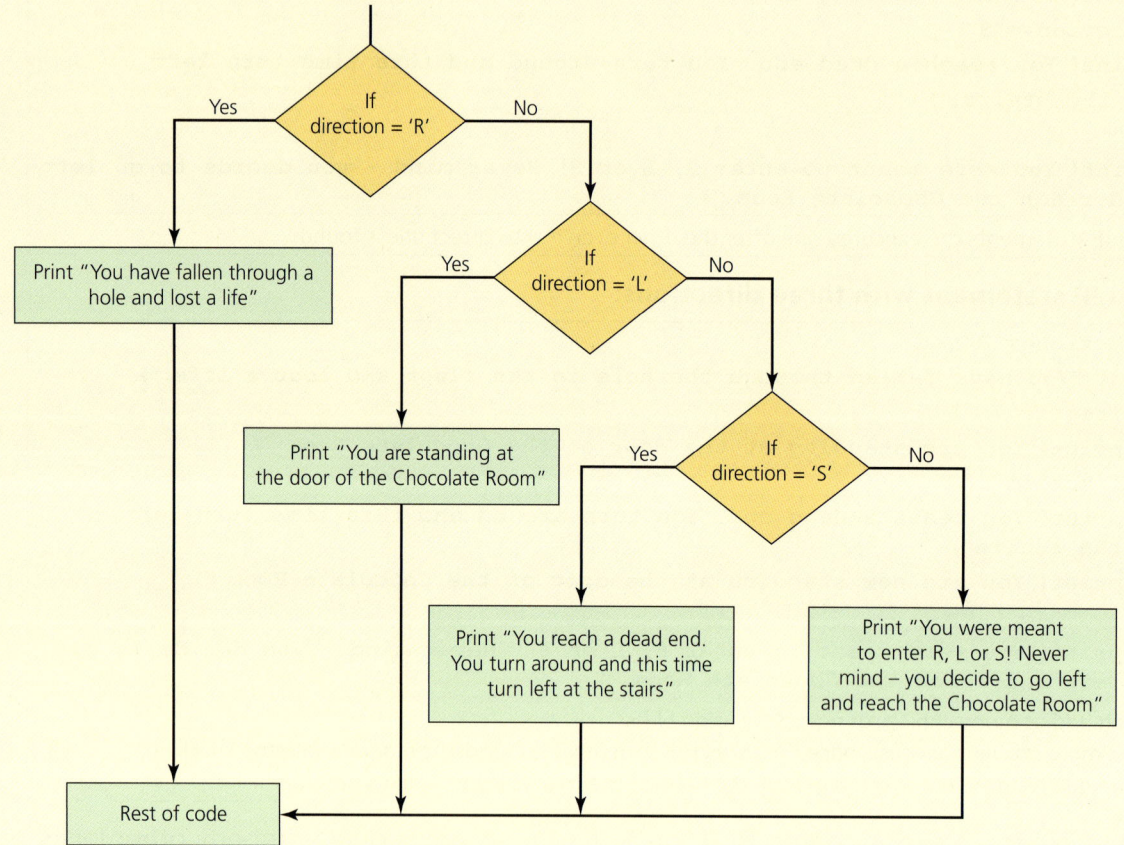

From the flowchart above, you can see that only one set of statements will be executed. So, if a player chooses to go to the left, only the instruction

print("You are standing at the door of the Chocolate Room.")

will be executed. After this, the program will exit out of the entire IF statement and continue with the rest of the code.

Decomposition

- Look at the code on the right. Discuss with a friend what the output would be if you enter the following values: **x=4, y=7**; **x=8, y=8**; **x=11, y=21**.

- Look at the code below on the right. Which message will be output if you enter the following values:

  x=5, y=4, z=11

  x=7, y=7, z=99

  x=12, y=21, z=0

- Create a set of values for **x**, **y** and **z** so that the message 'Hello world' is output.

```
File  Edit  Format  Run  Options  Window  Help
#elif3.py
x=int(input("Enter a value for x"))
y=int(input("Enter a value for y"))
if(x < y):
    message= "x is less than y"
elif (x == y):
    message= "x is same as y"
else:
    message="x is greater than y"
print(message)
#elif4.py
x=int(input("Enter a value for x"))
y=int(input("Enter a value for y"))
z=int(input("Enter a value for z"))
if(x < y)and (x < z):
    message= "Hello world"
elif (x == y) or (x == z):
    message= "Good afternoon"
else:
    message="Good morning"
print(message)
```

Practice

Open your version of **ad5b1.py**, provided by your teacher.

You are going to add the code for:

➤ when the user selects 'L' to go left at the top of the stairs
➤ when the user selects 'S' to go straight on at the top of the stairs.

You can use two separate ELIF statements for this. Add the ELIF statements in the position shown below.

If they select left, include the following print statement:

```
print("You are standing at the door of the Chocolate Room.")
```

If they select straight on, include the following print statements:

```
print("You reach a dead end. You turn around and this time turn left at
the stairs.")
```

```
print("You are now standing at the door of the Chocolate Room.")
```

```
if direction=="R":
    print("Oops....You have fallen through the hole in the floor and lost a life.")
    print("You climb the stairs again and select Left.  You are standing at the door of the Chocolate Room")
#add elif and condition here followed by :
    #add correct print statement here
else: print("You must enter R or L")
```

➤ Save and run the program.
➤ Look at the code below ELIF. What happens if a user tries to enter a value which is not 'R', 'L' or 'S'?
➤ Using the flowchart on the previous page, add a final ELSE statement to print a message if the user does not enter 'R', 'L' or 'S'.

Learn

Taking away a life

A variable is needed to keep track of the player's lives.

A variable called **playerlives** will be used. Each player starts with three lives, so **playerlives** will be set to 3 using an assignment statement:

playerlives=3

To increase the value stored in the variable by one, we use an assignment statement.

playerlives=playerlives+1

In this example:

➤ **playerlives** was assigned the value of 3
➤ add 1 to the current value of **playerlives**
➤ store the new increased value back in the variable **playerlives**
➤ print the new value of **playerlives**, which is now equal to 4.

Practice

➤ Open the file called **ad5c.py** provided by your teacher. You are going to write code to reduce the player's lives if they choose to go right.
The **playerlives** variable has been set to 3 at the start. That means every player has three lives to start with.

```
#Set player lives and chocolate
playerlives=3
chocolate=2
```

> Computers have to do things in simple steps. When performing this subtraction, we need to tell the computer to take the current value of **playerlives**, subtract one from it and then store the result of the calculation in the variable called **playerlives**, like this:
>
> **playerlives=playerlives-1**

➤ Now add a statement which will subtract a life from the player if they select 'R' for right in the program. Add the line of code where you see the comment.

```
if direction=="R":
    print("Oops....You have fallen through the hole in the floor and lost a life.")
    print("You climb the stairs again and select Left.  You are standing at the door of the Chocolate Room")
    #add a line of code here to subtract one from the playerlives variable
elif direction=="L":
    print("You are standing at the door of the Chocolate Room.")
```

➤ Add a print statement after your new line of code to tell the player that they have lost a life.
➤ Save the program.
➤ Run the program.
➤ Does it do what you expect it to?

Answer the robot's question

Learn

In the next stage of the game, the player meets the robot at the door of the Chocolate Room. The robot asks the player a question to make sure that they know about secure passwords.

The robot will ask the question then give the player a choice of 3 answers.

The player must guess by entering the numbers 1, 2 or 3.

➤ If the player gets the question right then the robot will give the player 2 bars of chocolate.

➤ If the player gets the question wrong the player will lose a life.

Decomposition and algorithmic thinking

The process of answering the question in the game can be broken into steps using decomposition. Then you can use algorithmic thinking to create a set of steps or a flow chart to solve the problem.

- ✪ Consider the steps involved in this process:

  The robot asks the question

  The player enters their answer

  The program checks the player's answer against the correct answer

  If the player's answer is correct

     the player gets 2 bars of chocolate

  if the player's answer is wrong

     the player loses a life

- ✪ Open the file called **ad5b3Start.py**, provided by your teacher.

- ✪ Go to the section **# Answer the robot's question**.

```
#Answer the robot's question
print()
print()
print("..............................................................")
print("The door opens and someone is standing there.  It is the robot "+robotname)
print("He tells you that you cannot enter unless you show that you know all about secure passwords.")
print("He asks you a question")
print()
print()
print("Hello " + playername +" Which of the following would be a good strong password?")
print("If you answer correctly he will give two bars of chocolate")
print("1 DigitalSweetShop, 2 Botty,  3 N*123MGx")

#enter a print statement which will tell the user to enter a number between 1 and 3

#enter an if statement to check if playeranswer is equal to 3
    #enter an assignment statement to increase chocolate by 2
    #enter a print statement to say "You have got two bars of chocolate, open the wrappers to see the two letters"
    # enter another print statement to say "You have letters A and R - memorise these"
#enter else:
    # enter a print statement to say "You have not guessed correctly so you have lost a life"
    # enter an assignment statement to subtract one from player lives
```

> Remember to indent the code as shown in the comments.

- ✪ In pairs look at the comments in this section and write down the lines of code required to replace the comments.
- ✪ Replace the comments in red in the code with the correct Python code.
- ✪ Save the program.
- ✪ Run the program and check to see if it works correctly.
- ✪ Check over the code for errors.

Validating user input

Learn

As the programmer of the game, you want to ensure that user input is acceptable and correct. Therefore, you should use validation.

You are going to check the user's response to the question at the start of the game:

'Do you enter the shop? Enter Y for yes and N for no.'

The program needs to ensure that only Y or N is accepted.

You can use a loop to make sure that the user enters a value that the program will accept.

While loop

The **while loop** repeats a series of programming commands while a condition is true. It is structured as follows:

```
while condition
    statement(s)
```

The following piece of code will keep looping until the user types 'Y' or 'N'. As soon as they type 'Y' or 'N', the program would move on to the next piece of code in the program (not shown in the screenshot).

```
#Use a loop to make sure the user enters Y or N
enterhouse=input("Do you enter the shop? Enter Y for yes and N for no ")
while enterhouse!="Y" and enterhouse!="N":
        enterhouse=input("Enter Y or N please")
```

A while loop can also be used to count using a **counter variable**. This is useful if a programmer wants to keep track of the number of times something happens in the game.

For example, to print out all of the numbers from 1 to 9, the following loop would be used:

```
#loop 1
number=1
while number<10:
    print(number)
    number=number+1

#loop 2
answer=int(input("Enter a value which is between 1 and 10"))
while answer>=1 and answer<=10:
    answer=int(input("Wrong - Enter a value between 1 and 10"))


#loop 3
userinput=input("Enter a letter in the range A - C")
while answer!="A" and answer!="B" and answer!="C":
    answer=input("Enter a letter in the range A - C")


#loop 4
times=int(input("Which times tables do you want to see"))
number=0
while number<=12:
    result=times*number
    print(str(times)+"*"+str(number)+"="+str(result))
    number=number+1
```

The variable **number** is used to count through the loop.

KEYWORDS

while loop: a loop which will continue to run while a condition is true

counter variable: a variable which is used to count the number of times a loop has been executed; it is usually increased by 1 each time the loop is executed

Practice

➤ Look at each of the loops on the right.
➤ With a partner discuss what will happen on screen when each loop is executed.
➤ **Loop 2** is not correct – can you suggest what needs to change to make it work?
➤ Open the file **whileloops.py** and run the program.
➤ Were your answers to the above questions correct?
➤ Did you get the answer to **loop 2** correct? If not you will find the correct code in **loop 5** in the program **whileloops.py**.

> Hint: The two conditions used are not correct.

```
#loop 1
number=1
while number<10:
    print(number)
    number=number+1

#loop 2
answer=int(input("Enter a value which is between 1 and 10"))
while answer>=1 and answer<=10:
    answer=int(input("Wrong - Enter a value between 1 and 10"))

#loop 3
userinput=input("Enter a letter in the range A - C")
while answer!="A" and answer!="B" and answer!="C":
    answer=input("Enter a letter in the range A - C")

#loop 4
times=int(input("Which times tables do you want to see"))
number=0
while number<=12:
    result=times*number
    print(str(times)+"*"+str(number)+"="+str(result))
    number=number+1
```

Go further

Consider how you could validate the user input for answering the robot's question about passwords on page 121. The input can only be between 1 and 3.

> Look back at page 122 to remind yourself about while loops.

You will need to break the problem down into a number of steps. To validate the input, you are going to create a while loop for the game.

◆ Open the file called **ad61.py**, provided by your teacher.
◆ Examine the code in the section **#Answer the robot's question**.
◆ Write a statement which will ask the user to enter a value between 1 and 3.

> Use the input statement to do this.

◆ Write a condition on paper, which will check to see if **playeranswer** is not between 1 and 3.
◆ Replace the two comments highlighted in the screenshot below with your two new lines of code. Do not forget to put a ':' at the end of the conditions otherwise an error will occur.

> You can do this by creating two conditions and using the OR logical operator. Condition 1: **playeranswer <1** OR Condition 2: **playeranswer >3**.

```
playeranswer=int(input("Enter a number between 1 and 3"))
#enter while statement with conditions here to make sure the player enter a number between 1 and 3
    #enter an input statement which will tell the user to enter a number between 1 and 3

if playeranswer==3:
    chocolate=chocolate+2
    print("You have got two bars of chocolate, open the wrappers to see the two letters")
    print("You have letters A and R - memorise these")
else:
    print("You have not guessed correctly so you have lost a life")
    playerlives=playerlives-1
```

◆ Save the code.
◆ Run the code.
◆ Ensure you correct any errors.

The Chocolate Room and ending the game

Challenge yourself

Once the player has answered the robot's question they enter the Chocolate Room, where they find the sweet shop owner. She will ask the player a question as follows:

'Which of the following could be used as a good password 1. Your pet's name. 2. Password123 3. A random set of numbers and letters.'

(The correct answer is 3)

If the player enters 3 they can pick one of two chocolate bars by entering a number 1 or 2.

➤ If the player picks chocolate bar 1 there is no information in it and they lose a life.
➤ If the player picks chocolate bar 2 the letter "T" is inside the wrapper.

If the player gives the wrong answer (1 or 2) to the owner's question they lose all their chocolate and lose a life.

Some of the code for the Chocolate Room has been completed for you.

With a friend look at the code.

Your challenge is to add the lines of code that are missing for the Chocolate Room.

```
#enter The Chocolate Room

print("Welcome to the Chocolate Room. I am the owner of this sweet shop, my name is "+ownername)
print("You must answer this question.")

#add an input statement to ask the question on the next line and store the response in a variable called answer
# "Which of the following could be used as a good password 1.  Your pet's name.  2.  Password123    3.  A random collection of numbers and letters?  "
# HINT : Use answer=int(input(...........................))

if answer==3:
        chocolatebar=int(input("Do you want chocolate bar 1 or 2? "))
        # add code to check if the chocolate bar is equal to 1
                #add code to print this message to the user "Hard luck, you lose a life and there is no information in that wrapper"
                #add code to subtract 1 from the player lives
        elif chocolatebar==2:
                print("OK - you can have the chocolate bar and the letter in the wrapper is T")

else:
        print("Wrong answer - you lose a life and all of your chocolate")
        #add code to set the chocolate value to 0
        #add code to subtract 1 from the player lives
```

➤ You can do this by opening the file **ad62.py**, provided by your teacher and add the required lines of code.

Ending the game

➤ Once the player has left the Chocolate Room the program will:
  o ask the player to try to remember any of the letters they were given in the game
  o ask the player to try to guess the password using the clue and the letters they already know
  o calculate and show the player their score.

```
# Guess password and output the score

#this loop clears the screen
for i in range(1,35):
    print()

bonus=0
numbercorrect=0

#the player must try to guess the password
print("Now you must enter each letter that you remember ")
print("You will be given 3 tries")

#add code here for a for a while loop using that counts from 1 to 3, so player has 3 guesses:
        letter=input("Try number "+str(i))
        #add an if statement here to check if the letter equals A, R or T:
                #add code to add 1 to numbercorrect
                #add code to print "Correct - well done"
        else:
                print("Wrong - sorry")

guess = input("Now try and guess the password **** - the clue is in this line four times.  Use the letters you were given to help")

if guess=="star":
    print("You are a star - you have opened the treasure chest of sweets and earned 1000 points")
    bonus=1000

score=(chocolate*50) + playerlives*50 + bonus

#add code here to output playername
#add code here to output the number of bars of chocolate the player has
#add code here to output number of lives the player has
#add code here to output number of bonus points the player has
#add code here to output the player's score
```

➤ Add the lines of code that are missing from this section of the program. You can do this by editing **ad63.py** provided by your teacher.
➤ Run the program and correct any errors.

Final project

You are going to create a game in Python, for 10–11 year olds to learn their times tables. Players will be asked 12 multiplication questions and their score will be calculated. You will use the skills you've learnt in this unit.

➤ Open the game **FINAL.py**, provided by your teacher, and look at the code. Use this code to look at when creating your new project.

The game should have the following features.

➤ An introductory screen with information about the game.

➤ A section of code, containing a while loop, to allow the user to input their name.

➤ A section of code, containing a while loop, to allow the user to input their age. The player's age must be between 10 and 11.

> Hint: look at the example of combining conditions on p106 to help you.

➤ A section of code to print a welcome message including the player's details onto the screen.

➤ A section of code which asks the child which times tables they want to try. Store this in a variable called **tables**.

➤ A while loop in which a variable called **number** goes from 0 to 12

- A section of code which prints out **number * tables** as an equation, with a question mark. For example: What is **5 * 5**?
- A section of code to calculate the result of multiplying the variable **number** by **tables**; use an assignment to store the result of this calculation in a variable called **result**.
- A section of code to allow the user to input their answer to the question, stored in a variable called **answer**. Do not forget to use **int()** with the input statement.
- A section of code, containing an IF statement, which checks to see if the **answer** equals the **result**. If the result and the answer are the same, then the player's score is increased by 1.

> Note that all of this code should be indented so that it is inside the while loop.

➤ A section of code to output the player's score and a message stating that the program has ended.

Run your game and correct any errors.

Evaluation

➤ Ask a friend to play your game and comment:
  o is it fun and enjoyable? (give two examples)
  o is it easy to use?
  o are the messages easy to understand?
  o are the final scores correct for the pupil? (they should check the calculations and keep a written record of each answer to see if the code is working correctly).

➤ Open your program and look at the code. Reflect on how you have used:
  o comments to improve readability
  o validation to ensure data is acceptable.

➤ Based on the evaluations, make a list of recommendations to improve your game.

Spreadsheet modelling: Model my merch

Spreadsheets

Spreadsheets can be used to help analyse data and improve how it is presented. A spreadsheet can perform calculations automatically and, if the values are changed, it can work out the new results automatically. This is an advantage because it means that you can try lots of values and see what the new results are. As the calculations are done so quickly, you can spend time looking at the new results and thinking about how changes to the data can affect it. In other words, you can predict what would happen if you made certain changes. Spreadsheets can be used to collect and store large amounts of data in rows and columns. We make use of abstraction techniques to view necessary data. For example, the data can be searched, sorted or filtered so that unnecessary data is hidden and only relevant data is displayed on the screen.

Big Data is collected by the many devices on the Internet of Things (IoT). The devices generate a lot of data that can be used to make them useful but it can also be analysed for other purposes. For example, your mobile phone constantly broadcasts information about your location. Smart watches collect information about fitness levels and exercise patterns. Most data collected by the IoT is stored in a form that can be used in a spreadsheet. The data can then be analysed to provide information. For example, business owners may want to know the number of users of their website, smart city lighting may collect data on electricity usage, and data about our spending habits can be analysed so that we receive messages on our smartphone about products we like.

In this unit you will learn to:

→ use the features of a spreadsheet to solve problems
→ use the following advanced features of a spreadsheet: **absolute cell references**, **conditional formatting**, validation, **named cells**
→ build more sophisticated formulas and use in-built functions to carry out calculations
→ use aspects of **data modelling** including **IF statements** and **lookup statements**
→ use **nested IF statements**
→ validate input using **presence**, **length**, **range** and **type** checks.
→ **sort** and **filter** contents of a spreadsheet

KEYWORDS

absolute cell reference: a cell reference that remains constant even if it is copied to other cells

conditional formatting: applying formatting such as colour to a cell based on certain criteria

named cell range: giving one cell or a set of cells a name; the cells can be referred to using the name assigned

data modelling: using mathematical functions and calculations on data to predict or model what may happen in the event of certain changes

IF statement: a statement which evaluates a condition and places one value in the cell if the condition is true and another value in the cell if the condition is false

lookup statement: Used to search through a table of data for a value and then return results if that value is found

→ link data between worksheets using formulas
→ create and use **macros** to automate tasks
→ understand how spreadsheets can be used as a modelling tool to support basic decision making.

KEYWORDS

sort: to change the order of data; for example, data can be sorted in alphabetical order or numerically
filter: A spreadsheet feature which allows the user to apply certain criteria and exclude or show certain data
macro: a small program which is used to automate a task

Microsoft Excel 2016 has been used to complete the examples in this unit. You can also complete the examples in a spreadsheet application of your choice, such as *Google Sheets* or *LibreOffice Calc*.

SCENARIO

You are a new employee in a local skate park, called Wreck Deck Skate Park. The owners, Văn and Hoa have just opened a merchandise store and want you to create a spreadsheet to help them keep track of the sale of goods. The store is going to stock a small selection of products including T-Shirts, skateboards and scooters. As you have some knowledge of spreadsheets, the owners have asked you to prepare a spreadsheet which will help them make decisions about their business.

Do you remember?

Before starting this unit you should be able to carry out the following in *Microsoft Excel*:
✔ Select an appropriate data type for data in a spreadsheet.
✔ Format data to improve its presentation.
✔ Write simple formulas to help analyse the data.
✔ Display a spreadsheet in formula view.
✔ Use the chart feature to create visual information.

KEYWORDS

nested IF statement: an IF statement which is embedded in another IF statement
presence check: a validation check which is used to ensure that there is a value entered. A length check can be used to do this; for example, a check to ensure that the value entered has at least one character
length check: a validation check which is used to ensure that the value entered has a particular number of characters; for example, a check to ensure that a name has at least five characters
range check: a validation check which is used to ensure that the value entered lies within a given range; for example, 1–100
type check: a validation check which is used to ensure that the value entered is of a certain data type; for example, a check to ensure data is numeric

Using conditional formatting and validation

Learn

Conditional formatting allows you to create rules for a range of cells so that they are formatted in a certain way depending on their value. This is useful if you want to highlight key data in the spreadsheet. This is a form of abstraction as conditional formatting can filter out data by making it less visible to the user.

For example, you can make a cell appear bold if the value of the cell is greater than 20, or you can make a cell appear red if it contains the word 'T-Shirt'. Being able to format data in this way makes it easier for the user to draw conclusions and make decisions.

A copy of the products sold in the shop is shown below.

	A	B	C
1		Wreck Deck Skate Park	
2		Product List	
3			
4	Product Code	Product Description	Cost Price
5	1000	Helmet	$ 40.99
6	1001	Pads	$ 28.99
7	1002	Gloves	$ 15.00
8	1003	T Shirt Large	$ 12.00
9	1004	T-shirt Medium	$ 14.00
10	1005	T-Shirt Small	$ 16.00
11	1006	Hoody Large	$ 35.00
12	1007	Hoody Medium	$ 37.00
13	1008	Hoody Small	$ 39.00
14	1009	Gloves	$ 12.50
15	1010	Mega Skate	$ 99.99
16	1011	Wreck Skate	$ 110.00
17	1012	Mega Wreck Skate	$ 120.00
18	1014	Mega Scooter	$ 59.99
19	1015	Wreck Scooter	$ 75.00
20	1016	Mega Wreck Scooter	$ 90.00
21			

Conditional formatting applies the specified formatting only when certain conditions met. It can be used to visually show when data is following or breaking a rule.

For example, the spreadsheet below shows a simple timesheet for Hoa's staff and highlights any staff member who is working more than 40 hours per week, as the company does not permit this.

Staff ID	First Name	Surname	Hours worked this week
123	L.	Chang	32
124	M.	Ng	41
125	R.	Wan	42
126	D.	Chang	

You can also compare rows based on a single value. For example, the table below shows staff with the name 'Chang' highlighted.

Staff ID	First Name	Surname	Hours worked this week
123	L.	Chang	32
124	M.	Ng	41
125	R.	Wan	42
126	D.	Chang	

Hoa wants to see all of the items that cost more than $20.00 because he is worried about the shop's profit. Conditional formatting can help to do this. In this case the rule would be: 'cells greater than $20.00'.

To do this:

1 Home Tab » Style group » Conditional Formatting dropdown » Highlight Cell rules » Greater Than…

2 Enter $20.00 in the Format cells box and click OK.

3 After clicking OK, the cells with values more than $20.00 are highlighted with Light Red Fill and Dark Red Text.

There are a number of different ways to use conditional formatting.

Data Bars show data values relative to each other as data bars. This is useful to see how each value compares to the largest value.

Top/Bottom Rules allow the user to highlight the top and bottom values, for example, the top 10%.

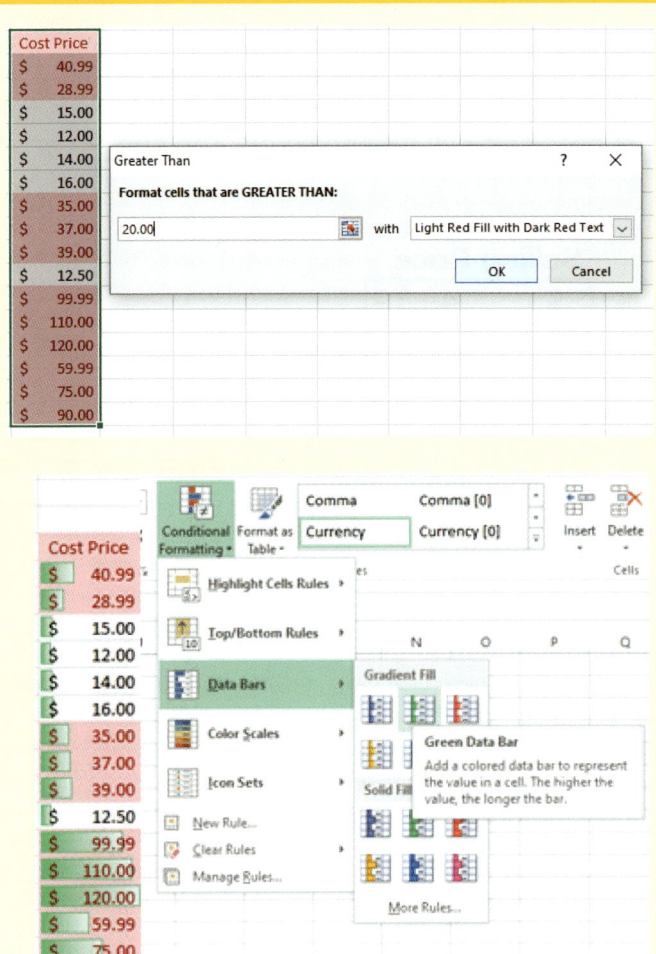

Practice

You are going to add some data about the products for sale in the shop. This data is needed so that products can be kept in stock and re-ordered when needed. Each product has its own re-order level and re-order quantity. If an item falls below its re-order level then it must be re-ordered. For example, 30 Large T-shirts must be ordered if the quantity in stock falls to 40 or below. Conditional formatting could help Hoa see immediately all of the items which need to be re-ordered.

➤ Open the file **WDSP1.xlsx**, provided by your teacher.

➤ Go to cell D5 and enter a formula in the formula bar for the Selling Price of a Helmet. This is calculated by multiplying the Cost Price by 1.2. Remember to enter the '=' symbol first. If you have done this correctly, the value $49.19 will appear in cell D5.

➤ Copy the formula down to each of the cells from D6 to D20. To copy the formula, go to cell D5 and drag down.

➤ Look at the formula in each of the cells D5 to D20. *Microsoft Excel* has automatically adjusted the cell reference in the original formula for each cell. Relative addresses are used. For example, in cell D5, the formula is based on cell C5, in cell D6 the formula is based on cell C6 and so on. The correct answers will automatically appear in column D 'Selling Price'.

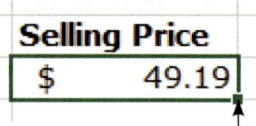

Selling Price
$ 49.19

drag the formula down through the cells using the fill handle at the bottom of cell D5

The fill handle is a small dot or square in the bottom right corner of the active cell; it can be used to copy the contents of a cell to adjacent cells, fill cells with numbers or labels, and copy formulas.

➤ Enter the following text and values in columns E, F, G and H.

	A	B	C	D	E	F	G	H
1		Wreck Deck Skate Park						
2		Product List						
3								
4	Product Code	Product Description	Cost Price	Selling Price	Quantity in Stock	Re-Order Level	Re-Order Quantity	Re-Order Yes/No
5	1000	Helmet	$ 40.99	$ 49.19	50	20	20	
6	1001	Pads	$ 28.99	$ 34.79	35	30	20	
7	1002	Gloves	$ 15.00	$ 18.00	100	100	50	
8	1003	T Shirt Large	$ 12.00	$ 14.40	45	40	30	
9	1004	T-shirt Medium	$ 14.00	$ 16.80	33	50	30	
10	1005	T-Shirt Small	$ 16.00	$ 19.20	12	10	10	
11	1006	Hoody Large	$ 35.00	$ 42.00	19	20	20	
12	1007	Hoody Medium	$ 37.00	$ 44.40	32	35	30	
13	1008	Hoody Small	$ 39.00	$ 46.80	21	25	20	
14	1009	Gloves Special	$ 12.50	$ 15.00	33	34	30	
15	1010	Mega Skate	$ 99.99	$ 119.99	12	15	15	
16	1011	Wreck Skate	$ 110.00	$ 132.00	15	16	20	
17	1012	Mega Wreck Skate	$ 120.00	$ 144.00	19	15	15	
18	1014	Mega Scooter	$ 59.99	$ 71.99	12	10	20	
19	1015	Wreck Scooter	$ 75.00	$ 90.00	16	15	20	
20	1016	Mega Wreck Scooter	$ 90.00	$ 108.00	20	25	20	

➤ The owners of the shop want to see which products are not selling well. Use conditional formatting to highlight, in green, all the items where the Quantity in Stock is greater than 30.
  o Highlight cells E5 to E20.
  o Select Conditional Formatting and use the Highlight Cells Rules.

➤ Selling prices are to be reviewed this year and the owners want to know about the highest and lowest priced items. Use the Top/Bottom rules to highlight the highest selling price for an item and the lowest selling price for an item.

➤ Văn needs to check the re-order quantity and he needs to compare them to each other. Use the Data Bars conditional formatting to give Văn a visual representation of this information.

➤ Look at the spreadsheet with conditional formatting. Is it easier to understand?

Data validation

Learn

Data validation allows you to set up rules which control the values or text that can be entered into a cell. When you use validation it prevents the entry of data which is unacceptable. The validation feature also allows you to provide helpful error or feedback messages to the user. This can help them to enter data in the correct form. Data validation can provide the following checks:

KEYWORD

data validation: the process of checking data entered to ensure that it is acceptable

Range check	Ensures that data entered is in the correct range.
Type check	Ensures that data entered is the correct type. For example, a text value cannot be entered if a number is required.
Presence check	To ensure that data is entered.
Length check	To ensure that the data entered has a certain number of characters.

Văn knows that the maximum cost of the products that are sold in the shop is $150.00. He wants you to create a validation rule that will ensure that no values outside of the range $0.00–$150.00 can be entered into cells B5 to B20. Văn needs a range check.

To create a validation rule:

1 First select the cells that you wish to create the rule for, B5:B20.

2 Choose Data Tab » Data Tools » Data Validation

The Data Validation dialog box will be displayed.

3 There are three parts to this box: Settings, Input Message, and Error Alert.

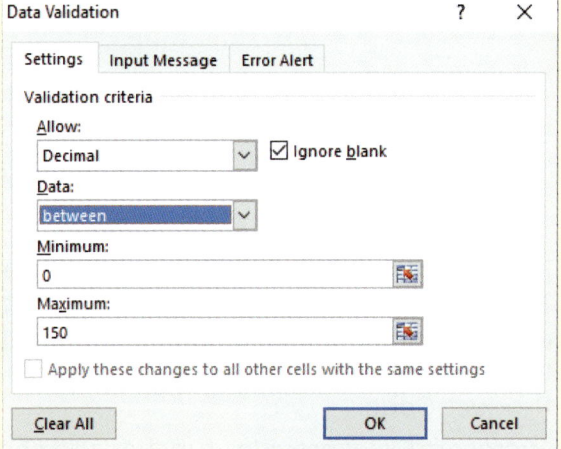

Settings is where you enter the validation criteria or rules.

➤ Choose an option from the Allow drop-down menu – in this case we allow decimal values. A decimal value is a number containing a decimal point. For example, 20.9.

➤ Choose an option from the Data drop down menu – in this case we select 'between' as we are creating a check for a range of values

➤ The Minimum and Maximum boxes will allow us to enter the range (0–150) for the acceptable values.

Input Message allows you to set a message here which will help the user when entering the data. The input message will appear when the cell is selected.

Error alert allows you to specify an error message using the Error Alert. The message will appear in a message box.

KEYWORDS

input message: a user defined message which will appear when the user is entering data into a cell

error alert: a user defined message that will appear when the user enters data that breaks the validation rule

Give an example of an error alert message you recently received.

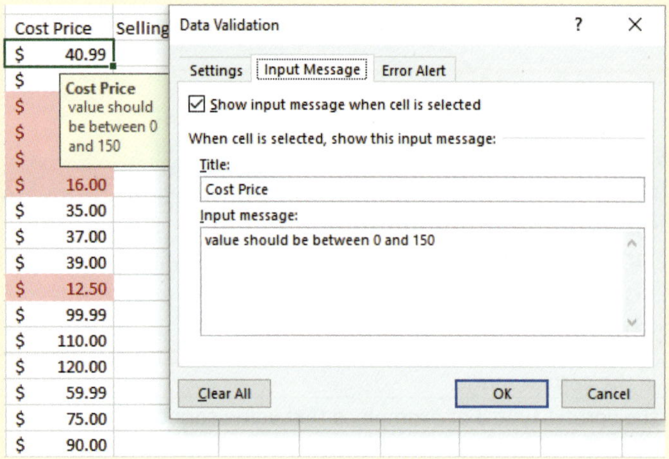

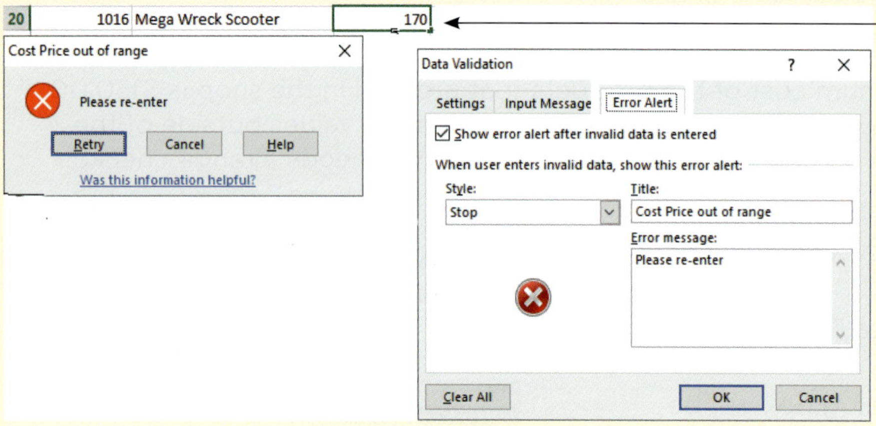

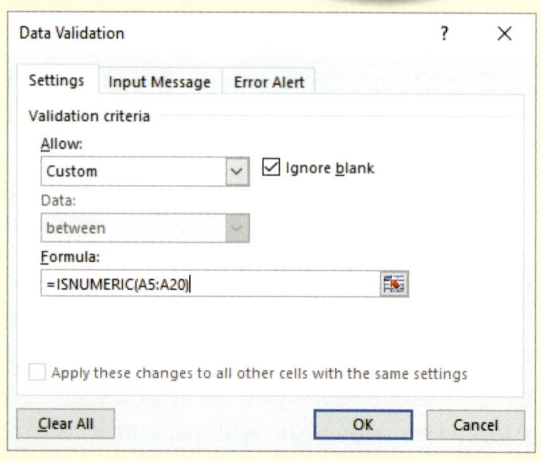

It is important that data entered is of the correct data type. To do this you can create a custom validation rule which will check for different data types. For example, in the case of the product code you would not want to have letters in the Product Code.

Microsoft Excel provides functions to check for data types, two of which are

ISNUMERIC(), which checks a cell value to ensure it is numeric. It returns a value of TRUE if the cell value is numeric and FALSE if it is not.

ISTEXT(), which checks a cell value to ensure it contains text. It returns a value of TRUE if the cell value is numeric and FALSE if it is not.

To add a data type validation for Product Code:
➤ select custom in the Allow drop-down menu
➤ add the formula **=ISNUMERIC(A5:A20)**
➤ add suitable input and error messages.

> Functions are small programs which are written to carry out a specific task. A function will return a value which can be used to control what happens next in a program.

Entering a value of 170 will trigger the error alert.

Practice

➤ Continue using the file **WDSP1.xlsx**, provided by your teacher.
➤ Create a validation rule for the Re-Order Level cells so that they are always between 0 and 100.
  o Highlight all of the values in the column.
  o Then select Data Tab» Data Tools » Data Validation.
  o Complete the three sections of the data validation dialog box.
➤ Create a further validation for the Re-Order Quantity cells to ensure that the value entered is always between 10 and 50. You should highlight all of the cells and complete all of the sections of the data validation dialog box.
➤ Test your validation rules by trying to enter the following:
  o Go to cell F7 and change 100 to 150. What happens?
  o Change the value in F7 back to 100.
  o Go to cell G7 and change 50 to -5. What happens?
  o Change the value in G7 back to 50.
➤ Create a validation rule for cells B5:B20, which contains a length check to ensure that the Product Description is at least four character's in length and no more than thirty characters in length. You can do this by selecting Text length from the Allow drop down menu and adding the maximum and minimum length in the validation criteria. Do not forget to add suitable input and error messages.

➤ Select cells B5:B20.
➤ Add a validation rule by:
  o selecting 'Text Length' in the 'Allow' box
  o entering the Minimum and Maximum length for the product description.
➤ Test your validation rule by:
  o changing the text in B6 from 'Pads' to 'Pad' (what happens?)
  o changing the text in B6 back to 'Pads'.
➤ Add a type check validation for the Product Description to ensure that only text can be entered. Remember to select cells B6:B20 first and use the `ISTEXT()` function. Test your validation rule to see if it works.

Using absolute cell references and named cell ranges

Learn

Using named cells in formulas

Named cells or cell ranges can be used as an alternative to cell references. In a formula, a named cell is the same as a cell reference but it is normally used for values that are used a number of times in different formulas.

When we use named cells it is similar to using a variable in a program. The computer will set aside an area in memory for the named cell and its value. Just like variables, if we want to use the value in the named cell we simply use the cell name.

Look at the formula in the cells, right. The **Selling Price** is calculated by multiplying the **Cost Price** by a value, which we will call the Markup Rate.

The Markup Rate is currently 1.2.

That means the Selling Price is 20% greater than the Cost Price.

> To display the formulas on a spreadsheet select Formulas Tab » Formula Auditing Group » Show Formulas.

What if the Selling Price is now calculated by multiplying the Cost Price by 1.3 instead of 1.2? How many changes would have to be made to the formulas on the spreadsheet?

You would need to change all of the formulas in the Selling Price column. Using a named cell can help improve the efficiency of the spreadsheet when making changes.

If the Markup Rate is held in a named cell, only one change would be needed. The Markup Rate is entered in cell C24 and given the name Markup, as shown.

Selling Price
=C5*1.2
=C6*1.2
=C7*1.2
=C8*1.2
=C9*1.2
=C10*1.2
=C11*1.2
=C12*1.2
=C13*1.2
=C14*1.2
=C15*1.2
=C16*1.2
=C17*1.2
=C18*1.2
=C19*1.2
=C20*1.2

> To create a named cell, click on the cell you want to name (in this case C24) and type the name in the space where the cell reference appears.

KEYWORDS

named cell: a name given to an individual cell in a spreadsheet
selling price: the price at which a product is sold to customers
cost price: the price at which a product is bought by the store owner

Update the formula in cell D5 so that it reads:

=C5*Markup

Using the fill handle, this formula is copied down to each cell in the column. When the formula is copied down, the reference to the named cell does not change.

The formulas in column D now look like the screenshot, right.

If the value in cell C24, now called Markup, is changed all of the values in the column are automatically adjusted. If the markup changes in the future, then only one change to the spreadsheet is needed – this is much more efficient.

Absolute cell reference

Absolute cell references are another way of referencing individual cells in a formula.

Văn wants to estimate the tax paid on each item. At present tax is paid at a rate of 10% on the Cost Price. The tax rate of 0.1 has been added to the spreadsheet in cell C25. A new column Tax Paid is added to column I.

Selling Price
=C5*Markup
=C6*Markup
=C7*Markup
=C8*Markup
=C9*Markup
=C10*Markup
=C11*Markup
=C12*Markup
=C13*Markup
=C14*Markup
=C15*Markup
=C16*Markup
=C17*Markup
=C18*Markup
=C19*Markup
=C20*Markup

	Product Code	Product Description	Cost Price	Selling Price	Quantity in Stock	Re-Order Level	Re-Order Quantity	Re-Order Yes/No	Tax Paid
1		Wreck Deck Skate Park							
2		Product List							
3									
4	Product Code	Product Description	Cost Price	Selling Price	Quantity in Stock	Re-Order Level	Re-Order Quantity	Re-Order Yes/No	Tax Paid
5	1000	Helmet	$ 40.99	$ 49.19	50	20	20		$ 4.10
6	1001	Pads	$ 28.99	$ 34.79	35	30	20		$ 26.09
7	1002	Gloves	$ 15.00	$ 18.00	100	100	50		$ 60.00
8	1003	T Shirt Large	$ 12.00	$ 14.40	45	40	30		$ -
9	1004	T-shirt Medium	$ 14.00	$ 16.80	33	50	30		$ -
10	1005	T-Shirt Small	$ 16.00	$ 19.20	12	10	10		$ -
11	1006	Hoody Large	$ 35.00	$ 42.00	19	20	20		$ -
12	1007	Hoody Medium	$ 37.00	$ 44.40	32	35	30		$ -
13	1008	Hoody Small	$ 39.00	$ 46.80	21	25	20		$ -
14	1009	Gloves Special	$ 12.50	$ 15.00	33	34	30		$ -
15	1010	Mega Skate	$ 99.99	$ 119.99	12	15	15		$ -
16	1011	Wreck Skate	$ 110.00	$ 132.00	15	16	20		$ -
17	1012	Mega Wreck Skate	$ 120.00	$ 144.00	19	15	15		$ -
18	1014	Mega Scooter	$ 59.99	$ 71.99	12	10	20		$ -
19	1015	Wreck Scooter	$ 75.00	$ 90.00	16	15	20		$ -
20	1016	Mega Wreck Scooter	$ 90.00	$ 108.00	20	25	20		$ -
21									
22									
23									
24		Markup Rate	1.2						
25		Tax Rate	0.1						
26		Euro Conversion Rate	$ 0.90						
27		Delivery Charge	$ 4.00						
28									
29									

Note that when the formula is copied, the answers are incorrect.

To calculate the tax paid on a helmet, the following formula is used in cell I5:

= C5*C25

However, when this formula is copied down to cells I6 to I20, the results are incorrect. Look at the formulas, right. What is wrong with them?

Each formula should be multiplied by the tax rate which is held in cell C25. However, *Microsoft Excel* has automatically changed the cell reference for each row. Read the section on relative cell references above to remind you about this.

In this case we do not want the cell reference to change so we must use an **absolute cell reference**. This is done by adding a $ symbol to the row and column of the cell reference (or pressing F4). So, in cell I5, the reference to C25 becomes $C$25. The formula in cell I5 is now:

=C5*$C$25

Tax Paid
=C5*C25
=C6*C26
=C7*C27
=C8*C28
=C9*C29
=C10*C30
=C11*C31
=C12*C32
=C13*C33
=C14*C34
=C15*C35
=C16*C36
=C17*C37
=C18*C38
=C19*C39
=C20*C40

> The formulas in column I are now correct. To see the results of the calculations simply turn off the formula view: Formulas Tab » Formula Auditing Group » Show Formulas.

When a formula containing an absolute cell reference is copied or dragged down, the absolute cell reference will not change.

Both named cells and absolute cell references make spreadsheets more efficient as they reduce the number of changes to formulas. They allow users to change one value and all the cells that use that value are automatically updated. This means that they can instantly see how changes of values affect the overall results in the data. For example, Văn and Hoa could try changing the Markup value to predict the effect this would have on the selling price for each item. This is a form of data modelling.

> If the tax rate changes then only the value in cell C25 needs to be changed. All of the results in the 'Tax Paid' column will be updated automatically.

Tax Paid	Tax Paid
=C5*$C$25	$ 4.10
=C6*$C$25	$ 2.90
=C7*$C$25	$ 1.50
=C8*$C$25	$ 1.20
=C9*$C$25	$ 1.40
=C10*$C$25	$ 1.60
=C11*$C$25	$ 3.50
=C12*$C$25	$ 3.70
=C13*$C$25	$ 3.90
=C14*$C$25	$ 1.25
=C15*$C$25	$ 10.00
=C16*$C$25	$ 11.00
=C17*$C$25	$ 12.00
=C18*$C$25	$ 6.00
=C19*$C$25	$ 7.50
=C20*$C$25	$ 9.00

Practice

The shop at Wreck Deck Skate Park is becoming very popular and Văn is thinking about selling on a website. He wants look at how different currencies would affect the selling price. Also, if he is selling online, he will have to charge postage. Văn has produced the following information:

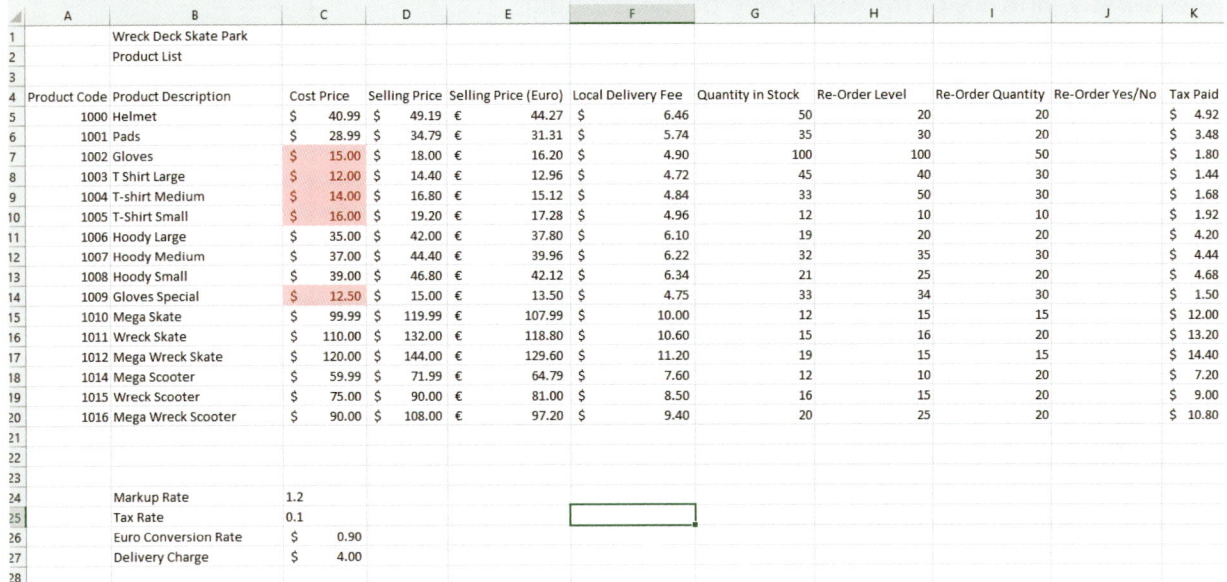

	A	B	C	D	E	F	G	H	I	J	K
1		Wreck Deck Skate Park									
2		Product List									
3											
4	Product Code	Product Description	Cost Price	Selling Price	Selling Price (Euro)	Local Delivery Fee	Quantity in Stock	Re-Order Level	Re-Order Quantity	Re-Order Yes/No	Tax Paid
5	1000	Helmet	$ 40.99	$ 49.19	€ 44.27	$ 6.46	50	20	20		$ 4.92
6	1001	Pads	$ 28.99	$ 34.79	€ 31.31	$ 5.74	35	30	20		$ 3.48
7	1002	Gloves	$ 15.00	$ 18.00	€ 16.20	$ 4.90	100	100	50		$ 1.80
8	1003	T Shirt Large	$ 12.00	$ 14.40	€ 12.96	$ 4.72	45	40	30		$ 1.44
9	1004	T-shirt Medium	$ 14.00	$ 16.80	€ 15.12	$ 4.84	33	50	30		$ 1.68
10	1005	T-Shirt Small	$ 16.00	$ 19.20	€ 17.28	$ 4.96	12	10	10		$ 1.92
11	1006	Hoody Large	$ 35.00	$ 42.00	€ 37.80	$ 6.10	19	20	20		$ 4.20
12	1007	Hoody Medium	$ 37.00	$ 44.40	€ 39.96	$ 6.22	32	35	30		$ 4.44
13	1008	Hoody Small	$ 39.00	$ 46.80	€ 42.12	$ 6.34	21	25	20		$ 4.68
14	1009	Gloves Special	$ 12.50	$ 15.00	€ 13.50	$ 4.75	33	34	30		$ 1.50
15	1010	Mega Skate	$ 99.99	$ 119.99	€ 107.99	$ 10.00	12	15	15		$ 12.00
16	1011	Wreck Skate	$ 110.00	$ 132.00	€ 118.80	$ 10.60	15	16	20		$ 13.20
17	1012	Mega Wreck Skate	$ 120.00	$ 144.00	€ 129.60	$ 11.20	19	15	15		$ 14.40
18	1014	Mega Scooter	$ 59.99	$ 71.99	€ 64.79	$ 7.60	12	10	20		$ 7.20
19	1015	Wreck Scooter	$ 75.00	$ 90.00	€ 81.00	$ 8.50	16	15	20		$ 9.00
20	1016	Mega Wreck Scooter	$ 90.00	$ 108.00	€ 97.20	$ 9.40	20	25	20		$ 10.80
21											
22											
23											
24		Markup Rate	1.2								
25		Tax Rate	0.1								
26		Euro Conversion Rate	$ 0.90								
27		Delivery Charge	$ 4.00								
28											

➤ Open the spreadsheet **WDSP3.xlsx**, provided by your teacher.

➤ Văn thinks that he could sell the merchandise to some European countries and wants to know about the Euro (€) conversion rate. Use the internet to research today's Dollar to Euro conversion rate.

➤ Văn decides to use 0.90 as the Dollar to Euro conversion rate. Enter this value in cell C26.

➤ Create a formula in cell E5 which will calculate the Selling Price in Euros for each product.

➤ Change the formula in cell E5 so that C25 is an absolute cell reference.

➤ Copy the formula in cell E5 into cells E6 to E20.

➤ Check your answers against Văn's information.

➤ Format the cells in E5 to E20 as currency.

➤ Try changing the Euro conversion rate and observe the effect on the values in cells E5 to E20.

A number of local customers have asked Hoa about having products delivered to them. She has a small truck and she thinks that she could deliver to customers within a 5 kilometre radius. She wants to see what she would have to charge for delivery. After talking to Văn they decide that they would charge $4 for delivery plus 5% of the cost of the item.

➤ Enter $4 into cell C27.

➤ Name cell C27 'DeliveryCharge'. You can do this by clicking on cell C27 and typing the words 'DeliveryCharge' into the name box.

Decomposition

- ✪ You will use decomposition to break problems down into smaller problems.
- ✪ You will have to create a formula which completes both aspects of the calculation.
  - o Firstly, find 5% of the cost price of the product.
  - o Secondly, add $4 to this cost.
- ✪ Create a formula in cell F5 which will calculate the Local Delivery Fee for a Helmet. Use the named cell 'DeliveryCharge' in your formula.
  - o Copy the formula to cells F6 to F20.
  - o Change the value in cell C27 'Delivery Cost' to $5. Look at the impact that this has on the values in column F.
  - o Change the value of the Tax Rate so that Hoa pays at least $10.00 tax on every item.
  - o What value did you reach for the Tax Rate?
  - o Compare this with the Tax Rate used by a classmate. Why are your values different?
  - o Set the Tax Rate back to 1.2.

Using built-in functions to carry out calculations

Learn

Microsoft Excel has many **built-in functions** which can be incorporated into formulas. Some of the most common functions include the SUM function which adds up the values in a cell range and the AVERAGE function which will find the average value in a cell range.

Most functions in *Microsoft Excel* require some information to carry out their task. The information which you give to the function is called an **argument**. A function generally returns a value that can be used later.

For example, the SUM function requires a cell range as an argument. In the formula:

`=SUM(C5:C20)`

the argument for the `SUM` function is the cell range `C5:C20`.

The general format of a function call is:

`FUNCTIONNAME(argument1, argument2,.....)`

There are two stages to complete when inserting a function: Stage 1: Select the function you want to insert, and Stage 2: Add the Function Arguments.

KEYWORDS

built-in functions: functions that exist within the software for use by the user

arguments: values that are passed to the function in the brackets that follow the function name; these values are used within the function

Stage 1: Select the function you want to insert

Click on the f_x symbol in the formula bar. The '=' symbol will be inserted automatically and the Insert Function window will appear.

You can then search for a function or select from a list of functions.

Stage 2: Add the Function Arguments

An argument is an actual value that is passed to the function at the time when it is called. An example of this is the cell range which it has to search through. (In programming, data can also be passed into functions or procedures using parameters. Parameters are variable names rather than actual values.)

For example, to find the maximum number in the cell range I5:I22, insert the MAX function. The function arguments are the cell range which will be used by the function. This screenshot shows how.

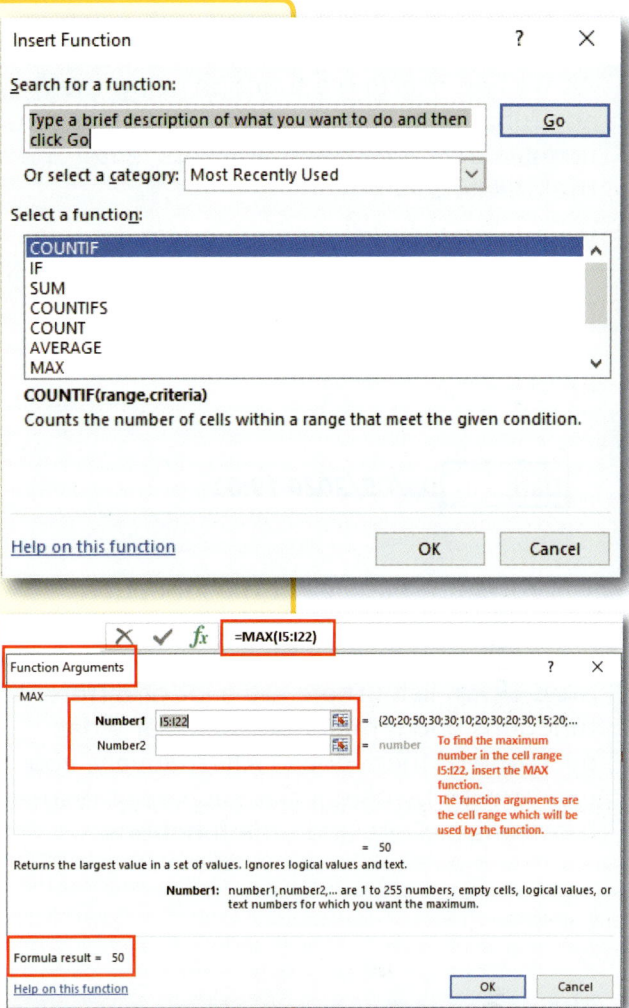

Algorithmic thinking

How would the Maximum function work in pseudocode?

```
SET MAX= 0

For each CELL in the range I5 TO I22

        IF VALUE IN CELL > MAX

            MAX = CELL VALUE

        ENDIF

END FOR

RETURN MAX
```

Another way of inserting a function

As well as inserting a function using the f_x symbol, you can use any function by entering its name after the '=' symbol in the formula bar. Then open brackets, enter the argument and close the brackets.

Whilst many functions have one or more arguments, some functions do not have any.

For example, the NOW() function which returns the current date and time does not need any arguments.

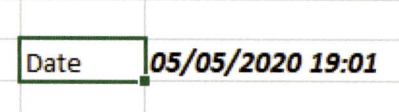

Date	05/05/2020 19:01

To browse through all of the functions available in *Microsoft Excel*, click on the f_x symbol and select All from the category drop-down list. (There are a lot of different functions and it might not be clear what each one of them does.) Alternatively, you can browse by categories such as Statistical functions or Date and time functions.

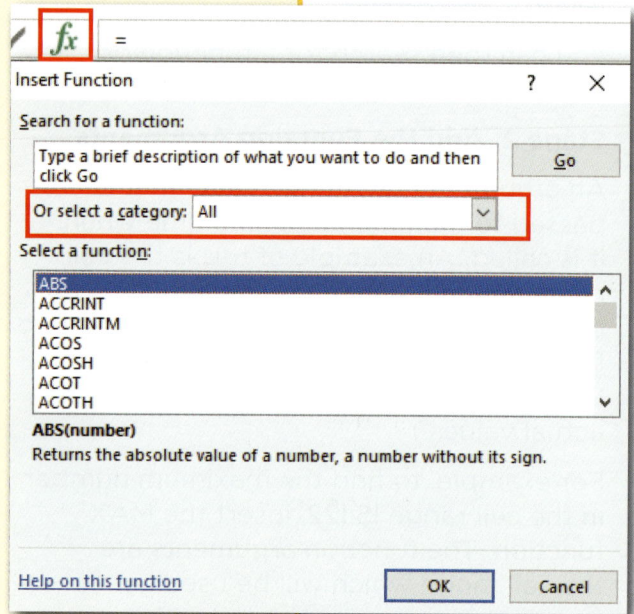

Practice

The owner of the shop wants to use some summary data relating to the spreadsheet. He needs average prices and wants to know how much money the stock is worth.

➤ Open the spreadsheet called **WDSP4.xlsx**, provided by your teacher.
➤ Using the insert function feature add the following:
   o In cell C21, a formula to find the average Cost Price.
   o In cell D21, a formula to find the average Selling Price.
   o In cell F21, a formula to find the average Local Delivery Fee.

Hoa is worried about the amount of stock that is stored at the shop. She wants to know how much the stock is worth in total and has asked you to calculate this value. The value is calculated by multiplying the Selling Price by the number of items in stock. For example, the stock value for Helmets is:

$49.19*50 = $2459.40

➤ Go to cell L5 and enter a formula which will calculate the Stock Value for Helmets.
➤ Copy the formula down to cells L6 to L20.
➤ Go to cell L21 and insert a formula containing the Sum function which will calculate the total value of the stock in the shop.
➤ Save the changes to the file **WDSP4.xlsx**.

Testing conditions using the IF function

Learn

The IF function can put one of two values in a cell depending on the outcome of evaluating a **condition**.

Relational operators in *Microsoft Excel*	
Equal to	=
Not equal to	<>
Less than	<
Greater than	>
Less than or equal to	<=
Greater than or equal to	>=

> Look back at section 8.4 to remind yourself about IF statements. These are used to select which statements will be executed.

In order to keep the store stocked properly, you need to know which items need to be re-ordered. Văn has told you that when the quantity in stock for a product falls below its re-order level, it must be re-ordered at the next possible opportunity.

You need to include a formula in the spreadsheet to identify those items that need to be re-ordered based on how many of them are in stock. Consider creating this formula for the Helmets in row 5. Column J will contain the IF function determined by the condition:

Quantity in Stock is less than or equal to the Re-Order Level

In terms of cell references this condition is:

G5<=H5

If the condition is true (the number of helmets in stock is less than or equal to the re-order level), then the formula should place a Yes in the relevant cell.

If the condition is false (the number of helmets in stock is greater than the re-order level), then the formula should place a No in the relevant cell.

➤ To enter the formula for a Helmet, make sure the active cell is J5.

➤ Using the insert function feature, select the IF function.

➤ In the Logical text box enter the condition **G5<=H5**.

➤ In the Value if true box, place the value that you wish to appear in the cell if the condition is true. In this case, Yes.

➤ In the Value if false box, place the value that you wish to appear in the cell if the condition is false. In this case, No.

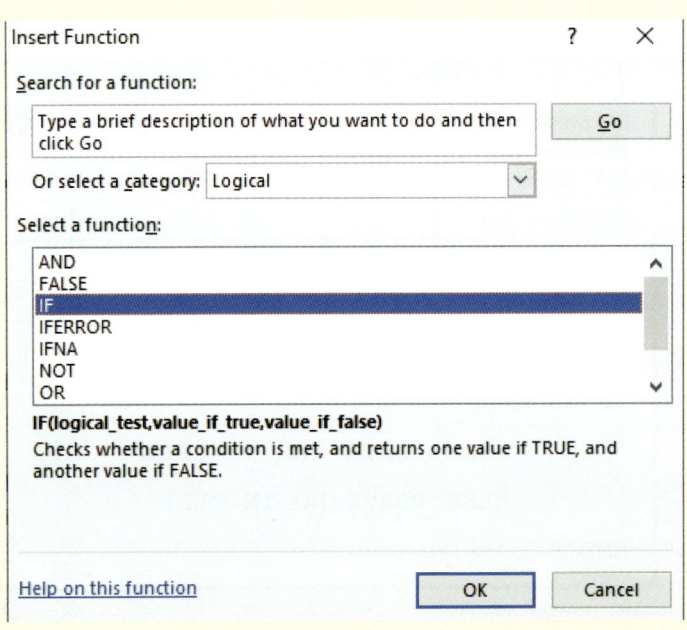

141

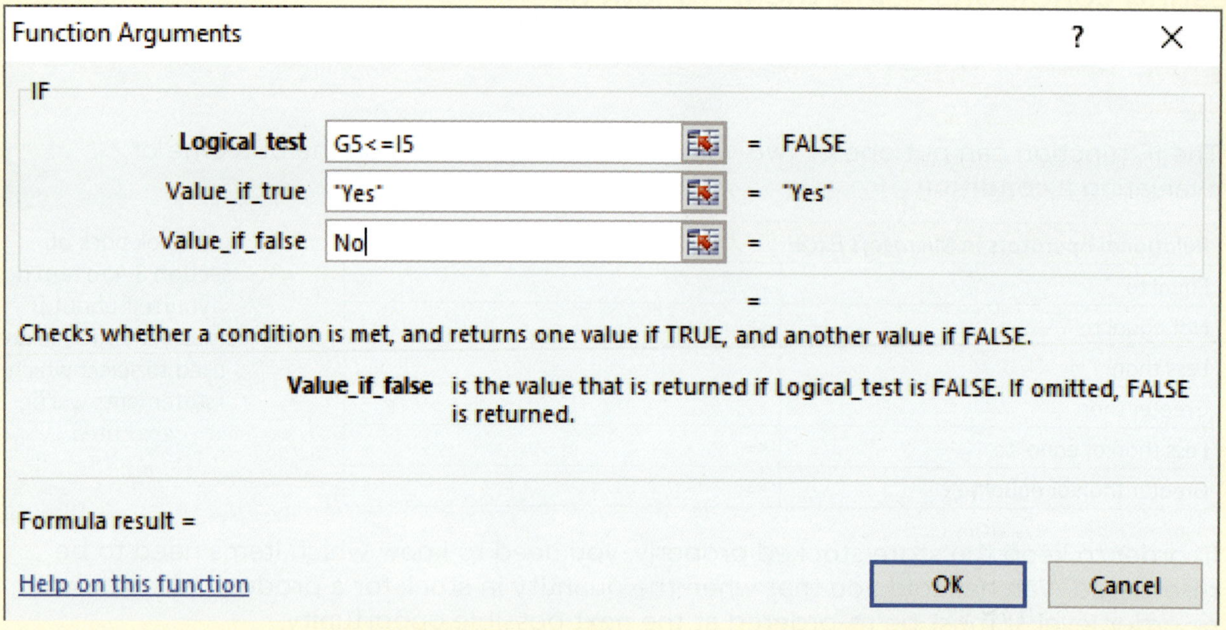

Function Arguments   ?   ✕

IF

Logical_test	G5<=I5	▦	=	FALSE
Value_if_true	"Yes"	▦	=	"Yes"
Value_if_false	No	▦	=	

=

Checks whether a condition is met, and returns one value if TRUE, and another value if FALSE.

         Value_if_false   is the value that is returned if Logical_test is FALSE. If omitted, FALSE is returned.

Formula result =

Help on this function   OK   Cancel

➤ Note that quotation marks are added to the text automatically. Click OK.

The IF statement appears in the formula bar as shown. The outcome from the IF statement is now shown in cell J5.

J5   ✕ ✓ fx   =IF(G5<=I5,"Yes","No")

	A	B	C	D	E	F	G	H	I	J
1		Wreck Deck Skate Park								
2		Product List								
3										
4	Product Code	Product Description	Cost Price	Selling Price	Selling Price (Euro)	Local Delivery Fee	Quantity in Stock	Re-Order Level	Re-Order Quantity	Re-Order Yes/No
5	1000	Helmet	$ 40.99	$ 49.19	€ 44.27	$ 6.46	50	20	20	No

Algorithmic thinking ⭐

The general format of an IF statement is

Algorithm	Spreadsheet equivalent
IF condition	IF logical test
THEN action 1	Condition if true
ELSE action 2	Condition if false
endif	-

The algorithm for this particular example could be

```
IF G5 <=I5
        THEN PLACE YES IN CELL
        ELSE PLACE NO IN CELL
ENDIF
```

The formula must now be copied down to cells J6 to J20.

Pattern recognition

When you copy a formula to other cells there are similarities between the formulas in each cell.

Re-Order Yes/No

| =IF(G5<=I5,"Yes","No") |
| =IF(G6<=I6,"Yes","No") |
| =IF(G7<=I7,"Yes","No") |
| =IF(G8<=I8,"Yes","No") |
| =IF(G9<=I9,"Yes","No") |

Look at the first few formulas in Column J. What are the similarities and differences between the formulas in each cell?.

Using nested IF statements

If you need to test for more than one condition, and then take one of several actions based on the result of the test, you can add multiple IF statements together in one formula. These are known as nested IFs because one IF function is contained within another.

Văn wants to keep track of the total stock value in the shop. He has decided to take action based on the value of the stock. Here is a table showing the actions he will take based on the total stock value.

Stock Value($)	Action
0–15999	No action
16000–21999	Check high value items and report
22000 and over	Reduce the number of high value items in store

Văn wants the actions to show on the spreadsheet when he opens it so that he doesn't forget about them. He has decided to put the message in cell B30.

We can use nested IF statements to solve this problem.

To build up a nested IF formula that will do this,

➤ Start by testing to see if the stock value is below 16000.

➤ If TRUE, we return 'No Action'. If FALSE, we move into the next IF function.

➤ Next test to see if the score is less than 22000.

➤ If TRUE, we return 'Check High Cost Items and Report'. If FALSE, we 'Reduce the number of high value items in store'.

The total stock value is held in L21. The formula to be entered into cell L25 will be:

`=IF(L21<16000,"No Action",IF(L21<20000,"Check High Value Items and Report","Reduce the number of high Value Items in store")).`

Algorithmic thinking

The algorithm to solve Văn's problem is:

```
IF TOTALSTOCKVALUE < 16000

    OUTPUT "No Action"

    ELSE IF TOTALSTOCKVALUE < 21999

        OUTPUT "Check High Value Items and Report"

        ELSE OUTPUT "Reduce the number of high

        Value Items in store"

    ENDIF

ENDIF
```

Match the algorithm to the formula.

Algorithm	Formula
1 IF TOTALSTOCKVALUE < 16000	=IF(L21<16000
2 THEN OUTPUT "No Action"	,"No Action"
3 ELSE IF TOTALSTOCKVALUE < 20000	,IF(L21<20000
4 THEN OUTPUT "Check High Value Items and Report"	,"Check High Value Items and Report"
5 ELSE OUTPUT "Reduce the number of high Value Items in store"	,"Reduce the number of high Value Items in store"))
In the formula, THEN and ELSE are represented as commas.	

It is important to move in one direction, either low to high, or high to low. This allows us to return a result whenever a test returns TRUE, because we know that the previous tests have returned FALSE.

Decomposition and Generalisation

You will use decomposition to break a large problem into smaller more manageable problems. You will use the experience that you have gained to help you solve these problems. This is generalisation, when you use your experience in one problem solving exercise to help you with another.

- ⚙ Continue using **WDSP4.xlsx**.
- ⚙ Hoa wants to classify the products in terms of the stock value.
    - ○ Products worth more than $1500 will be classified as High Value.
    - ○ Otherwise stock will be classified as Normal Value.
    - ○ With a partner, write down the condition that will solve this problem.
    - ○ Use cell references in your condition.
- ⚙ Review your condition and create an IF statement for cell M5 which will assign the correct value to the cell given the stock value for Helmets.
- ⚙ Go to cell M4 and enter the text 'Value'.

Hint: you must use a condition which checks to see if the value in the cell is greater than 1500.

- ❖ Go to cell M5. Enter your formula into cell M5.
- ❖ Check the value in cell M5 to ensure it is correct.
- ❖ Now copy the formula down to cells M6 to M20.
- ❖ Look at the spreadsheet in formula view and review column M. Identify the similarities and differences between the formulas in each of the cells M6 to M20.
- ❖ Văn wants to change the stock value boundaries for the actions he will take. He has come up with a new table. Add an IF statement to cell B30 which will place the correct message in this cell based on the new values.

Stock Value($)	Action
0–17049	No action
17050–19999	Check high value items and report
20000 and over	Reduce the number of high value items in store

Practice

You are going to use the COUNTIF function. This function counts the number of cells that meet certain criteria. For example, **=COUNTIF(A1:A20, "London")**, counts the number of cells with the word 'London' in cells A1:A20.

➤ Add a formula to cell H25 containing the COUNTIF function which will count the number of products which need to be re-ordered. (Hint: you need to consider the values in column J.)

➤ Add a formula to cell H26 containing the COUNTIF function which will count the number of high value products stored in the shop.

Filtering and sorting the contents of a spreadsheet

Learn

Filtering data

Filtering data in *Microsoft Excel* refers to displaying only the rows that meet certain conditions. The other rows get hidden.

Using the shop data, if you only want to see all the products which need to be re-ordered then you can set a filter to do this.

➤ Highlight cells A4 to M20

➤ Choose Data Tab » Filter to set filter. The drop-down arrows will appear beside the headings.

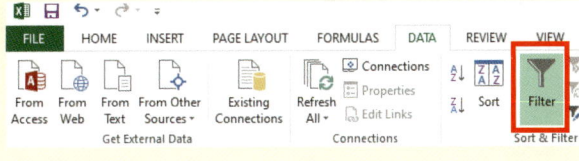

➤ Click the drop-down arrow in the Re-Order Yes/No column.

➤ Remove the check mark from Select All, which unselects everything.

➤ Then select the check mark for Yes which will filter the data and display only those products that need to be re-ordered.

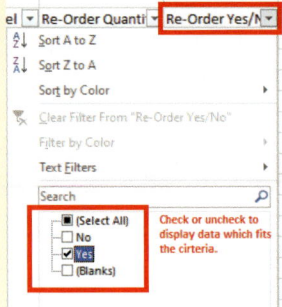

➤ Part of the spreadsheet is shown. Note that some of the row numbers are missing; these rows contain the filtered (hidden) data.

Product Co	Product Description	Cost Price	Selling Pri	Selling Price (Eur	Local Delivery Fee	Quantity in Stock	Re-Order Level	Re-Order Quanti	Re-Order Yes/N
1006	Hoody Large	$ 35.00	$ 42.00	€ 37.80	$ 6.10	19	20	20	Yes
1010	Mega Skate	$ 99.99	$ 119.99	€ 107.99	$ 10.00	12	15	15	Yes
1011	Wreck Skate	$ 110.00	$ 132.00	€ 118.80	$ 10.60	15	16	20	Yes
1014	Mega Scooter	$ 59.99	$ 71.99	€ 64.79	$ 7.60	12	10	20	Yes
1015	Wreck Scooter	$ 75.00	$ 90.00	€ 81.00	$ 8.50	16	15	20	Yes
1016	Mega Wreck Scooter	$ 90.00	$ 108.00	€ 97.20	$ 9.40	20	25	20	Yes

The drop-down arrow in the Re-Order Yes/No column now shows a different graphic – an icon that indicates the column is filtered.

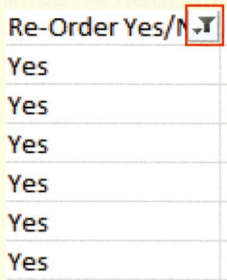

Using multiple filters

You can filter the data using multiple conditions. Suppose after the re–order list is shown, you want only to see those products that are classified as High Value. After setting the filter for Re-Order Yes/No, click the arrow at the top of the Value column and select the filter 'High Value' as shown.

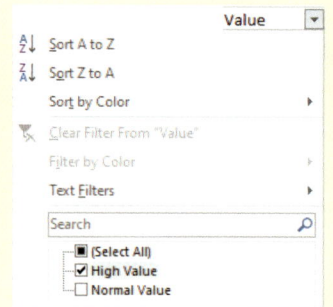

You can see the two columns which have been filtered as they have the filter icon beside the heading.

	Re-Order Quanti		Re-Order Yes/N	Tax Pa	Stock Valu	Value	
16	20		Yes	$ 13.20	$ 1,980.00	High Value	
25	20		Yes	$ 10.80	$ 2,160.00	High Value	

To clear the filters, choose Data Tab » Filter or tick "Select All" in the filtered columns.

146

Sorting data

Sorting data in *Microsoft Excel* rearranges the rows based on the contents of a particular column. For instance you may want to sort data in alphabetical or numerical order. To do this:

➤ Select cells A5:M20
➤ Choose either:
   • Data Tab » Sort, or
   • Home Tab » Sort & Filter

The dialog box below appears.

➤ Select the field (column name) on which you want to sort. In this case, we want to sort products according to their name, so choose Product Description.

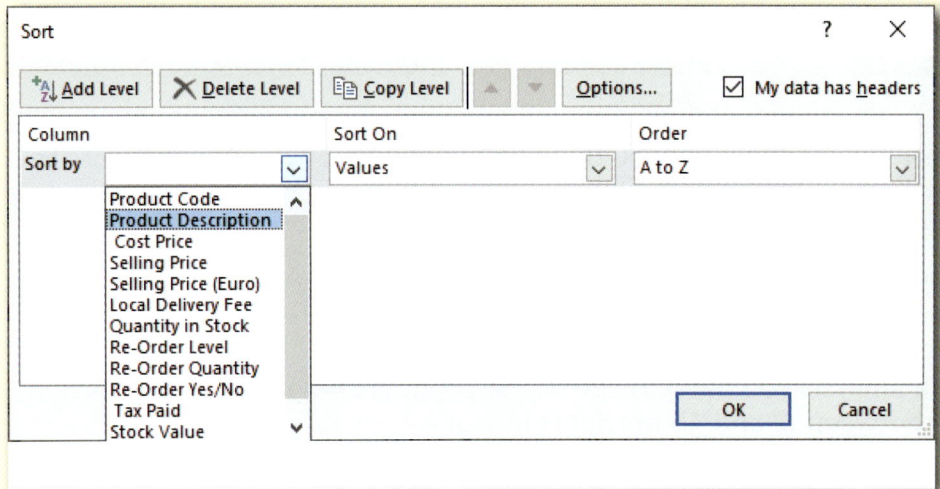

➤ Click OK. The data is now sorted on Product Description.

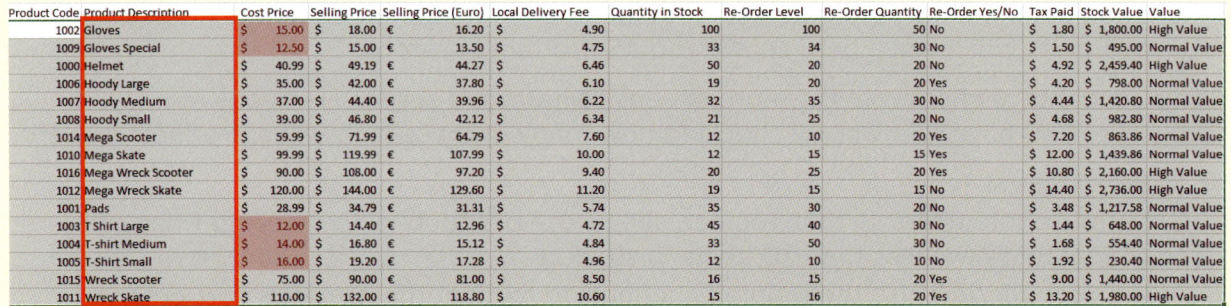

You can sort data on more than one column in a spreadsheet. For example Văn wants to see all items ordered by their Value and then Stock Value.

To perform a sort like this, we need two levels added to the sort. Level 1 will contain the first sort on Value, and level 2 will contain the second sort on Stock Value.

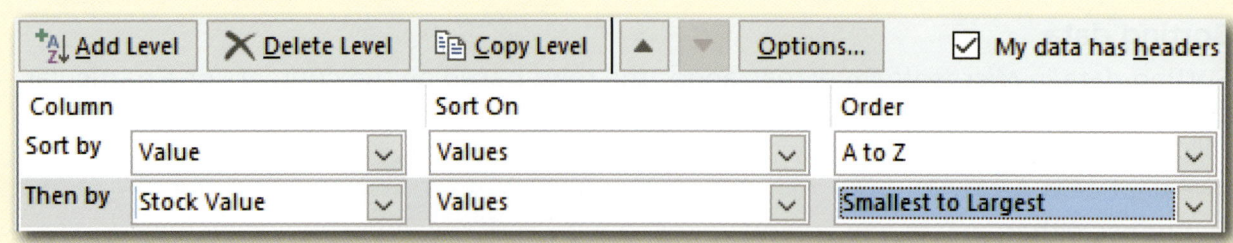

You can Sort based on the following conditions:

➤ Values (alphabetically or numerically)

➤ Cell color

➤ Font color

➤ Cell icon

Practice

You are going to review the data about stock that needs to be re-ordered. Văn wants to see which have the most stock left and which items have the lowest re-order level. He may stop selling these items as they may not be selling well.

➤ Open the spreadsheet **WDSP5.xlsx**, provided by your teacher.

➤ Sort the data by Quantity in Stock, then by Re-Order Level. Ensure the result shows the data in the order as required by Văn.

➤ As part of your data analysis you need to see all the products with a Cost Price less than $20 that have between 12 and 45 products in stock.

   o Set a filter on the Cost Price column, which will show only data for the cells shaded in pink.

   o To do this, you will use the "Filter By Colour" option on the filter menu.

   o Then set a filter on the Quantity in Stock column which will show only those products which have between 12 and 45 products in stock.

Văn also wants to check that the more expensive items are selling. He needs to know if items over $50 have sold well by checking how many of these high value products are left.

➤ Clear all filters.

➤ Set appropriate filters so that you can see all the products with a Selling Price of more than $50 that have less than 20 items in stock.

➤ In the Sort window, use the Delete Level button to clear the previous sort criteria.

➤ Sort the data so that it is sorted on Selling Price and then Stock Value.

Abstraction

Abstraction is the removal of data that is not necessary for solving the problem. You have provided Văn with more information about the prices of products. However he does not need to see all of the data to help him understand how the business is running. Filtering will remove unnecessary data to provide useful insights for Văn.

Using Lookup tables

Abstraction

Vertical Lookup (VLOOKUP) tables provide data in the form of a list or a table. The data can be searched and relevant information extracted from the table or list and returned. The data returned can then be used to put data into a cell or a calculation. The user is normally unaware of the VLOOKUP process that the software uses to perform the operation.

Learn

The information in a VLOOKUP table is structured like any other data stored in a database or in a file created by a program. Each column represents a different category of information, known as an **attribute**. Each row represents all the information about a single record in the table. The row is called a **tuple**.

Văn wants to classify products and will use their profit to do this. He will use the profit value to assign a profit rating to each product.

A VLOOKUP table can be used to for this. As Văn wants to monitor the profitability of his stock he has asked you to classify each product based on the amount of profit made. This is calculated by subtracting the Cost Price from the Selling Price of each product. He wants to classify the products using the following rules.

attribute

Profit	Profit Rating	
$0.00–$9.00	Little Profit	} tuple
$10.00–$19.00	Good Profit	
Over $20.00	Highly Profitable	

A lookup table has been created in cells L25 to M27 in **WDSP5b.xlsx**.

Column 1	Column 2
0	Little Profit
10	Good Profit
20	Highly Profitable

The **VLOOKUP** function allows you to set up a range search. It uses a value and compares the cell value to those in the table.

This is the VLOOKUP statement that will be used in cell O5 to assign a rating to each product. The profit for Helmets has been calculated and is stored in cell F5.

```
=VLOOKUP(F5,L25:M27,2)
```

KEYWORDS

Vertical Lookup (VLOOKUP) table: a table in a spreadsheet which is be used to lookup a value and return data to a cell in the spreadsheet

VLOOKUP: makes use of a lookup table of data to match the contents of a cell with a value in the lookup table

lookup value: the value used to search through the lookup table

table array: the set of data that will be searched using the lookup value

column index num: the column number of the data that will be returned if there is a match for the lookup value in the table array

The first argument in the VLOOKUP function is called the **lookup value**. In this case it is the profit made from the product in cell F5. The second argument is the **table array**, which is the table containing the lookup data. In this case the table array is located in cells L25:M27. The third argument is the **column index num**, which is the value we are looking for.

> There is a fourth argument which is set to True if returning a partial match and False if returning an exact match.

This VLOOKUP statement uses a value in cell F5 and checks through cells L25 to M27 to see if the value in cell F5 is present. If the value is found, the VLOOKUP function will return the matching value in column 2. But if the numeric value is not found, the statement will return the next value in the table which is smaller than the value being looked for.

Take care when copying the VLOOKUP formula:

`=VLOOKUP(F6,L26:M28,2)`

When the formula is copied down to cells O6 to O20 the results are incorrect. Open the spreadsheet **WDSP5b.xlsx**, provided by your teacher. Go to cell O5 and examine the formula which works perfectly.

Why do you think that the formula does not work in the other cells?

The lookup data is located in cells L25 to M27. Look at the formula shown. The reference to the lookup data is wrong. Remember, when a formula is copied, that *Microsoft Excel* automatically adjusts the cell references. How do we stop this from occurring?

We use absolute cell referencing. Change the formula in cell O5 to:

`=VLOOKUP(F5,$L$25:$M$27,2)`

Save this spreadsheet as you will use it in the practice exercise.

Then copy the formula down to cells O6 to O20. The results are now correct.

This VLOOKUP function can be used to help model different situations on the spreadsheet and to predict outcomes if the data is to change. For example, the VLOOKUP table can be used to determine profitability and the boundaries can be changed. Any changes made to the boundaries will be reflected in the Profitability Rating column immediately.

An advantage of using formulas and VLOOKUP tables in spreadsheets is that any changes to the data are reflected across all relevant calculations and functions.

Practice

➤ Use your updated version of the spreadsheet **WDSP5b.xlsx**.
➤ Go to the lookup table and make the following changes.

0	Little Profit
7	Good Profit
14	Highly Profitable
20	Extremely Profitable

➤ Modify the VLOOKUP statement in cell O5 to include the new category.

> Ensure that you have included the dollar symbols in the correct places in the formula.

➤ Copy the VLOOKUP statement in cell O5 to cells O6 to O20.
➤ Check that the results are correct.
➤ Try changing the boundaries in the lookup table and review the changes made to the data.
➤ Save the file.

Linking data between worksheets

Learn

You have been asked to include a further worksheet with sales data for each product.

The new worksheet called Sales has been added to the spreadsheet **WDSP6.xlsx**.

> Add a new worksheet by right clicking on the New Worksheet icon at the bottom of the spreadsheet.

The data for the products will be placed on the new Sales worksheet by linking to the Products worksheet. This will save re-typing the data and also means that any changes made to data in the Products worksheet will automatically be copied to the Sales worksheet.

To link data to the Sales worksheet:

➤ Click on the Sales worksheet and go to cell A5. This is the destination worksheet.

➤ Type the = symbol.

➤ Click on the Products worksheet and go to cell A5. This is the source worksheet.

➤ Press Enter.

Check the formula bar (which displays the contents of the selected cell) at the top of your workbook. For cell A5 in the Sales worksheet it should show the name of your source worksheet, followed by an exclamation mark:

This means that cell A5 in the Sales worksheet contains the value of cell A5 in the Products worksheet.

The formula in cell A5 of the Sales worksheet can now be copied to cells A6 to A20.

Linking data on worksheets helps save time and means that any changes in the Products worksheet will be updated wherever that data has been linked.

Practice

Văn is now coming to a decision about the products that should continue to be sold and those that he no longer wishes to sell. You are going to use VLOOKUP table to classify the different products to help Văn make his decision.

➤ Open the spreadsheet **WDSP6.xlsx** provided by your teacher.

➤ Go to the Sales worksheet.

➤ Go to cell A5 and copy the formula to cells A6 to A20.

➤ Go to cell B5 and create a link to the Products worksheet to display the product description in this cell. Review the instructions for linking data (above) to help you with this.

➤ Copy the formula in cell B5 to cells B6 to B20.

➤ A lookup table has been created in cells N5 to O8 with the following information:

0	Stop Selling
100	Check Sales Weekly
200	Good Seller
300	Best Seller

➤ Create a VLOOKUP statement in cell J5 which will return a Sales classification for Helmets based on the Total Sold in cell I5.

> Remember to use absolute cell referencing for the lookup table before copying the formula.

➤ Copy the formula in cell J5 to cells J6 to J20.

➤ Review the results.

➤ With a partner, discuss how the data in column J could help Hoa and Văn when selecting products to stock in their shop.

Challenge yourself

Create and use macros to automate tasks

A **macro** is a small program which is created to automate a repetitive task such as printing a spreadsheet. The macro recorder can record a particular on-screen action and then attach that action to a button. The button can then be placed on the spreadsheet and pressed when the action is to be carried out.

A macro is required which will create a chart showing the Cost Price of each product.

➤ Open the spreadsheet **WDSP8.xlsx**, provided by your teacher.

➤ Choose View Tab » Macro dropdown.

➤ Click on Record Macro.

➤ Give the macro the name 'CreateChart' and click OK.

➤ Select the cells B4 to C20 and Create a Column chart for the data.

> Select the Insert tab and select the icon representing a column chart, from the Charts group.

➤ Choose View Tab » Macro dropdown »Stop Recording.

➤ Choose View Tab » Macro dropdown. Look at the macro code generated by using the Record Macro feature.

Abstraction

When you record a macro you can only see the function name (CreateChart) but you cannot see the code behind the function. This is a form of abstraction as you only see the information relevant to solve the problem.

The screen shot below shows the code and explains what each line means.

Can you map each line to your actions when recording the macro?

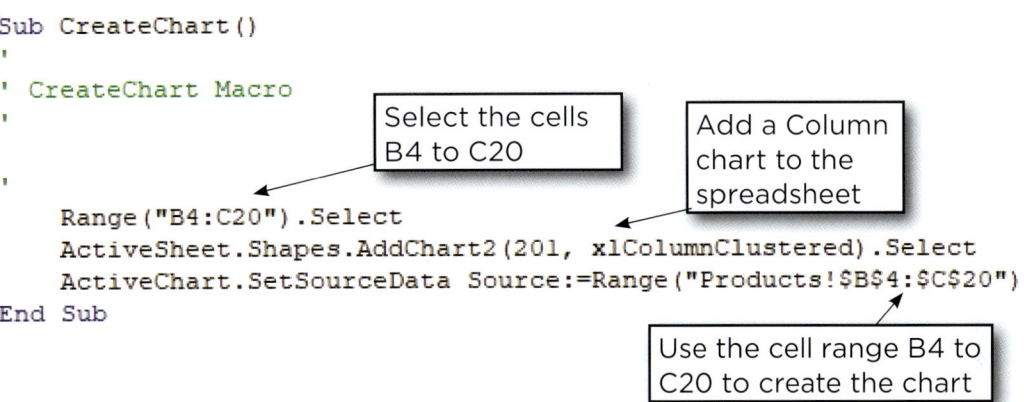

```
Sub CreateChart()
'
' CreateChart Macro
'

'
    Range("B4:C20").Select
    ActiveSheet.Shapes.AddChart2(201, xlColumnClustered).Select
    ActiveChart.SetSourceData Source:=Range("Products!$B$4:$C$20")
End Sub
```

Select the cells B4 to C20

Add a Column chart to the spreadsheet

Use the cell range B4 to C20 to create the chart

Now attach the Macro to a button.
➤ Choose Developer Tab » Insert dropdown.
➤ Click on Button (Form Controls).

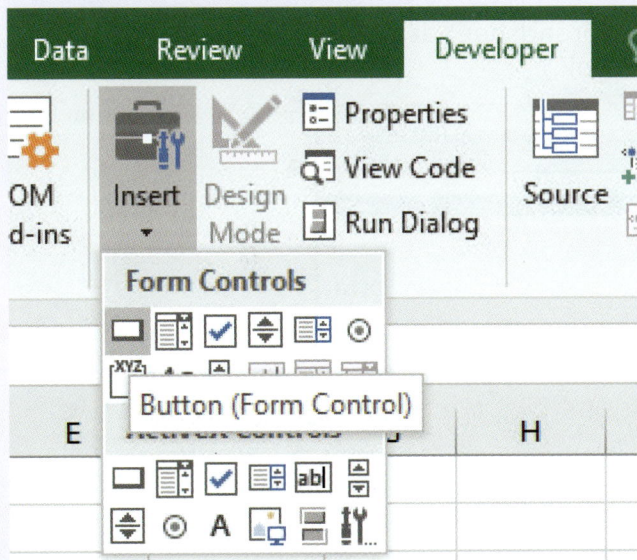

➤ A small black cross will appear. Use this to draw the button on the spreadsheet.
➤ When you have drawn the outline of the button, the Assign Macro window will open.

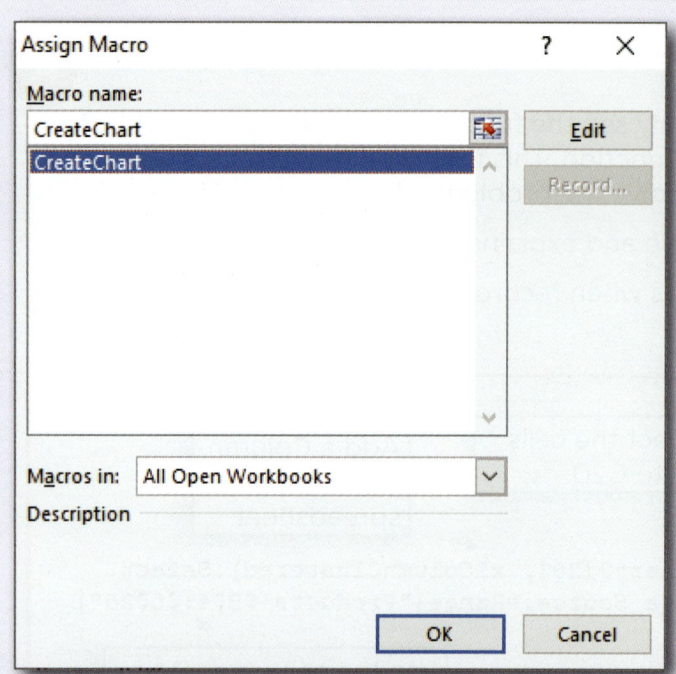

➤ Select the CreateChart macro and click OK. The Macro is now assigned to the button.
➤ The button will appear on the spreadsheet.
➤ Change the text on the button to say 'Create Chart'. To do this click on the text currently on the button.
➤ The chart will appear on the worksheet. You can delete the chart and recreate it using the button.
➤ Save the spreadsheet. (You must save the spreadsheet as a Macro enabled workbook as you have added a macro into the workbook.)

Go further

Using complex formulas

Open the spreadsheet **WDSP7.xlsx**, provided by your teacher.

Văn wants to calculate the income from each product using the sales figures. To do this you will have to use data from the Products worksheet and the Sales worksheet.

You need the sales price for each product from the Product worksheet. To do this you must set up a **named cell range** which is made up of the product data in cells A4 to O20.

◆ Highlight the cells in A4 to O20 in the Products worksheet.
◆ Whilst the cells are highlighted, type the word PRODUCTS into the name box. You have now created a named cell range. You can refer to this table of data by its name anywhere in the spreadsheet.

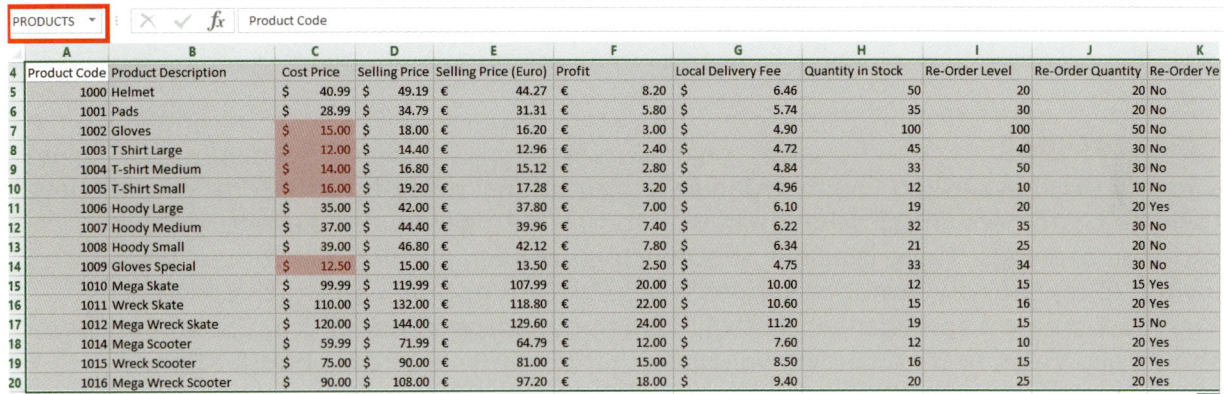

◆ To calculate the total income from each product you must break the problem down to create a formula which uses a lookup statement and multiplies the value returned by the lookup statement by another number.

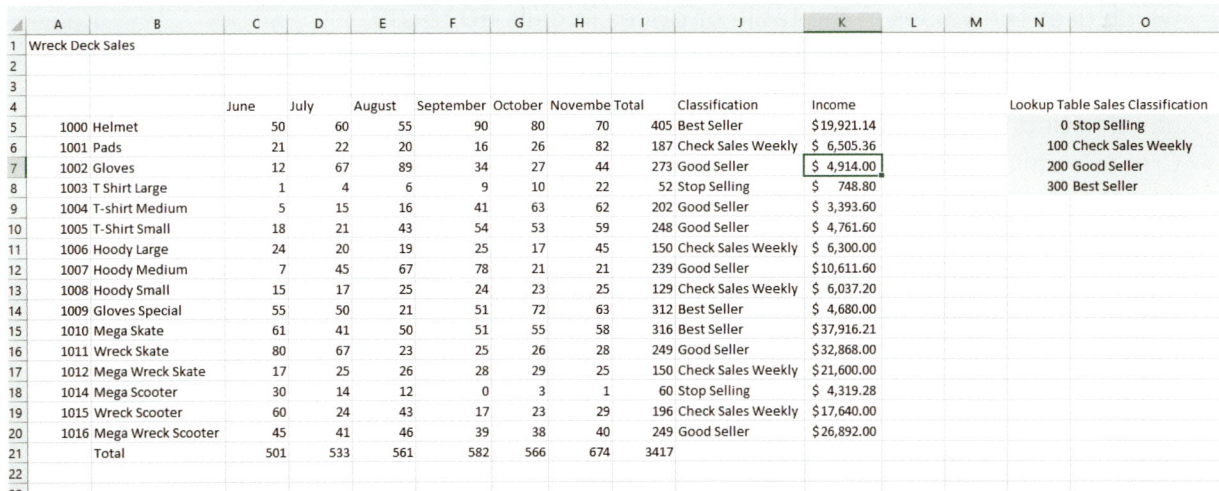

◆ Go to the Sales worksheet.
◆ Add the appropriate text to cell K4.
◆ Format column K as currency.

◆ Create a VLOOKUP statement in cell K5 which uses the Product ID in cell A5 to lookup the PRODUCTS table and return the selling price. From the data above, note that the selling price is in the fourth column.

```
=VLOOKUP(A5, PRODUCTS, _ _ _ _ _ _ _ )
```

◆ Ensure your results are correct by comparing them to the ones in the previous screenshot. Start by comparing your results in K5 to the results shown for K5.

◆ If you make any changes to the formula in cell K5, copy the formula down to cell K6 to K20.

◆ Create a chart showing the Income from each product.

◆ Discuss how charts can help shop owners to manage their business.

◆ Go to cell C24 on the Products worksheet. Change the Markup rate to 1.4.

◆ With a partner, examine the entire spreadsheet and look at the changes that have occurred as a result of making this change. Discuss how predictions can be made by changing certain values in the spreadsheet.

Final project

Văn and Hoa have asked you to organise a promotional event for the store. You will have to invite customers and provide them with food. There will be three events on three separate evenings. There is a limit of 80 customers each evening. Customers will be invited to try the new skateboards and will be given a goodie bag worth $6.00.

You must create a spreadsheet that will plan and manage expenditure. The spreadsheet should allow Văn to try changing values so that he can manage his budget tightly. He has a budget of $4000 for the three nights.

➤ Open the spreadsheet **BUDGET.xlsx**, provided by your teacher.

➤ Complete the totals for each column using appropriate functions.

➤ Complete the values in column B. To do this use a VLOOKUP statement which uses the values in the table of prices in cells I10 to J19.

> Remember you can use the SUM function to add the values in a range of cells.

➤ In the Number Required column, Văn has estimated how much of each type of food he will need. He knows that not every guest will like Potato Chips and has decided to order 40 bottles of water and 40 bottles of lemonade.

➤ Create a validation rule with suitable validation text which will ensure that the number entered in cells C2 to C16 is between 0 and 80.

➤ Complete the values in column D.

➤ Complete the values in column E and use an absolute cell reference in your formula. This will help with modelling later.

➤ Apply conditional formatting to all values in column E which are over $600.00. You should highlight them in red.

➤ Apply a filter to the data to show only the values which are over $600.00.

➤ Use an IF statement in cell E20 to determine if the party costs are over budget or not.

> An absolute cell reference contains $ symbols and does not change when copied.

➤ Record a macro which will create a Pie Chart of each item and the total cost for each item.

➤ Add a button to the spreadsheet and assign the macro the button.

➤ Save the spreadsheet.

Evaluation

Once you have created your spreadsheet you can see that Văn is over budget.

➤ You must look at the figures and make changes to the spreadsheet to ensure that Văn does not over spend.

➤ With a partner, discuss what changes you would make. Try modelling the changes in the spreadsheet so that Văn's spending does not exceed $4000.00.

➤ Together create a report, using a word processor, which will tell Văn what changes need to be made to keep him within budget. Your report should include:

o a short introduction telling Văn that he is over budget and by how much

o a section detailing the most expensive costs

o a section detailing your recommendation for change including two charts

o a conclusion explaining how much Văn will save.

➤ Share your report with another group. Ask them to read the report and comment on:

o how easy it is to understand

o how the graphs and charts help them understand.

➤ Based on the feedback you have received make changes to the report to improve its readability.

Relational databases: SegwayThere

Introducing relational databases

Databases are used by organisations to help them manage large quantities of data. The simplest databases look more like large tables of information organised under a set of headings.

For example, this table shows an extract from a database which records the details of some countries around the world.

Microsoft Access 2016 is used in the worked examples in this unit but other versions of Microsoft Access can also be used in this unit. Other examples of database software include ADABAS and IBM Db2.

Country name	Capital city	Country population	Continent	Continent size in square miles	Continent population
India	New Delhi	1,420,062,022	Asia	17,139,445	4,436,224,000
Brazil	Brasilia	209,737,513	South America	6,880,706	422,535,000
Nigeria	Abuja	200,962,417	Africa	11,677,239	1,216,130,000
Philippines	Manila	108,106,310	Asia	17,139,445	4,436,224,000
Vietnam	Hanoi	97,429,061	Asia	17,139,445	4,436,224,000
Germany	Berlin	82,438,639	Europe	3,997,929	738,849,000
France	Paris	65,480,710	Europe	3,997,929	738,849,000
United Kingdom	London	66,959,016	Europe	3,997,929	738,849,000
Saudi Arabia	Riyadh	34,140,662	Asia	17,139,445	4,436,224,000
Peru	Lima	32,933,835	South America	6,880,706	422,535,000
Canada	Ottawa	37,279,811	North America	9,361,791	579,024,000
Australia	Canberra	25,088,636	Australia	2,967,909	34,601,860
Taiwan	Taipei	23,758,247	Asia	17,139,445	4,436,224,0

The table above is an example of a **flat-file database**. A flat-file database is a database which uses only one table to store all of the data.

You can see in this extract from the database that the continent of Asia has been referred to a number of times. Compare the population of Asia in the last row of this database with the other references to Asia.

An error has been made when recording the population of Asia in this row of the flat-file database.

Relational databases can help prevent this type of error occurring. If we create a relational database we could use two tables to store this data.

Many developers will use a special code when naming parts of a database. This can help other developers tell one part of the database from the other. In this example, we will use _TBL to show these are tables.

> **KEYWORDS**
>
> **flat-file database:** a database which stores all data items using one table
>
> **relational database:** a database which stores data using two or more linked tables

158

country_TBL			
country_name	capital_city	country_population	continent
India	New Delhi	1,420,062,022	Asia
Brazil	Brasilia	209,737,513	South America
Nigeria	Abuja	200,962,417	Africa
Philippines	Manila	108,106,310	Asia
Vietnam	Hanoi	97,429,061	Asia
Germany	Berlin	82,438,639	Europe
France	Paris	65,480,710	Europe
United Kingdom	London	66,959,016	Europe
Saudi Arabia	Riyadh	34,140,662	Asia
Peru	Lima	32,933,835	South America
Canada	Ottawa	37,279,811	North America
Australia	Canberra	25,088,636	Australia
Taiwan	Taipei	23,758,247	Asia

continent_TBL		
continent	continent_size_(sq_miles)	continent_population
Asia	17,139,445	4,436,224,000
Africa	11,677,239	1,216,130,000
Europe	3,997,929	738,849,000
South America	6,880,706	422,535,000
North America	9,361,791	579,024,000
Australia	2,967,909	34,601,860

Notice how 'continent' appears on both tables. It is the **primary key field** of the Continent Table (continent_TBL) but also appears in the Country Table (country_TBL). The 'continent' field provides a link between the two tables. Most database developers do not include spaces in field names or table names; they use an underscore '_' instead.

When a continent name appears in the Country Table, the relational database will look up the other details about that continent in the Continent Table.

In this unit you will learn:
→ the differences between a relational and a flat-file database
→ how to describe the main features of a relational database
→ to create and edit a relational database
→ how to import data into an existing database structure
→ to create forms and reports to input and output data from a database
→ how to use queries (QBE) to extract useful data from a database
→ how to view and evaluate the SQL statements used to extract data from a relational database and be able to create simple SQL statements to extract data from a database.

KEYWORD

primary key field: a field used to uniquely identify a record in a database

DID YOU KNOW?

Databases are used to store large quantities of data and queries are used to locate information from database tables but queries can also be used to perform calculations! We will see how to do this later in this chapter.

SCENARIO

SegwayThere is a business renting Segways, electric scooters and safety equipment to tourists. Customers can also buy safety equipment if they wish.

SegwayThere uses a number of tables of data stored in a number of different text files to keep track of customers, bookings and equipment. Part of one of the text files used to store customer data is shown below.

```
cust_ID, Title, Surname, Firstname, address1, address2, address3, Country, ID_number, Age
1001,"Mr","Bisset","Nicolas","120 Rue Des Flerus","Bordeaux","Aquitaine","France","DL908789",21.00
1002,"Ms","Feliciano","Zelda","2916 Franklee Lane","PN","Pennsylvania","USA","PP656765",30.00
1003,"Mr","Ho","Ho","533 Ewald Crescent","Claudelands","Hamilton","New Zealand","ST487614",18.00
```

The owners were calculating bills for customers manually and giving them a handwritten ticket as a record of each item they have rented or purchased. This led to too many mistakes, was slow, and looked unprofessional. The owners have asked you to set up a database to store details of their bookings, customers and the items they have available for rental. They would like to be able to use this database to print a bill for customers. They would also like to be able to search the database for useful information.

> A text file used in this way is used only to record data which is typed in. The data stored in a text file cannot be processed in any way.

When a customer rents equipment, they must provide identification such as a passport, driving licence or student card. To make sure the different types of identification don't get mixed up, the company adds the letters PP to the beginning of all passport numbers, DL to all driving licence numbers and ST to all student cards when they store the details.

Equipment will only be rented to people over the age of 18 and it can be rented out for more than one day. The rental fee must be paid in advance.

Do you remember?

Before starting this unit, you should be able to:

✔ describe what a database is and some of the main uses of databases
✔ select appropriate **field names** and **data types** when creating database tables
✔ create an appropriate primary key field for a database table
✔ be able to view database objects such as **tables** and **queries**
✔ open an existing database and add a new field
✔ apply basic **validation** to database applications
✔ create and run simple queries to select data
✔ apply example **input masks** to ensure data is added in the correct format.

KEYWORDS

field names: names used to describe a piece of information about a single person or thing

tables: organised collection of related information

query: a process of searching for data in a database

input mask: a special control used to ensure data is entered in a specific format; for example, dates must be entered as mm/dd/yyyy

Why relational?

Learn

In databases, tables are used to store data in an organised way. Each table will have a number of fields. In a database table, data is organised under a set of headings called field headings. In the continent_TBL shown on page 159 we have three field headings.

Continent	continent_size_(sq_miles)	continent_population
Asia	17,139,445	4,436,224,000
Africa	11,677,239	1,216,130,000
Europe	3,997,929	738,849,000
South America	6,880,706	422,535,000
North America	9,361,791	579,024,000
Australia	2,967,909	34,601,860

three field headings

six records

Data stored in each table will be related in some way. For example, a table could hold details on each of the Continents as shown above, or a database could include a table which stores data on all of the customers of a shop, or all the products the shop sells.

Each row in a database table stores all of the data about a single person or thing. Each row is called a record. The continent_TBL has six records.

Each table will have a special field called a primary key field. A primary key field is used to uniquely identify each record. In contintent_TBL the field Continent could be used to uniquely identify each record in the table.

When database tables are being created, each field can be designed to store only a specific type of data such as text, numbers, date/time. To help reduce the chance of errors occurring when data is being entered into a database table, the database can also be designed to carry out validation checks. Validation checks help make sure that data being entered into the database table is, for example, of the correct data type, has the correct number of characters.

In some cases a special format check can be applied using an input mask which makes sure that data being entered follows a specific pattern. For example an input mask can be used to make sure a date is entered in the mm/dd/yyyy format.

Some data may need to be recorded more than once in a flat-file database. Unnecessary data duplication is called **data redundancy**. Storing data twice can cause problems in databases, such as taking longer to process data and output results, especially if the databases contain a lot of data.

Mistakes can easily happen when data is recorded more than once in a large database. Mistakes cause **data integrity** problems. In the example shown on the next page an error has been made when entering the continent for the last field in the table.

KEYWORDS

data redundancy: the unnecessary repetition of data in a database
data integrity: the correctness and accuracy of data in a database

country_name	capital_city	country_population	continent
India	New Delhi	1,420,062,022	Asia
Brazil	Brasilia	209,737,513	South America
Nigeria	Abuja	200,962,417	Africa
Philippines	Manila	108,106,310	Asia
Vietnam	Hanoi	97,429,061	Asia
Germany	Berlin	82,438,639	Europe
France	Paris	65,480,710	Europe
United Kingdom	London	66,959,016	Europe
Saudi Arabia	Riyadh	34,140,662	Asia
Peru	Lima	32,933,835	South America
Canada	Ottawa	37,279,811	North America
Australia	Canberra	25,088,636	Australia
Taiwan	Taipei	23,758,247	Azia

A search for all of the records relating to Asia would not return this record, and so the results displayed would be inaccurate.

Data tables can be linked by including the primary key field from one table as a data field in another table.

Relational databases have two main advantages.

➤ Data is stored only once – this reduces data redundancy and means the database will need less storage space.

➤ Data integrity is improved – there are fewer chances for input errors as data items need only be entered once.

Some redundancy is always necessary; for example, in the continents and country example shown previously, the continent field must appear in both tables to show how the data is linked.

Abstraction

Most flat-file databases can be converted to a relational database format.

On the next page, you can see some of the data used by SegwayThere; the data is shown in table format so it is easy to read. The first table, called Booking_Purchases_TBL, is used to store details of customers and bookings. The second table, called Equipment_TBL, is used to store details of the equipment they have available.

✔ With a friend, examine the Booking_Purchases_TBL structure. Decide how you can split this table into two separate tables to reduce data duplication. Use the process of abstraction to identify two separate groups of data in the flat-file shown. Think how these two groups of data could be stored in two separate tables. What would the tables be called?

✔ What would the primary key field be?

✔ What field would you use to link the second table to the first table?

Booking_Purchases_TBL

> Look carefully at the data items that have been repeated. Think about what we did with the data items in our Country–Continent table at the start of this unit.

Cust Number	Title	Surname	Firstname	Address 1	Address 2	Address 3	Country	ID Number	Age	Product ID	Date Out	Date Back
1001	Mr	Bisset	Nicolas	120 Rue Des Flerus	Bordeaux	Aquitaine	France	DL908789	21	SW111	21/03/2020	24/03/2020
1002	Ms	Feliciano	Zelda	2916 Franklee Lane	PN	Pennsylvania	USA	PP656765	30	SW334	22/03/2020	22/03/2020
1003	Mr	Ho	Louis	533 Ewald Crescent	Claudelands	Hamilton	New Zealand	ST487614	18	SC009	22/03/2020	25/03/2020
1004	Mr	Lue	Benton	Avendano 87	Alesanco	La Rioja	Spain	PP028597	29	SW097	22/03/2020	28/03/2020
1005	Mrs	Iola	Tovar	2132 St-Jacques Est	Princeville	Quebec	Canada	DL546763	20	SC128	23/03/2020	29/03/2020
1005	Mrs	Iola	Tovar	2132 St-Jacques Est	Princeville	Quebec	Canada	DL546763	20	HEL122	23/03/2020	29/03/2020
1005	Mrs	Iola	Tovar	2132 St-Jacques Est	Princeville	Quebec	Canada	DL546763	20	GLV675	03/04/2020	05/04/2020
1006	Miss	Sloan	Romona	Alcide De Gasperi 39	Arten	Belluno	Italy	PP723456	18	SW765	23/03/2020	24/03/2020
1004	Mr	Lue	Benton	Avendano 87	Alesanco	La Rioja	Spain	PP028597	29	SW097	01/04/2020	02/04/2020
1002	Ms	Feliciano	Zelda	2916 Franklee Lane	PN	Pennsylvania	USA	PP656765	30	SW334	02/04/2020	10/04/2020
1005	Mrs	Iola	Tovar	2132 St-Jacques Est	Princeville	Quebec	Canada	DL546763	20	SC128	03/04/2020	05/04/2020
1005	Mrs	Iola	Tovar	2132 St-Jacques Est	Princeville	Quebec	Canada	DL546763	20	HEL122	03/04/2020	05/04/2020
1005	Mrs	Iola	Tovar	2132 St-Jacques Est	Princeville	Quebec	Canada	DL546763	20	GLV675	03/04/2020	05/04/2020

Practice

You have split the Booking_Purchases_TBL into two tables. Equipment_TBL lists the equipment for rent:

Equipment_TBL

Product ID	Product	Description	Daily Rate	Purchase Fee
SW111	Segway	Segway Pro	$49.99	$0.00
SW334	Segway	Segway i2 SE	$45.99	$0.00
SC009	e-Scooter	Razor E90	$20.99	$0.00
SW097	Segway	Segway Pro	$49.00	$0.00
SC128	e-Scooter	Razor E90	$20.99	$0.00
SW765	Segway	Navboard LME-S1	$35.99	$0.00
HEL122	Helmet	Small	$4.99	$24.00
GLV675	Gloves	Med	$1.99	$5.99
SJ234	Safety Jacket	Med	$4.99	$20.99

You will now have a total of three tables in your database.

➤ Make a list of the attributes / field headings each table will contain.

➤ Select a suitable name for each of the new tables. (Hint: do not include capital letters or spaces; instead of a space, use an underscore '_'.)

> Think carefully about what field must be included in both tables to create the links shown.

➤ Copy and complete the diagram below, filling in the fields for each table to show how the three tables will be linked.

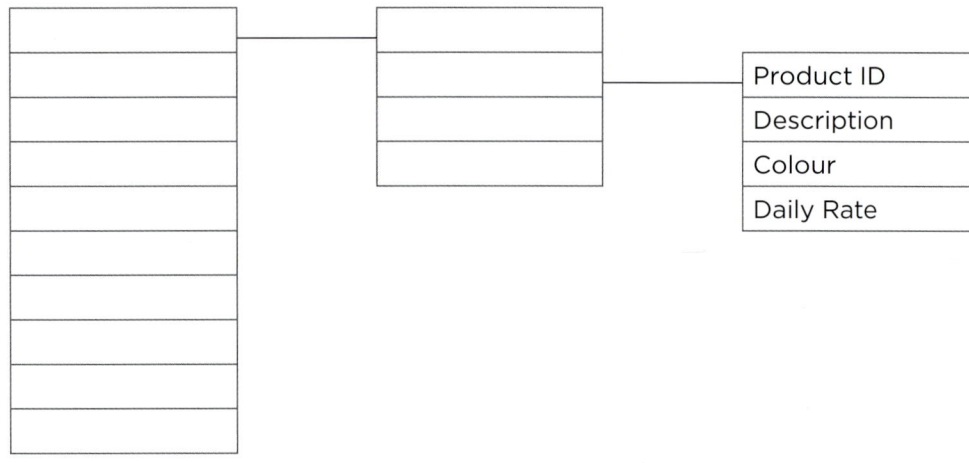

| Product ID |
| Description |
| Colour |
| Daily Rate |

Relational databases – designing and linking tables

Learn

Before data can be added to a relational database, the tables being used to store the data must first be created.

Database designers will first produce a **data dictionary** which, among other things, will contain:
➤ details of any **entities** represented in each table in the database; an entity is an individual person or thing about which data is stored in a database
➤ **attributes** associated with each entity; attributes represent the characteristics of each person or thing stored in the database; field names are used to describe each attribute
➤ data types for each attribute / field name (in other words, text, numbers, dates…)
➤ field lengths (in other words, how long each piece of data can be); for example, the Customer Number in the previous example has a field length of four (only four characters are used to store each Customer Number)
➤ validation checks to help reduce the chance of errors occurring when data is entered; we will look at validation in more detail later in this chapter.

This table shows a data dictionary for our Countries–Continents database on page 159.

Table	Attribute Name	Data Type	Field Length	Validation Check	Required	Notes
country_TBL	Country_Name	Text	60	Presence check	Yes	Primary Key field
country_TBL	Capital_City	Text	60	Presence check	Yes	
country_TBL	Country_Population	Integer		Range check	Yes	Must be >0
country_TBL	Continent	Text	12	Lookup list	Yes	Africa, Asia, Australia, Europe, South America, North America
continent_TBL	Continent	Text	60	Presence check	Yes	Primary Key field
continent_TBL	Continent_Size_(Sq_miles)	Integer		Range check	Yes	Must be >0
continent_TBL	Continent_Population	Integer		Range check	Yes	Must be >0

You will notice from this table and from the diagram on page 159 that the attribute 'Continent' appears in both country_TBL and continent_TBL. It is being used to create a link between the two tables. Continent is a primary key field in the continent_TBL table. Since it appears in country_TBL to help create a link between the two tables it is known as a **foreign key** in country_TBL.

Database applications use **relationships** to link tables together.

> **KEYWORDS**
>
> **data dictionary:** a document used to describe the main parts of a database and how each of the main database parts are linked
>
> **entity:** an individual person or thing about which data is stored in a database
>
> **attribute:** represents a characteristic of a person or thing stored in the database, described using a field name
>
> **foreign key:** a field in one table which appears in another table, creating a link between the two tables
>
> **relationship:** the link between two tables in a database application, created using a field that appears in both tables

There are three types of relationships in database design:

➤ one-to-one

➤ one-to-many

➤ many-to-many.

Database designers use a special diagram called an **entity relationship diagram (ERD)**, to show how each of the entities in the relational database are linked.

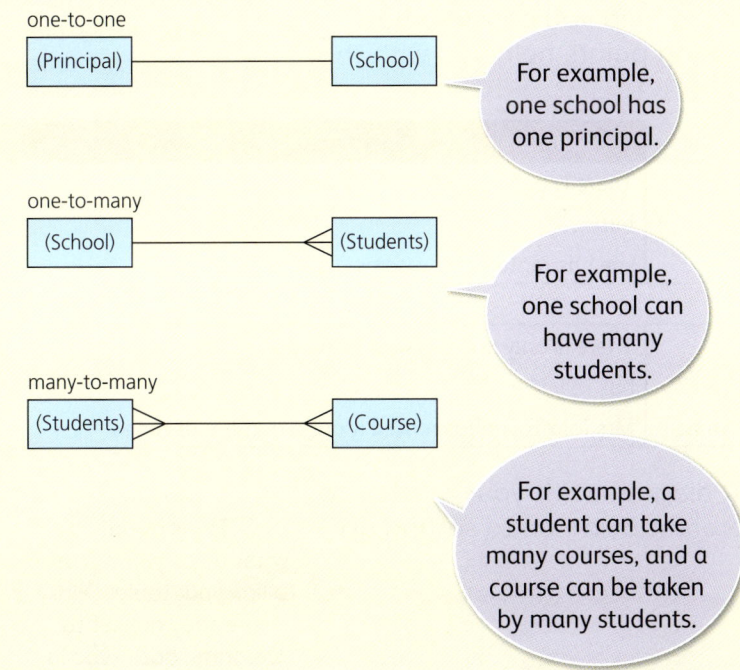

one-to-one
(Principal) — (School)

For example, one school has one principal.

one-to-many
(School) — (Students)

For example, one school can have many students.

many-to-many
(Students) — (Course)

For example, a student can take many courses, and a course can be taken by many students.

> **KEYWORD**
>
> **entity relationship diagram (ERD):** a diagram used to illustrate the relationship between two entities in a relational database

Practice

Using the list of fields and tables you produced in the practice task on page 163–4:

➤ create a similar data dictionary for each of the three tables you will use in your 'SegwayThere' database

➤ think carefully about the field headings you will use for the attributes in each table; try to select field headings which are easy to remember but that still describe the attributes they represent

➤ identify the primary key fields and foreign key fields in each table.

> Think carefully about how you can control the number of characters being entered into a field, how you can make sure data within certain values can be entered into a field or how you can use input masks to control the format of data entered into a field.

> One table will have two foreign key fields. It will be used to link the other two tables.

> Remember it is good practice not to include spaces or capital letters in your field headings.

Abstraction

Think carefully about the relationships that must exist between your three tables in order to reduce data duplication. Now produce an ER diagram to illustrate the links between your three tables.

What information should only be stored once to help reduce the chance of errors being made when data is recorded?

Look at the data in each of the tables to help you consider how the tables would be linked. The following points help you with this.

> Think carefully – a customer's personal details should only exist once, but a customer might rent more than one product at a time.

	For example:
Each customer can only exist once but ... each customer can have many bookings.	There is only one Mrs Iola Tovar but ... she has rented many items.

| Each item can only exist once but ... each item can be rented out many different times. | There is only one physical Razor Ego scooter but ... Mrs Iola Tovar has rented it out a number of times. |

Discuss your data dictionary and ER diagram with your teacher to make sure your design is correct before moving on to setting up your database.

> Think about what fields you will use to link your tables. Make sure they are set to the same data type in each table in your data dictionary.

Database structures

Learn

Like other computer applications, relational databases receive input data, store and process it, before producing output for the end user. The diagram below shows how the linked tables in a relational database interact with the other objects in the database.

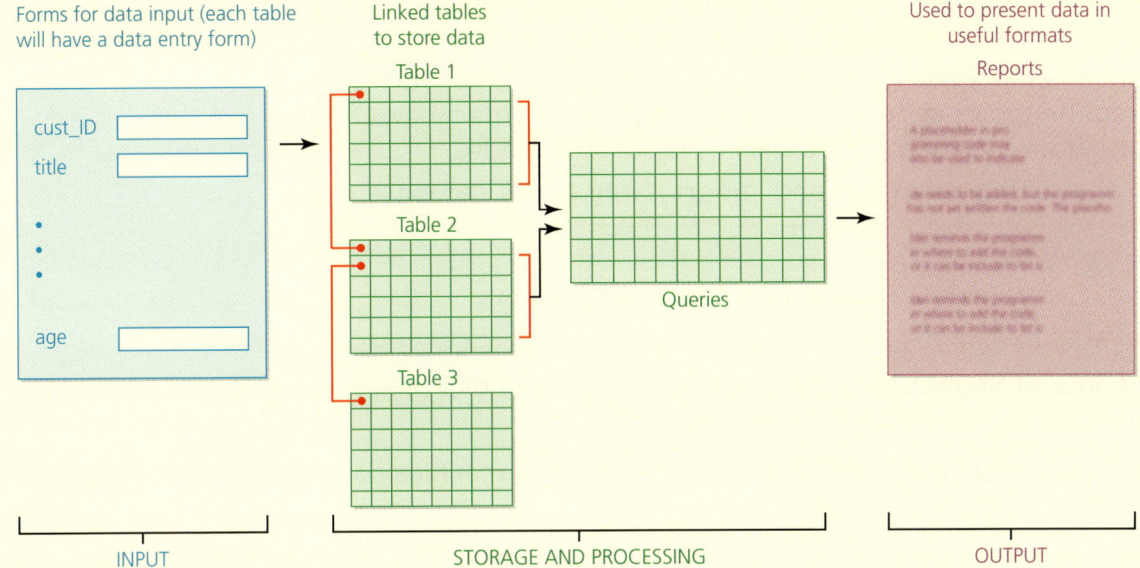

Forms for data input (each table will have a data entry form)

Linked tables to store data

Used to present data in useful formats

Table 1

Table 2

Table 3

Queries

Reports

cust_ID

title

age

INPUT

STORAGE AND PROCESSING

OUTPUT

Forms:
➤ Used to input data by users of the database.
➤ Data is transferred from the form to the correct table in the database.

Queries
➤ Used to search for data.
➤ Can be used to search for and display data from more than one table at a time.
➤ Can be used to perform calculations.

Reports
➤ Used to display data in a useful format onscreen and as a printout.

You should have already used simple queries to search for data. In this unit we will look at more complex queries.

Populating databases

Learn

We know from our previous work with databases, and from what we have studied in this unit so far, that databases use tables to store data.

Adding data to a database table is known as **populating the database**. This can be done in a number of ways.

➤ Create an empty database structure. The user can then add data to the tables as required; for example, each time a new customer arrives, or a new rental or purchase is made.

➤ Take an existing data table and import it into a new database.

KEYWORD

populating a database: the process of adding new data to a database or integrating existing data into a database

Practice

The manager of SegwayThere has looked at your data dictionary and has restructured his original tables to meet your new design.

The owner has copied the data into three *Microsoft Excel* files so you can import the data into the new relational database.

Your teacher will give you a copy of three *Microsoft Excel* files called **customer_TBL**, **booking_TBL** and **product_TBL**.

Your first task is to:

➤ import each of these files into a blank database and select appropriate data types (text, integers, dates, and so on)

➤ open a new blank database using *Microsoft Access* by clicking on *Blank desktop database*

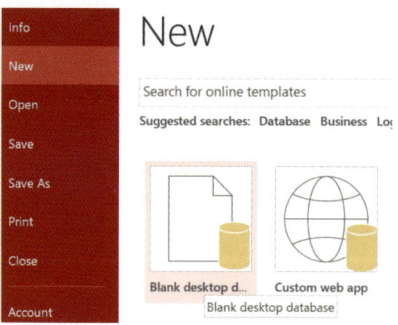

➤ give the database an appropriate name; for example, **SegwayThereDB** and click Create.

First we will import the data for customer_TBL.

➤ Click on the External Data tab and then the Excel icon to Import data from a *Microsoft Excel* file.

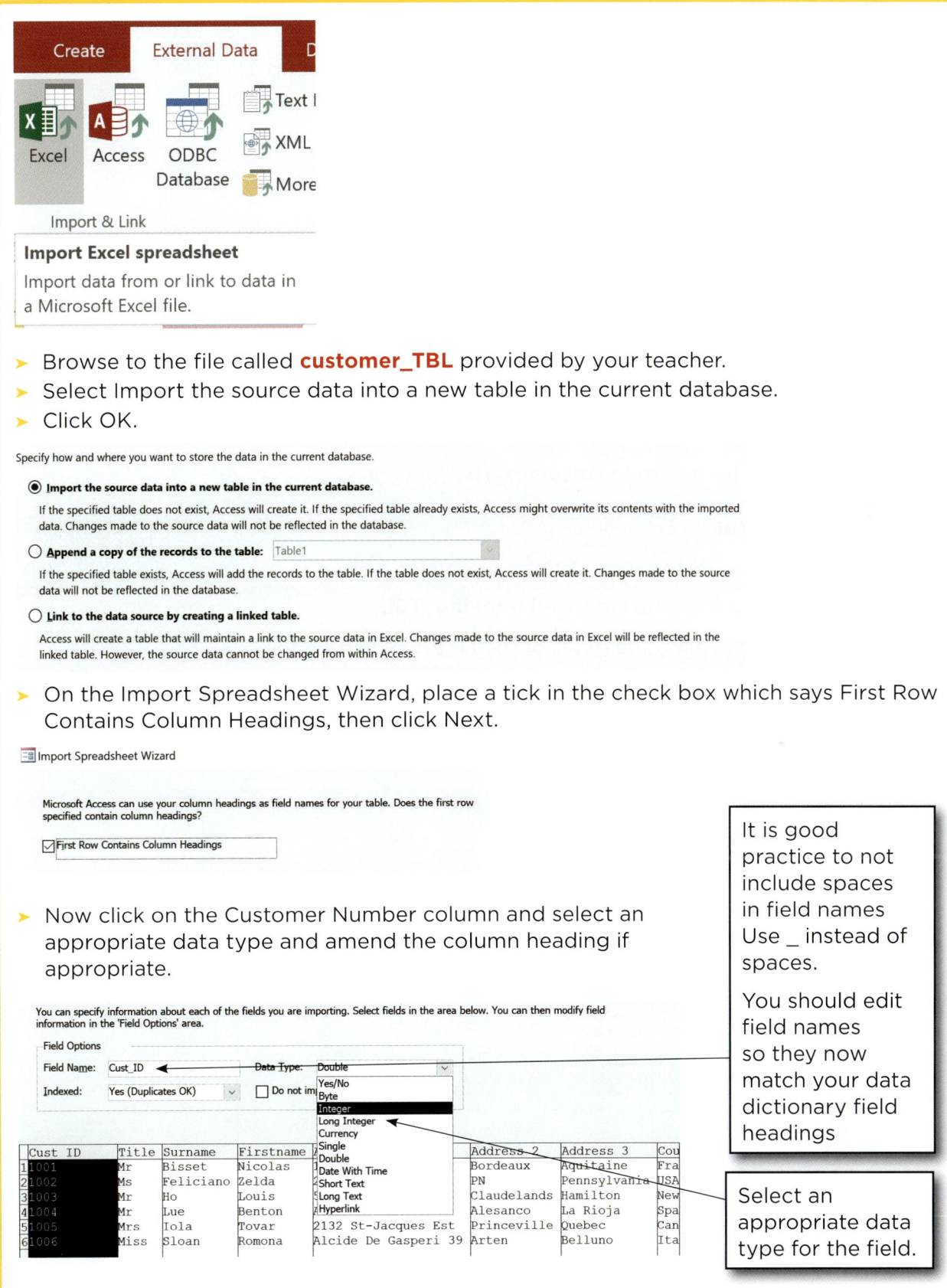

➤ Browse to the file called **customer_TBL** provided by your teacher.
➤ Select Import the source data into a new table in the current database.
➤ Click OK.

Specify how and where you want to store the data in the current database.

◉ **Import the source data into a new table in the current database.**
If the specified table does not exist, Access will create it. If the specified table already exists, Access might overwrite its contents with the imported data. Changes made to the source data will not be reflected in the database.

○ **Append a copy of the records to the table:** Table1
If the specified table exists, Access will add the records to the table. If the table does not exist, Access will create it. Changes made to the source data will not be reflected in the database.

○ **Link to the data source by creating a linked table.**
Access will create a table that will maintain a link to the source data in Excel. Changes made to the source data in Excel will be reflected in the linked table. However, the source data cannot be changed from within Access.

➤ On the Import Spreadsheet Wizard, place a tick in the check box which says First Row Contains Column Headings, then click Next.

Import Spreadsheet Wizard

Microsoft Access can use your column headings as field names for your table. Does the first row specified contain column headings?

☑ First Row Contains Column Headings

➤ Now click on the Customer Number column and select an appropriate data type and amend the column heading if appropriate.

It is good practice to not include spaces in field names Use _ instead of spaces.

You should edit field names so they now match your data dictionary field headings

Select an appropriate data type for the field.

➤ Click on each column in turn and repeat this process for every field in **customer_TBL**.

➤ When all fields from **customer_TBL** have been correctly set up, click Next.

You will now be able to select a primary key field for your database table.

Microsoft Access will automatically try to create a primary key field for you. Be sure to set cust_ID as your primary key field as shown below.

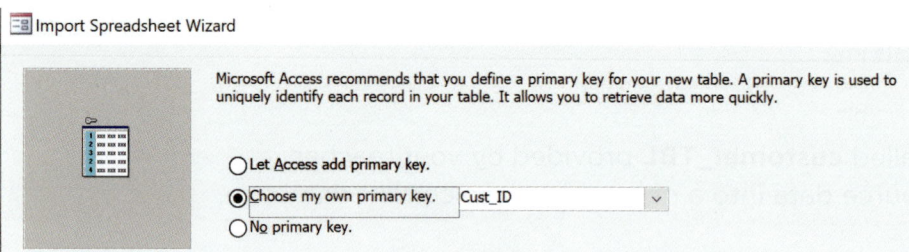

> Remember to select currency format for daily fee and purchase fee.

➤ Click Next and enter the name **customer_TBL** for your database table.

➤ Save **customer_TBL**.

Repeat the above process to import data from **product_TBL**.

Now import the data from the file called **booking_TBL**.

> Look carefully at the data in this table. Why would Product ID be the most suitable primary key field?

➤ Edit the field names and data types of the first two fields in the table to match **customer_TBL** and **product_TBL**.

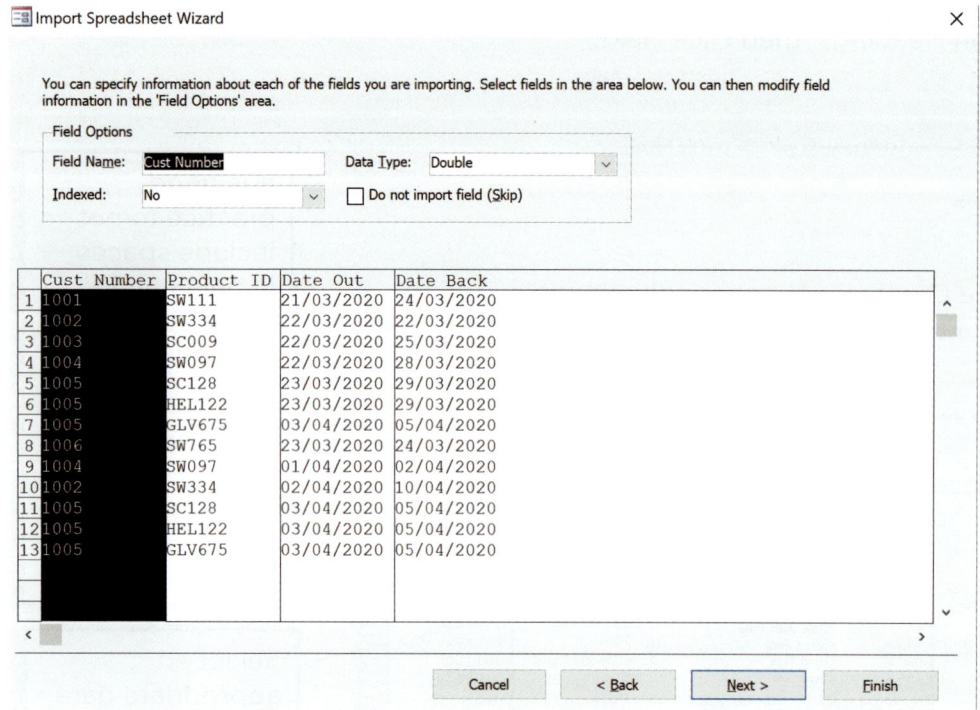

➤ Once you are happy with the field names and data types, click Next.

Click on 'Let Access add primary key for this table'. The first field heading in this table is Customer Number. The same customer number has been entered many times so this would not provide a unique identifier for each booking.

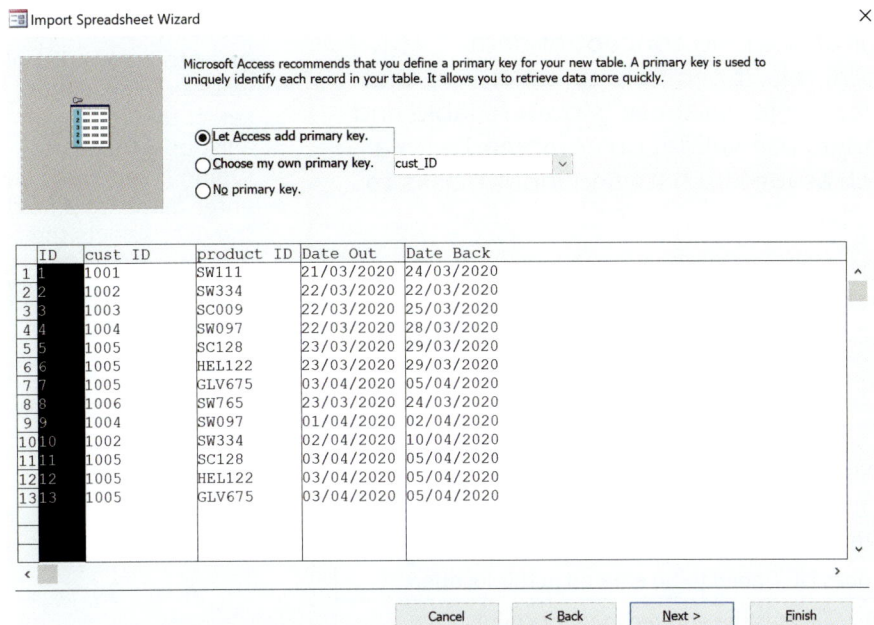

When you have completed the import process view the table in design view and rename the primary key in this table to Booking_ID.

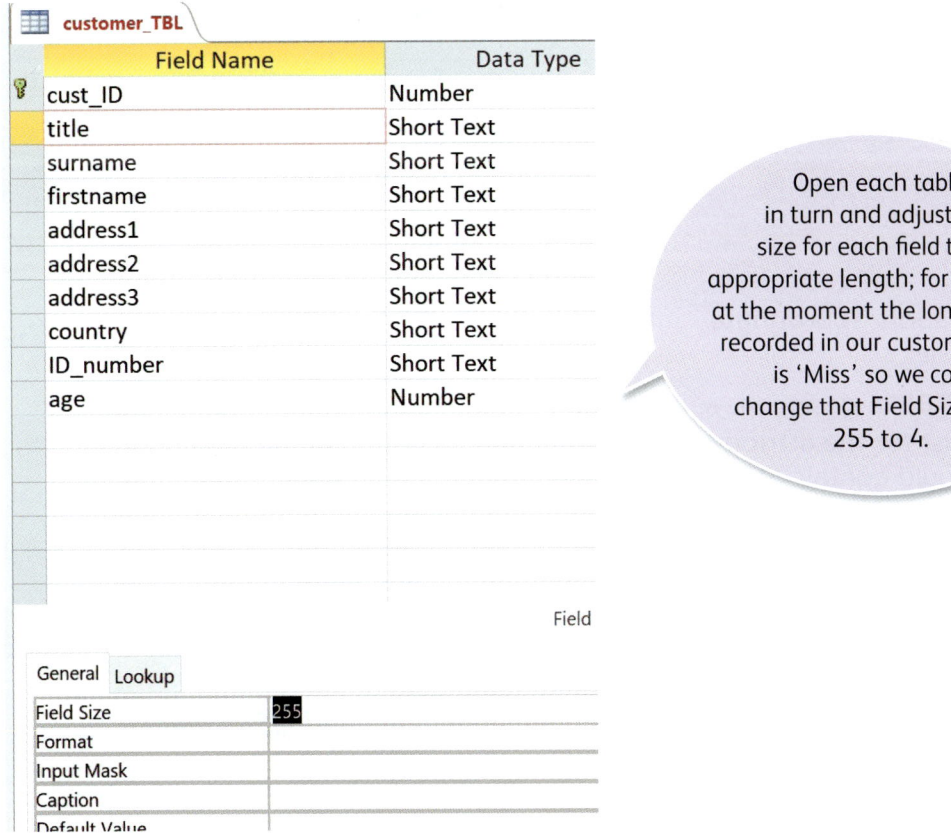

Open each table in turn and adjust the size for each field to an appropriate length; for example, at the moment the longest title recorded in our customer_TBL is 'Miss' so we could change that Field Size from 255 to 4.

Accurate data entry

Learn

You should already be familiar with the concept of data validation and how important it is. It can help to make sure that the data entered into an electronic database is both reliable and accurate. Database developers use validation combined with a range of other controls such as **lookup lists** and input masks to help with data reliability.

Input masks can be used to make sure data entered contains capitals, letters and numbers in the right place. The table below shows some of the common input mask controls used in *Microsoft Access*.

0	0 to 9 can be entered. A value must be entered in this location
9	0 to 9 or SPACE can be entered. A value does NOT need to be entered in this location
L	A–Z can be entered. A value must be entered in this location
?	A–Z can be entered. A value does NOT need to be entered in this location
A	A–Z or 0–9 can be entered. A value must be entered in this location
a	A–Z or 0–9 can be entered. A value does NOT need to be entered in this location
&	Any character or space can be entered. A value must be entered in this location
C	Any character or space can be entered. A value does NOT need to be entered in this location
>	All characters following this symbol will be displayed as upper case
<	All characters following this symbol will be displayed as lower case

Practice

Your next task is to apply appropriate validation to the tables.

➤ Open **customer_TBL** in design view.
➤ Create a lookup list for the attribute Title (your list should contain Mr, Miss, Ms, Mx, Mrs – you can add other appropriate titles if you wish).
  • Select Lookup Wizard.
  • Select 'I will type the values that I want' and click Next.
  • Enter the values you wish to appear in your lookup list.

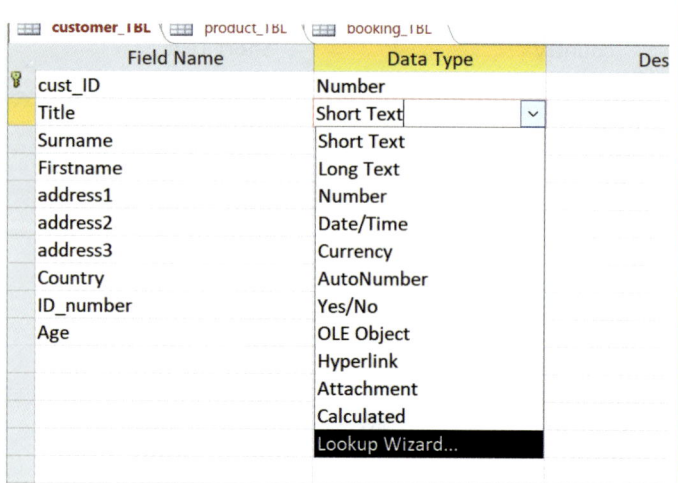

Lookup Wizard

What values do you want to see in your lookup field? Enter the number of columns you want in the list, and then type the values you want in each cell.

To adjust the width of a column, drag its right edge to the width you want, or double-click the right edge of the column heading to get the best fit.

Number of columns: 1

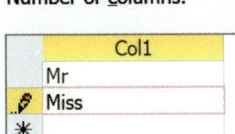

> **KEYWORD**
>
> **unit testing:** the process of testing individual parts or components in a computer based solution

- Click Next and then Next again.
- Click Finish to set up your lookup list.
- View the table again in Datasheet View and test your lookup list by clicking on the title field for one of the existing records. A lookup list should appear as shown.

cust_ID	Title	Surname	Firs...
1001	Mr	Bisset	Nico
1002	Mr	Feliciano	Zelda
1003	Miss	Ho	Ho
1004	Ms	Lue	Bent
1005	Mrs	Iola	Tova
1006	Mx	Sloan	Rom

➤ Surname and Firstname fields should be no longer than 30 characters long. In Design View, add an appropriate validation rule using the LEN function to these fields. Also, add validation text for both fields.

> Add the following to the Validation Rule to both Surname and Firstname: e.g. Len([Username]).

➤ Use the LEN function to add a length check to the Title attribute (it should be>0).

➤ Customers cannot rent equipment from the company unless they are 18 years old or above. Add an appropriate validation check and text to the Age attribute.

➤ Using the input mask controls we looked at earlier, for the input mask for Title would be: **>L<L??.** Add this input mask to the Title field in your customer_TBL.

➤ Save your database by selecting File and then Save. (When you save a database file in *Microsoft Access*, it automatically saves all parts of your project; you do not have to save each table individually.)

> This is an example of **unit testing**, where we are testing each table as a standalone unit / object in the database to make sure it works correctly on its own. Only after we are sure each table works will we begin to test the full database.

Use a similar test plan layout to the one shown below to test your Title input masks

Test	Reason for test	Value	Expected Outcome	Actual Outcome	Does Expected Outcome match Actual Outcome? (Y/N)
1	Invalid title	98W	Error message		
2	No Data Entered	leave Title blank	Error message		
3	Valid Title entered	Mr	Accepted		
4					

Pattern recognition

- ✪ Identify the pattern used when recording ID number. Once you have recognised the pattern create an input mask for this field.
- ✪ Design and create appropriate validation checks and/or input masks for the remaining text fields in your customer_TBL.
- ✪ Test all of your validation checks and input masks in customer_TBL using a similar test plan layout to the one you used for the Title field.

Abstraction and generalisation

Open the other two tables in turn.
- ✪ Discuss with a friend where and how you could apply any validation methods and input masks to the fields created in each table.
- ✪ Add any validation checks and/or input masks you have discussed with your friend to each table in turn.

> Remember you will need to look for patterns in the data first of all before deciding on the input mask format. Not all fields will need an input mask.

- ✪ Create a test plan similar to the one used with customer_TBL to ensure all of your validation checks and/or input masks operate correctly.
- ✪ Save all of your work.

Linking tables

Practice

Now that the tables have been designed, created and tested as individual objects, it is time to create and test the relationships between the tables.

- ➤ Open the file **SegwayThereDB**.
- ➤ Click on the Database Tools tab and click on the Relationships icon.
- ➤ The Show Table dialog box will appear. Select on each table in turn and click Add.
- ➤ Organise your display in the relationships window so your tables appear as shown. Notice that the primary/ key fields are labelled with a key icon.

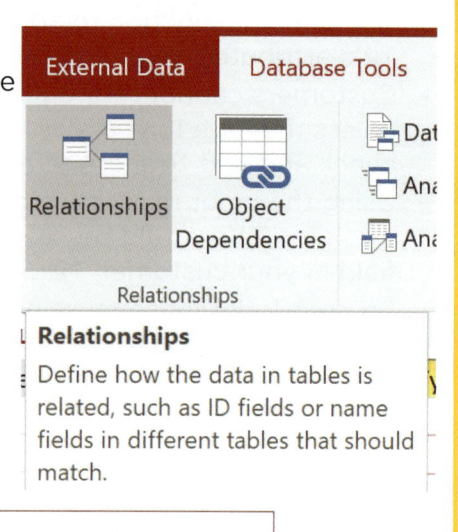

customer_TBL
- cust_ID
- title
- surname
- firstname
- address1
- address2
- address3

booking_TBL
- booking_ID
- cust_ID
- product_ID
- date_out
- date_back

product_TBL
- product_ID
- product_type
- description
- daily_rate
- purchase_fee
- product_image

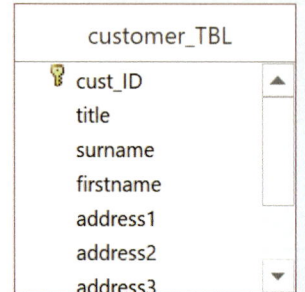
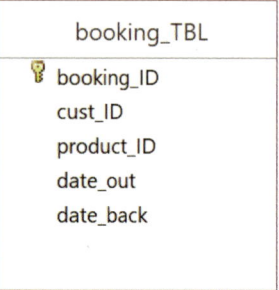
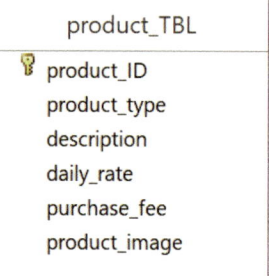

➤ Click on cust_ID (the primary key) for customer_TBL.

➤ Drag this field over to cust_ID on booking_TBL.

➤ We wish to **cascade delete** records in all tables and enforce **referential integrity**. Place a tick beside Enforce Referential Integrity and Cascade Delete Related Records.

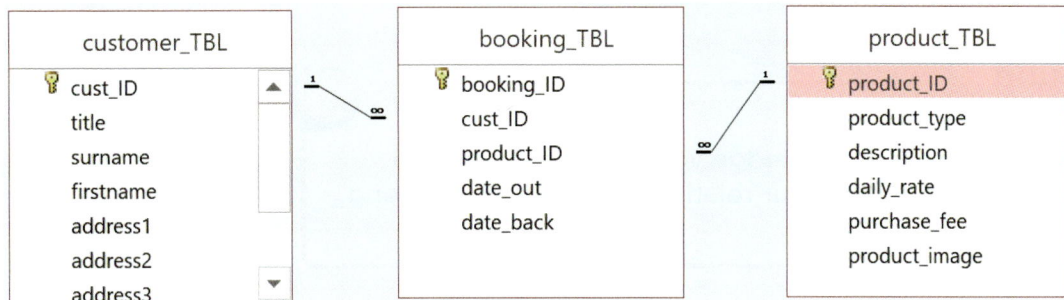

☑ Enforce Referential Integrity ◄——— Ensures that a booking cannot be made for a customer if that customer does not exist in customer_TBL.

☐ Cascade Update Related Fields

☑ Cascade Delete Related Records ◄——— Ensures that if a customer is deleted from customer_TBL all of their related records in booking_TBL will also be removed.

➤ Create a similar relationship between booking_TBL and product_TBL using product_ID.

customer_TBL	booking_TBL	product_TBL
🔑 cust_ID	🔑 booking_ID	🔑 product_ID
title	cust_ID	product_type
surname	product_ID	description
firstname	date_out	daily_rate
address1	date_back	purchase_fee
address2		product_image
address3		

➤ Notice that the relationships between the fields in different tables are denoted with link lines shown in the Relationships window.

➤ Save your file.

KEYWORDS

cascade delete: a feature of relational databases which means that, for example, if a customer is deleted from the customer table, all of the bookings linked to that customer will also be removed from the booking table

referential integrity: a feature of relational databases which means for example that a booking cannot be added for a customer who does not exist in the customer table

Practice

➤ Open **SegwayThereDB**.

➤ Double click on booking_TBL to open the table in Datasheet View.

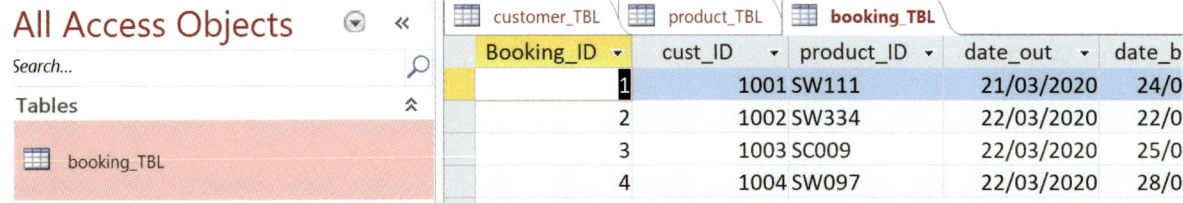

All Access Objects

Search...

Tables

booking_TBL

Booking_ID	cust_ID	product_ID	date_out	date_b
1	1001	SW111	21/03/2020	24/0
2	1002	SW334	22/03/2020	22/0
3	1003	SC009	22/03/2020	25/0
4	1004	SW097	22/03/2020	28/0

> ➤ Try to enter a booking for a customer.
> 1007, Miss Dancia McLeod, 817 Rose Lane, West End, London, UK, driving licence number DL991276, aged 27
> ➤ She would like to book a Segway Pro (Product ID) SW097 from 3/5/23 to 5/5/23.
> ➤ Discuss with a partner the message you received when you tried to enter this booking.
> ➤ Discuss the steps you need to take to correct this problem and then add the booking to the database.

> Click on the (New) row at the bottom of the table to add a new record.

> Check customer_TBL to see if customer 1007 exists in the database.

Generalisation

With your partner use the knowledge you have developed to create a similar test to check your relationship between booking_TBL and product_TBL.

> Try adding a booking for cust_ID 1003 but with a product that is not listed in product_TBL.

Creating input forms

Learn

Databases provide users with forms to enter data, modify a record or to view a single record on screen.

Data entered into a form will automatically be added to the correct table in the relational database.

Practice

> ➤ Open the file **SegwayThereDB**.
> ➤ Highlight customer_TBL in the Objects panel at the left hand side of the screen.
> ➤ Click on the Create tab and then Form Wizard.

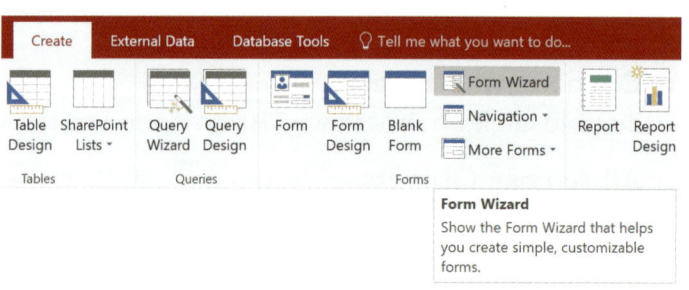

➤ Click the double chevron icon to move all Available Fields across to Selected Fields

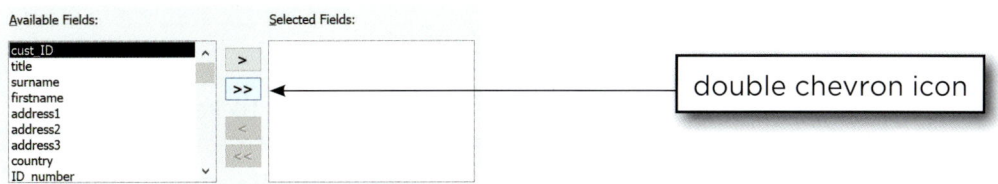

double chevron icon

➤ Click Next and select Column layout, before clicking Next again.
➤ Give the form an appropriate name, such as customer_FRM and then click Finish.

The form will display with the first customer record from customer_TBL.

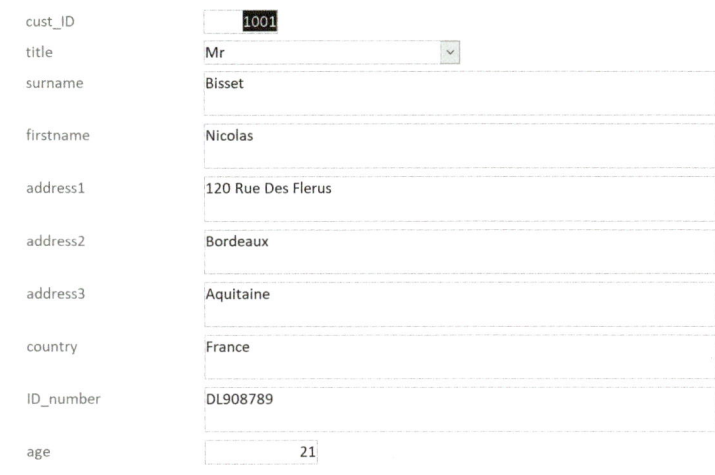

cust_ID	1001
title	Mr
surname	Bisset
firstname	Nicolas
address1	120 Rue Des Flerus
address2	Bordeaux
address3	Aquitaine
country	France
ID_number	DL908789
age	21

Generalisation and evaluation

Use the form **wizard** to create a similar form for booking_TBL, called booking_FRM.
Do not worry about creating a form for product_TBL just yet.

With a partner, discuss the design and layout of the forms you have created.
In your discussion, you should consider:

- Does the form look professional?
- Do the field headings easily describe the attributes being recorded?
- How can you improve the forms?
- Would special instructions help the user complete any attribute?
- How might colour improve the presentation of the form?
- Is the text large enough on screen?

Does it look like a form that could be printed out and shown to a customer?

A more relevant form title would help describe the form's use.

Data must be entered in a specific format, the form could include an example to help the user

KEYWORD

wizard: a software tool which takes users step-by-step through the completion of a task

Input form design and layout

Learn

Most databases will have more than one form. Database designers try to keep the database looking professional. They can do this by making sure forms:

➤ are consistent; for example, all the same colour, use the same font, have form titles in the same place

➤ use field headings which clearly describe each attribute being recorded

➤ include instructions to help the user; for example, if data is being recorded, they may give an example of the layout such as dd/mm/yyyy

➤ provide easy-to-understand feedback to users.

> Good use of validation rules and validation text when creating the tables can help with this.

Practice

Using the feedback from your discussions with your partner, improve the presentation of customer_FRM and booking_FRM to make it more professional.

➤ Open each form in Design View.

➤ Click on the text in the form header 'customer_TBL' and edit this to read 'Customer Details Form'. Use the text formatting tools to amend the size, font and colour of this title to a design of your choice.

➤ Click on each attribute label and edit the label to make it more **user friendly**; for example, instead of cust_ID the first attribute label could read Customer Number.

> You can click on any object, such as a text box, on a *Microsoft Access* form and edit the properties. The properties window is often displayed at the right hand side of the database window. If it is not displayed automatically, right click on the object and select Properties from the menu displayed on screen.

KEYWORD

user friendly: something that is not difficult to learn or understand

Property Sheet ✕

Selection type: Label

Label20 ⌄

Format	Data	Event	Other	All

Caption	Customer Details
Visible	Yes
Width	7.688cm
Height	1.709cm
Top	0.101cm
Left	0.101cm
Back Style	Transparent
Back Color	Background 1
Border Style	Transparent
Border Width	Hairline
Border Color	Text 1, Lighter 50
Special Effect	Flat
Font Name	Calibri (Detail)
Font Size	20
Text Align	General
Font Weight	Normal
Font Underline	No
Font Italic	No
Fore Color	Text 1, Lighter 50
Line Spacing	0cm
Hyperlink Address	
Hyperlink SubAddress	
Hyperlink Target	

> For example, editing text format using the properties window.

➤ Edit the font, size and style of each of the attribute labels so they are more user friendly.
➤ Right click on any part of the form to edit the background colour.

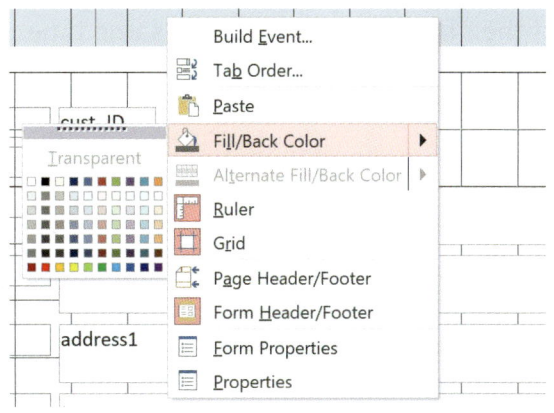

> You can also right click on any text box or label in the form to edit background.

➤ In design view, you can move text boxes and labels around to make the form more user friendly. For example, you may wish to display title, firstname and surname in one line as that is the way someone would normally write their name.

➤ Click on the surname text field and label and drag it to another position on customer_FRM.

➤ You will notice that they both move at the same time.

➤ Separate the label and the text field by right clicking on the label and selecting Edit – Cut.

➤ Select Edit and then Paste to add the label back onto customer_FRM.

➤ You can now move both parts around separately.

➤ Edit the layout of customer_FRM so it looks similar to the one shown, right.

➤ Edit your booking_FRM so it has a similar layout.

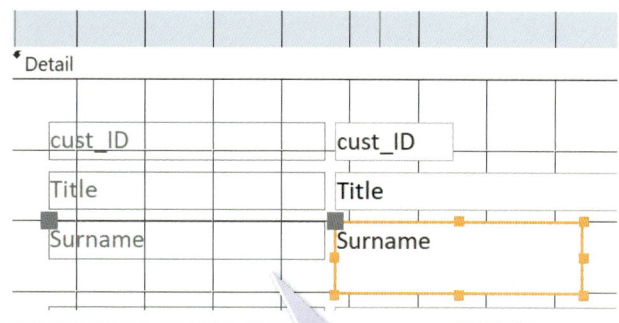

> The grid lines shown in design view act as good markers when moving objects around. You can also view your form in layout view and move the fields and labels around so you can see what the final form looks like after each change you make.

Customer Details Form

Customer ID	1001

Title	Firstname	Surname
Mr	Nicolas	Bisset

Select from Mr, Miss, Ms, Mrs

Address Line 1	120 Rue Des Flerus
Address Line 2	Bordeaux
Address Line 3	Aquitaine
Country	France

Age	21

Identification	DL908789

PP= Passport, DL = Driving Licence, ST = Student Card
e.g. PP123456

Abstraction

Often the way a database is presented to the user is not the way it is stored or organised. In this example, **SegwayThereDB** has three tables but the owner of SegwayThere would like to be able to see each customer's details and all of their booking details at the same time.

This level of abstraction can be achieved in a relational database by using a data entry form which can combine data from more than one source.

✪ The owner of SegwayThere would like a single form which allows them to add customers and bookings at the same time.
  o Click on the Create tab again and select Form Wizard.
  o Select and add the fields from customer_TBL as before.
  o Select and add all fields from booking_TBL (do not add customer_ID).

> This field will already be on the form.

✪ Before completing all of the steps on the Form Wizard and clicking Finish, with a friend think what this form might look like and how it might operate.
  o Test the form by adding the details of someone you know as a customer.
  o Add two bookings for this person.
  o Close the form and open **customer_TBL** to check their details were added correctly.
  o Open **booking_TBL** to check the two bookings were also added correctly.

QBE v SQL

Learn

Most relational databases use **Structured Query Language (SQL)** to access the data stored in the data tables.

Previously, you may have used a method called **Query by Example (QBE)** to extract data from a database. A QBE interface provides the user with a grid. The user adds the fields and search criteria and the software creates the SQL to actually process the query.

> Remember: clicking the double chevrons allows you to add all fields. If all fields are not needed click on each field in turn and click the single chevron to move the fields over one at a time.

To create a simple QBE to search for the details of all of the Segways in product_TBL:

➤ click on the Create Tab and select Query Wizard

➤ select Simple query Wizard and click OK

➤ add all fields from product_TBL into the selected fields panel

➤ click Next to give the query a name, segwayQRY

➤ select Modify the query design

➤ under criteria for product_type, enter Segway, and run the query.

> Remember: the exclamation mark is used to run queries.

In *Microsoft Access* you can view the SQL behind any queries.

➤ Double click on segwayQRY.

➤ Click on the Home tab and then View and select SQL view.

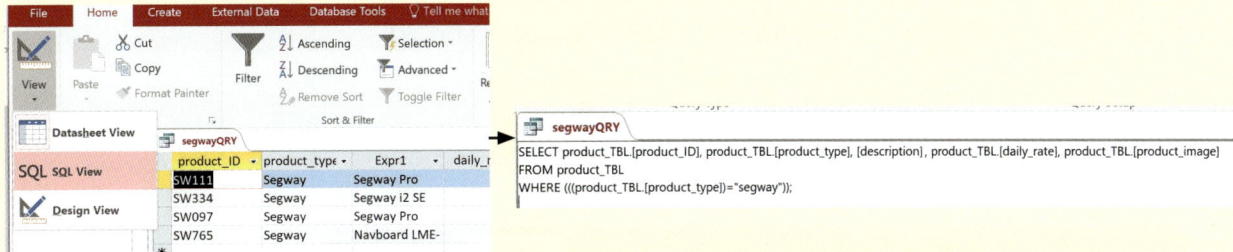

The above example shows that SQL statements have three main parts:

➤ SELECT – used to specify the data/fields to be displayed in the query.

➤ FROM – used to identify the source or table the data is to be selected from.

➤ WHERE – used to identify the criteria used to select the data.

KEYWORDS

Structured Query Language (SQL): a specialised language used with relational databases to input or retrieve data

Query By Example (QBE): an interface that allows users to add fields and criteria to a grid and then the software creates the SQL needed to process the data

Pattern recognition and algorithmic thinking

With a friend try to analyse the SQL statement created.

✪ Rewrite the statement in a pseudocode format to make it more efficient and easier to understand.

✪ Edit the statement in SQL view to remove the product image from the query results.

✪ Run the query to check the how results are now displayed.

> product_TBL is identified on the FROM line; remove it from the SELECT and WHERE line.

> Delete ",product_TBL.[product_image]" from the SQL.

Practice

Microsoft Access can also be used to create your own SQL queries.

Create an SQL query, using booking_TBL, to search for the details of all of the bookings made by customer 1005. The query should display product_ID, date_out and date_back only.

➤ Click Create and then Query Design.
➤ Close the Show Table dialogue box that appears on screen.
➤ Click View and then select SQL view.

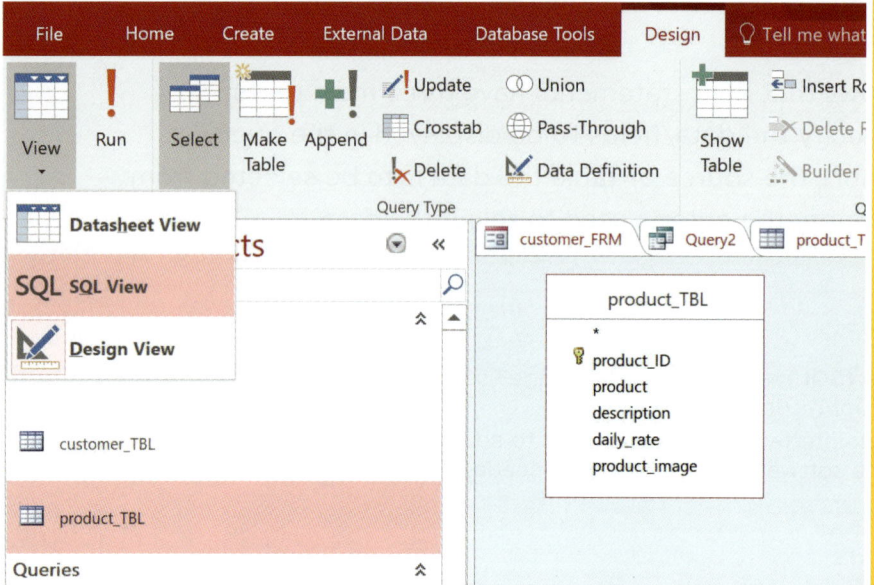

➤ Copy and complete the following SQL statement for this query and then run the query to test that it works correctly
SELECT [product_ID], [_____], [_____]
FROM _____
WHERE ((([cust_ID])= _____);

> Notice that cust_ID is not included in the SELECT part of the statement as we do not want to display it in the results.

> Think carefully about the data type used to store cust_ID; if it is a numeric value it does not need "".

➤ Test your Query by clicking on the Run icon. The following results should be displayed.

product_ID	date_out	date_back
SC128	23/03/2020	29/03/2020
HEL122	23/03/2020	29/03/2020
GLV675	03/04/2020	05/04/2020
SC128	03/04/2020	05/04/2020
HEL122	03/04/2020	05/04/2020
GLV675	03/04/2020	05/04/2020
*		

➤ Close the query results. You will be asked do you want to save the changes to the design of your query. Click Yes and name your query 1005Bookings.

Use the example completed above to help you create your own SQL statement to SELECT and display the product_ID, product, description and daily_rate FROM product_TBL all products with a daily_rate of <$25.00.

Examine the following SQL statements with a friend and predict the outcome of running each statement.

```
SELECT product_ID, product, description, daily_rate
FROM product_TBL
WHERE product="e-Scooter";
```

```
SELECT product_ID, date_out, date_back
FROM booking_TBL
WHERE product_ID=HEL122;
```

> Think about replacing '=' in the WHERE line with the '<' symbol to help with this task

> SQL statements do not need a criterion. By leaving out the WHERE line, the query will display all of the fields listed in the SELECT statement.

➤ Create an SQL statement using each of the examples shown above.
➤ Run each query and check if your predictions were correct.
➤ Try running one of the queries without including the WHERE statement to see how this alters the results displayed.

The following SQL queries have been created but are not returning the expected results. Discuss each query with a friend and try to identify any errors.

```
SELECT product_ID, product, description, daily_rate
FROM customer_TBL
WHERE product_ID="SC-009";
```

```
SELECT cust_ID, secondname, firstname, country
FROM customer_TBL
WHERE country ="USA"
```

Go further

Inserting images

The owner of SegwayThere would like to use the database to produce a report which contains images of all of the equipment available for rental.

Before they can do this they have asked you to help them source some images to help show what each product looks like.

◆ Use an advanced internet search to locate appropriate images of Segways and e-Scooters, and each of the other products referred to in your database.
◆ Open your file called **SegwayThereDB**.
◆ Keep a note of the websites you used as sources for each of your images.
◆ Open **product_TBL** in Design View and add a new field called product_image.
◆ Set the data type to **Object Linking and Embedding Object (OLE Object)**.

product_TBL	
Field Name	**Data Type**
product_ID	Short Text
product	Short Text
description	Short Text
daily_rate	Currency
product_image	OLE Object
	Short Text
	Long Text
	Number
	Date/Time
	Currency
	AutoNumber
	Yes/No
	OLE Object
	Hyperlink
	Attachment
	Calculated
	Lookup Wizard...

◆ Use the Form Wizard to create a form for product_TBL.
◆ Save the form as product_FRM.
◆ Edit the form in Design and Layout view so it has the same professional look as the other forms in your application.

Remember, these images belong to someone else and you can't use someone else's material without their permission. You must always give attribution (credit) to the original owners or creators of a digital artefact if you are using it in a document you have created.

If you have permission from others in your class you could add a new field to the customer_TBL called customer_image and include photographs of other students and use them to represent the customers in your database. However you must have permission from each student.

OLE Object data types are used in *Microsoft Access* to allow you to attach other files to your database, in this case we will attach images.

KEYWORD

Object Linking and Embedding Object (OLE Object): used to allow the linking of existing files to other programs and applications

◆ Open the form in data view and right click on the OLE place holder. Select insert and browse to the location where your have stored your image for that product.

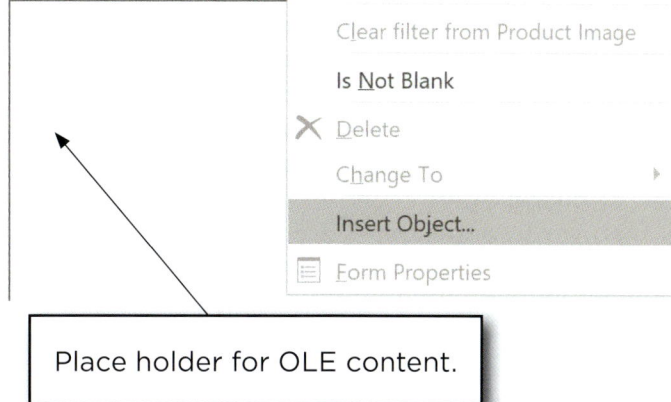

Place holder for OLE content.

◆ Click on the Next Record button at the bottom of the data entry form to move on to the next product.

Next record

◆ Repeat the process until you have added an OLE image for each product in the database.
◆ Save your work.
◆ Finally, do not forget, the owner would like you to create a report which shows all of the products available for rental. The report should include:
  ❏ images of each product
  ❏ names of each product underneath the image
  ❏ a text box at the bottom of the report listing the sources of the images.

Challenge yourself

More advanced SQL

The SQL statements created earlier in this chapter allowed us to search for and display data from one table, using specific data.

SQL statements can also be created to allow the user to:
➤ enter their own criteria to search a database
➤ display data from more than one table.
Use what you have learned about SQL to create a new SQL query that will display the following from customer_TBL.
➤ Create a new query and display the query in SQL view.
➤ Enter the SQL statement shown below to first of all display the cust_ID, surname, firstname and country of all customers from USA.

```
SELECT cust_ID, surname, firstname, country
FROM customer_TBL
WHERE country="USA";
```

KEYWORD

parameter query: a query which asks the user to enter search criteria

➤ Save and test your query to ensure it works correctly.

SegwayThere has customers from many different countries. It would be better if they have one query that allows the user to enter the country for themselves. Instead of giving exact criteria in the WHERE statement we can use [ ] to ask the user to enter the search criteria.

> A query which asks the user to enter the data in this way is known as a **parameter query**.

➤ Edit the WHERE statement to read WHERE country = [Enter Country];.

➤ Save and run the query to see how this changes how the query now works.

The owners of SegwayThere would like to display any bookings shown in booking_TBL that have been made by customer 1001. But they would like the firstname and surname of the customer to be displayed also.

This will involve selecting data from two tables, customer_TBL and booking_TBL.

> cust_ID is the primary key field in customer_TBL but also appears in booking_TBL and a relationship has been created between the two tables using this field.

To select data from two tables it is important that the two tables are already linked. In this example, booking_TBL and customer_TBL are already linked using cust_ID.

➤ Create a new query and display the query in SQL view.

➤ Enter the following SQL statement.

```
SELECT booking_TBL.booking_ID, booking_TBL.cust_ID, booking_
TBL.product_ID, booking_TBL.date_out, booking_TBL.date_back,
customer_TBL.firstname, customer_TBL.secondname
FROM customer_TBL, booking_TBL
WHERE customer_TBL="1001"
```

> Notice how in this query you need to specify the table each field is being taken from.
>
> You can do this by typing the table name before each field in the select line.

➤ Run your query and with a friend examine the results displayed. The results displayed at first are not correct.

booking_ID	cust_ID	product_ID	date_out	date_back	firstname	
1	1001	SW111	21/03/2020	24/03/2020	Nicolas	1
2	1002	SW334	22/03/2020	22/03/2020	Nicolas	1
3	1003	SC009	22/03/2020	25/03/2020	Nicolas	1
4	1004	SW097	22/03/2020	28/03/2020	Nicolas	1
5	1005	SC128	23/03/2020	29/03/2020	Nicolas	1
6	1005	HEL122	23/03/2020	29/03/2020	Nicolas	1
7	1005	GLV675	03/04/2020	05/04/2020	Nicolas	1
8	1006	SW765	23/03/2020	24/03/2020	Nicolas	1
9	1004	SW097	01/04/2020	02/04/2020	Nicolas	1
10	1002	SW334	02/04/2020	10/04/2020	Nicolas	1
11	1005	SC128	03/04/2020	05/04/2020	Nicolas	1
12	1005	HEL122	03/04/2020	05/04/2020	Nicolas	1
13	1005	GLV675	03/04/2020	05/04/2020	Nicolas	1

> The query is displaying the first and second name of cust_ID 1001 to every booking contained in booking_TBL.

- ➤ Remember that cust_ID appears in both customer_TBL and booking_TBL. The SQL statement must include an instruction to also search booking_TBL for cust_ID 1001
- ➤ Edit the WHERE statement to now read WHERE customer_TBL.cust_ID=1001 AND booking_TBL.cust_ID=1001;
- ➤ Run and test the query again to ensure the correct results are displayed this time.
- ➤ Save the query as **bookingnamesQRY**.

Create your own SELECT statement to now display the contents of booking_TBL, this time with the product and description fields included from product_TBL. Use product_ID SC128 as your search criteria.

Final project

The owners of SegwayThere have decided to start giving lessons in using Segways and e-Scooters to under 18s. They have recorded some details of students and lessons in a new database called **lessons_DB**. Your teacher will give you a copy of this file.

- ➤ Open the file called **lessons_DB**.
- ➤ Produce a data dictionary which can be used to describe the contents of both tables in the database. Include details of primary keys, validation rules and input masks you will apply to each field.
- ➤ Some comments have been included in the description column for some fields to help you with this task.
- ➤ Apply the validation rules and input masks you have designed to each of the tables in the database.
- ➤ Produce a test plan and test the validation rules in each table.
- ➤ Produce an entity relationship diagram to show how the two tables are related.
- ➤ Create a one to many relationship between student_TBL and lessons_TBL.
- ➤ The owner would like each student to have a card with their name and photograph on it so the tutor can easily remember their name.
  - ● Add a new field called student_picture to student_TBL. Set this field as an OLE object. Add a picture to student_TBL for each student.
  - ● Produce a report called student_card_RPT which can be used to print a student's full name and their photograph.

> You can search for images from the internet.

- ➤ The owner would also like to have one form which allows them to enter data into student_TBL and lesson_TBL at the same time. Create a form which is appropriate for this task.

> Remember to create a parameter query first which asks the user to enter student_ID.

- ➤ With a friend evaluate your form layout to determine how professional it is. You should discuss:
  - ● text style, size, font and colour used
  - ● use of background colours
  - ● how well the field headings describe each attribute
  - ● use of special instructions to help the user.
- ➤ Create an SQL statement that allows the user to search for and display all of the data on all lessons on the 28 April 2020.

> Use the form wizard to add details from both tables, one after the other. Remember that student_ID need only be included once.

➤ The results of this query should be displayed in a report called lessonRPT. Results should be grouped by vehicle type and sorted by lesson_time.

➤ Create an SQL statement that displays the student firstname and surname from student_TBL along with details of the lessons recorded in lesson_TBL. The query should use student_ID as the search criteria.

➤ Display the results of this query in a report called lesson_namesRPT.

Evaluation

➤ Ask a friend to test your database solution against each of the following requirements which say that the database should contain:
   o easy to use interface with links to all forms, queries and reports.
   o A single data entry form to enter data into both tables at the same time.
   o Queries and reports to:
      • allow user to print a list of lessons each day (grouped by vehicle type and sorted by time)
      • print a bill for the user.

➤ Ask your friend to evaluate your form and report layouts to determine how professional they are. You should discuss:
   o text style, size, font and colour used
   o use of background colours
   o how well the field headings describe each attribute
   o use of special instructions to help the user.

➤ Write down any improvements your friend recommended and then describe in a short written report any changes you made to your database and why.

Glossary

Key Term Definition

absolute cell reference a cell reference that remains constant even if it is copied to other cells

accessibility providing support for the individual needs of all users, for example by including audio output of content for users with visual difficulties

American Standard Code for Information Interchange (ASCII) a standard code used to represent text on computers and other electronic devices

analogue a continually varying signal, for example a sound signal

analogue to digital converter (ADC) used to convert analogue signals, such as the human voice, to digital signals

arguments values that are passed to the function in the brackets that follow the function name; these values are used within the function

arithmetic operators +, − , *, / and other symbols which can be used for arithmetic

arithmetic shift a process of shifting binary digits left or right to help perform complex calculations

artificial intelligence (AI) the study of machines and application of algorithms designed to carry out tasks in a way which mimics the thought processes normally associated with human beings

assignment statements a statement which assigns a variable a value; for example, x = 3

attribute (database) represents a characteristic of a person or thing stored in the database, described using a field name

attribute (web page) used to define how the text, images and other content is to be displayed on a web page, normally added to the opening tag of an element; for example, <p align = 'left'>This is left aligned</p>

backup the process of making a copy of a program or file. This allows the developer to restore work if the original file becomes damaged in some way

base 10 another term for decimal as it is based on 10 digits

base 16 another name for hexadecimal because it is based on 16 characters

big data the large volume of data that is created by digital devices and websites every day; it is analysed using computer programs

binary a number system which uses combinations of two digits (0 and 1) to represent all other values. Used to represent data in computer systems

binary digit 0 or 1, the smallest unit of data represented by a computer

binary number format numbers represented using 1s and 0s

bit short for binary digit

bit depth the number of bits used to store a single sound sample

built-in functions (*Microsoft Excel*) functions that exist within the software for use by the user

built-in functions (Python) functions that can be used in the Python language without adding any additional code

byte a group of 8 bits, often used to represent a single character in a computer

cascade delete a feature of relational databases which means that, for example, if a customer is deleted from the customer table, all of the bookings linked to that customer will also be removed from the booking table

case-sensitive can distinguish between capital and small letters

cell single square or rectangle in a table used to contain an item of data or a table header

character set the set of characters that can be represented on any device

chatbot a computer program designed to mimic a human conversation

class attribute an attribute which can be used to define styles for other elements with the same name so they all have the same style

cloud storage online storage space for files and documents

column index num the column number of the data that will be returned if there is a match for the lookup value in the table array

comments (HTML) text used to explain your code; they can be seen by anyone viewing the HTML code but are not displayed in the browser window

comments (Python) text entered by the programmer to improve the readability of the code; they start with the # symbol in Python

communications protocol an agreed standard or set of rules for sending or receiving data on a network

condition an expression which evaluates to true or false; for example, X<10?

conditional formatting applying formatting such as colour to a cell based on certain criteria

copper cable has a core of copper wires which is covered in plastic or rubber; the wires can be twisted together; data transmission is through the use of electrical signals; copper cable is cheaper than fibre optic cabling but the speed of data transmission is much slower

cost price the price at which a product is bought by the owner of the store

counter variable a variable which is used to count the number of times a loop has been executed; it is usually increased by 1 each time the loop is executed

CSS (Cascading Stylesheets) the language used to describe how content on a web page should be displayed in the browser window

CSS property the attribute you want to change using CSS

CSS style rules the actual rules used to define how items described using HTML will be displayed in the browser window

CSS value the new value you wish to assign to the property identified in a CSS style tag

cyber crime a malicious attack on a computer system

cyber security the different ways in which we protect networks, programs and data from attack and unauthorised access

data dictionary a document used to describe the main parts of a database and how each of the main database parts are linked

data integrity the correctness and accuracy of data in a database

data modelling using mathematical functions and calculations on data to predict or model what may happen in the event of certain changes

data redundancy the unnecessary repetition of data in a database

data security protecting data

data types the different ways in which data can be stored; for example, number, string, date

data validation the process of checking data entered to ensure that it is acceptable

decimal number system number system using the digits 0, 1, 2, 3, 4, 5, 6, 7, 8, 9

dedent move the Python code out by four spaces

digital footprint the digital data held about a person as a result of their online activity

distributed denial of service (DDoS) a malicious attack on a network that can prevent users from logging on to access their data

div tag a tag <div> </div> used to group sections of HTML elements together for further formatting; for example, using CSS

domain hosting service a service where users can upload their own website and make it available on the internet

domain name the address of the server which holds the email

ELIF a statement which is part of an IF statement but provides an alternative pathway. There can be multiple ELIF statements in one IF statement

emoji a graphic which is a visual representation of an emotion

empathy the ability to understand the feelings of another person

encrypted data encoded in some way to protect it

encryption a process which scrambles data so that it cannot be read by unauthorised users

encryption key the key which will decode the data so that it can be read by a receiving computer

entity an individual person or thing about which data is stored in a database

entity relationship diagram (ERD) a diagram used to illustrate the relationship between two entities in a relational database

error alert a user defined message that will appear when the user enters data that breaks the validation rule

execute another word for running a program

external CSS a separate document is written containing the CSS for a website. Each page in the website contains a link to that file inside the <head> </head> tags at the start of an HTML document

fibre optic cable a cable with a glass or Perspex core used to link networks together; data transmission is via light signals and the speed of data transmission is very fast

field names names used to describe a piece of information about a single person or thing

file server the main computer on the network; it is more powerful than all of the other computers with a large amount of RAM and hard disk space

filter a spreadsheet feature which allows the user to apply certain criteria and exclude or show certain data

firewall hardware or software which monitors and filters data entering and leaving the network

fixed length having a set number of bits to represent a value; for example, numbers in binary are normally shown using 8 bits

flat-file database a database which stores all data items using one table

foreign key a key field in one table which appears in another table, creating a link between the two tables

hackers individuals who try to gain unauthorised access to computer systems to damage them or steal data

hertz a unit of measurement which tells us how many sound samples were taken in a single second

hexadecimal (hex) a number system which uses 16 characters 0–9 and A–F; often used by programmers to simplify long strings of binary numbers

high bandwidth bandwidth refers to the amount of data that can be transferred on a communications line in a given time

homepage the start-up page of a website, the page that loads first when the website is displayed in a web browser

HTML elements the opening tag, closing tag and content to be added to an HTML document; for example, <p>This is a paragraph</p> is an HTML element

hypertext clickable links on a web page

Hypertext Markup Language (HTML) the language used to create web pages

IDLE interface Python's Integrated Development and Learning Environment which provides features for creating, editing and running programs

IF statement a statement which evaluates a condition and places one value in the cell if the condition is true and another value in the cell if the condition is false

indent move the Python code in by four spaces

initialise setting a variable to a starting value. For example, x=0

inline CSS CSS which is applied to a single element in the <body> section of an HTML document

input a function which Python uses to capture string data from users

input mask a special control used to ensure data is entered in a specific format; for example, dates must be entered as mm/dd/yyyy

input message a user defined message which will appear when the user is entering data into a cell

integer whole number

interactive mode the Python shell allows commands to be entered and run immediately

interactive web page a web page containing content the user can engage with, for example through the use of buttons to make selections, including videos and sounds for the user to play, or games for the user to play

internal CSS the style definition would be included as part of the <head> </head> tag at the start of an HTML document

internal style CSS definitions which have been included in the <head> tags of an HTML document

internet service provider (ISP) a company who provides users with an internet connection for a subscription fee

interpreter the feature of Python which translates the Python code into language that the computer can understand, line by line

keylogger a malicious software application which will collect the keystrokes that a person is typing at the computer; typically used to find out peoples' passwords

Least Significant Bit (LSB) the digit to the right hand side of the number; the bit with the smallest place value

length check a validation check which is used to ensure that the value entered has a particular number of characters; for example, a check to ensure that a name has at least five characters

levels of access limiting the activities different users can perform on the computer system, based on their role in the organisation

local area network (LAN) a network spread over a small geographic area like a building

logic error when the program does not do what the programmer wanted it to

lookup list make use of a drop-down list of values (the user can select the value from a list onscreen – no typing is required) to enter data into a field; the user selects the value from a drop-down list

lookup statement used to search through a table of data for a value and then return results if that value is found

lookup value the value used to search through the lookup table

machine code the language that a computer uses to carry out instructions

macro a small program which is used to automate a task

malware software designed to damage a computer system or its data

meta tags a coding statement that describes some of the content on the web page; this can be used by search engines to help identify if the page should be returned in a search

metadata data about other data; for example, the use of style definitions in an HTML document used to describe how web page content is to be displayed

microphone an input device used to enter sound into a computer

Most Significant Bit (MSB) the digit to the left hand side of the number; the bit with the largest place value

multimedia a mixture of sound, video, animation and text

named cell a name given to an individual cell in a spreadsheet

named cell range giving one cell or a set of cells a name; the cells can be referred to using the name assigned

navigational structure the pathway the user can follow when visiting the various web pages on a website

nested IF statement an IF statement which is embedded in another IF statement

nibble a 4 bit number

nonverbal communication communication made without speaking such as gestures.

Object Linking and Embedding Object (OLE Object) used to allow the linking of existing files to other programs and applications

ordered list a list where each item on the list is given a place value such as '1', 'a', 'A', 'i' or 'I'

parameter query a query which asks the user to enter search criteria

parental controls rules, set by parents, which govern the websites that are allowed to be viewed on a computer

peripherals hardware connected to a network such as printers and scanners

pharming redirecting users to bogus websites to capture personal details

phishing sending bogus emails to capture personal details

place value the numerical value a digit has as a result of its position in a number; for example, the number 24_{10} actually represents $(2 \times 10) + (4 \times 1)$

podcast a digital audio file that is made available on the internet and can be listened to online or downloaded to a computer

populating a database the process of adding new data to a database or integrating existing data into a database

presence check a validation check which is used to ensure that there is a value entered. A length check can be used to do this; for example, a check to ensure that the value entered has at least one character

primary key field a field used to uniquely identify a record in a database

print statement a Python statement used to output text or values onto the screen

program code the Python code created in the IDLE

Python shell the Python interactive mode, where commands can be typed directly

query a process of searching for data in a database

Query By Example (QBE) an interface that allows users to add fields and criteria to a grid and then the software creates the SQL needed to process the data

range check a validation check which is used to ensure that the value entered lies within a given range; for example, 1–100

ranking the position in which the company's website sits when a search is done. The higher the ranking the more popular the website is

referential integrity a feature of relational databases which means for example that a booking cannot be added for a customer who does not exist in the customer table

relational database a database which stores data using two or more linked tables

relationship the link between two tables in a database application, created using a field that appears in both tables

repetition repeating sections of code in a loop

robot a machine designed to automatically carry out a pre-programmed task without human intervention

Roman numerals for example, i, ii, iii, iv

router a piece of networking equipment that shares a network connection between devices; it can be wired or wireless and allows a LAN to connect to the internet

sample rate the number of sound samples taken each second

satellite link a radio link between one station transmitting on Earth and another through a satellite

script mode Python's text editor which allows programmers to enter a list of commands and they are executed together

selection selecting statements based on a decision

selling price the price at which a product is sold to customers

social influencers individuals who make use of social media and whose opinions and actions can influence other users of social media

social media websites that allow users to create and share content or to participate in social networking

solo adventure game a game in which the player assumes the role of the main character

sort to change the order of data; for example, data can be sorted in alphabetical order or numerically

sound card a hardware device inside a computer which can convert analogue sound signals to digital data

spam email that is sent as part of a large set of messages; the email is not wanted by the receiver

special characters symbols and other characters (aside from standard letters, numbers and punctuation symbols) which can be created using a standard keyboard, such as #, ~, %

spyware software that aims to gather information about a person or organisation without their permission. The software is usually downloaded without the user's knowledge

standalone computers computers which are not connected to a network

storyboard a set of line drawings which provide a basic outline of the content of pages of an application

string data type data which is made up of letters, numbers or any characters on the keyboard

structure diagram a diagrammatic illustration of the pathway through the pages of a website

Structured Query Language (SQL) a specialised language used with relational databases to input or retrieve data

style information information relating to how an item will be presented on an HTML document when it is opened in a browser window

style tag used to contain information or rules which will define how items described using HTML will be displayed in the browser window

suite a section of code which has been indented at the same level

syntax rules the rules of a programming language which determine how its instructions are written

table array the set of data that will be searched using the lookup value

table header data used to describe the contents of each column in an HTML table

tables organised collection of related information

tags hidden key words in a web page which describe the content to be displayed in the browser window; for example, <p> is an opening tag which is used to describe a paragraph, </p> is the closing tag for the paragraph

telecommunications link using technology like fibre optic cables, computers are linked to the internet; the link is the channel that allows communication between computers and the internet

test plan a document containing information about how the program will be tested and the data used to test it

transistor a tiny switch that can be activated by electrical signals. If the transistor is ON it represents 1, when it is OFF it represents 0

type check a validation check which is used to ensure that the value entered is of a certain data type; for example, a check to ensure data is numeric

unit testing the process of testing individual parts or components in a computer based solution

unordered list a list of text appearing on a web page with no special order or sequence

user friendly something that is not difficult to learn or understand

user identifier the part of the email address which uniquely identifies the user

user-defined functions functions defined and created by the programmer

validation ensuring that the data entered by the user is acceptable

variable a named memory location used to store data of a given type during the program execution; a variable can change value as the program runs

variety the number of different types of data generated

velocity the speed of data processing

Vertical Lookup (VLOOKUP) table a table in a spreadsheet which is be used to lookup a value and return data to a cell in the spreadsheet

video conferencing using the internet to transmit pictures and sound between computers

virus a program which gains access to a computer and seeks to damage the computer system or collect data

VLOOKUP makes use of a lookup table of data to match the contents of a cell with a value in the lookup table

Voice over Internet Protocol (VoIP) using the internet to make telephone calls

volume the amount of data generated

web browser software which allows the user to view web pages on the world wide web

web browser application a software package used to view website content

website developers individuals or groups of individuals responsible for the end-to-end coding of websites

website filtering software which enables websites to be allowed or blocked based on their content

while loop a loop which will continue to run while a condition is true

wide area network (WAN) a network spread over a large geographic area such as a country

wizard a software tool which takes users step-by-step through the completion of a task

worm a malicious software application which spreads across computer networks; typically used when an email attachment is opened and the program is activated

# Index